A Fundamental Law of the European Union

The Spinelli Group, Bertelsmann Stiftung

A Fundamental Law of the European Union

Verlag BertelsmannStiftung

Bibliographic information published by the Deutsche Nationalbibliothek

The Deutsche Nationalbibliothek lists this publication in the Deutsche Nationalbibliografie; detailed bibliographic data is available on the Internet at http://dnb.d-nb.de.

Responsible: Thomas Fischer, Joachim Fritz-Vannahme
Production editor: Christiane Raffel
Cover design: Elisabeth Menke
Cover illustration: Shutterstock/Adisa
Typesetting and Printing Hans Kock Buch- und Offsetdruck GmbH, Bielefeld
ISBN 978-3-86793-537-1

www.bertelsmann-stiftung.org/publications

A Fundamental Law

The unity of Europe is vital if global challenges are to be met and European values and interests promoted. But how should the new polity of the European Union be governed?

The present constitutional architecture is hardly fit for the purpose. Executive authority is dispersed and democratic accountability weak. Expedient measures needed to address the financial and economic crisis have stretched the present EU treaties close to their limits.

The Union's system of governance must be reformed if it is to deliver much needed public goods at home and decisive leadership abroad. In the face of hostile public opinion, the national governments of its Member States fear to give the EU the powers and resources it needs. National parties and parliaments fail to embrace the European dimension of politics.

So the European Union needs to assert itself. European challenges can be met only in a European way.

This proposal for a Fundamental Law of the European Union is a comprehensive revision of the Treaty of Lisbon (2007). Replacing the existing treaties, it takes a major step towards a federal union. It turns the European Commission into a democratic constitutional government, keeping to the method built by Jean Monnet in which the Commission drafts laws which are then enacted jointly by the Council, representing the states, and the European Parliament, representing the citizens. All the reforms proposed are aimed at strengthening the capacity of the EU to act.

The Union reformed along the lines established in the Fundamental Law will be more efficient and effective, more transparent and accountable. The Spinelli Group of MEPs recommends the Fundamental Law for consideration by the Convention which will soon be called upon to amend the EU treaties.

Table of Contents

Foreword

A Fundamental Law of the European Union is elaborated under the auspices of the Spinelli Group whose board comprises Elmar Brok, Dany Cohn-Bendit, Andrew Duff, Isabelle Durant, Sylvie Goulard, Roberto Gualtieri, Jo Leinen and Guy Verhofstadt. A working party of MEPs was established under the coordination of Andrew Duff.

While all support its publication as an important contribution to the debate on the future of Europe, members of the Spinelli board are not bound individually by all aspects of the draft treaty.

The writing of *A Fundamental Law* has been shaped by discussions in the wider group of Spinelli MEPs and in the Union of European Federalists. A number of officials from the EU institutions, who remain anonymous, have helped us with sound advice, as have our own collaborators: Matteo Adduci, Philip Drauz, Maria Laura Formisano, Daniel Freund, Guillaume McLaughlin, Fabian Pescher, Maxime Rolland-Calligaro, Miriam Schoeps, Pierre-Jean Verrando, Christian Wenning and Sietse Wijnsma. Pier-Virgilio Dastoli gave us the benefit of his long experience in the federalist circles. From outside the institutions, we thank Christophe Hillion and René Repasi, and our many interlocutors in governments and parliaments, think-tanks and academic circles who, perhaps unwittingly, have shaped our approach.

We thank the Bertelsmann Stiftung, which shares with the Spinelli Group the leitmotif for a federal Europe, for its support. The Bertelsmann Stiftung publishes the *Fundamental Law* as a major contribution to the debate on the future of Europe.

How to Read the Text

The text of the *Fundamental Law of the European Union* postulates a general revision of the Treaty of Lisbon (2007). It amalgamates the Treaty on European Union (TEU) and the Treaty on the Functioning of the European Union (TFEU), and updates and amends them. It integrates the Charter of Fundamental Rights (CFR). It incorporates the essence of the Euratom Treaty (1957) and of the Fiscal Compact Treaty (2012). The 1976 Act on the direct election of the European Parliament, as amended, is transported into a protocol.

There are 437 articles in eight parts, plus a preamble, and 18 protocols. Each chapter is preceded by a short explanatory comment summarising its main features.

Part I (Articles 1–144) contains all the constitutional and institutional provisions.

Part II (Articles 145–198) is the Charter.

Part III (Articles 199–217) concerns the finances of the Union.

Part IV (Articles 218–246) is the policies and organisation of economic and monetary union.

Part V (Articles 247–376) lays out the sectoral policies of the Union.

Part VI (Articles 377–398) deals with the area of freedom, security and justice.

Part VII (Articles 399–405) covers the association of overseas territories.

Part VIII (Articles 406–437) provides for the external affairs of the Union.

The new treaty is laid out in the right-hand column. Equivalent clauses from the TEU, TFEU and CFR are laid out in the left-hand column.

No change is indicated by '.....' in both columns. Words emboldened seek to draw attention to the more important changes and novelties. In stylistic changes, 'Member States' become 'States', and 'national parliaments' become 'State Parliaments'.

The official text of the current treaties and the Charter is found at: http://register.consilium.europa.eu/pdf/en/08/st06/st06655-re07.en08.pdf

Finally, a table of equivalences marries the old and the new.

A Fundamental Law of the European Union: Why Europe Needs a New Constitutional Treaty

Commentary

The financial and economic crisis has exposed many shortcomings in the way the European Union is run. Confidence that the experiment of European integration is 'condemned to succeed' has been shaken. The hope that the introduction of the euro would lead smoothly to the greater integration of Europe's national economies has been dashed. The cohesion of the eurozone and the wider internal market is at risk. Growth has stalled and the drive to greater competitiveness is frustrated. Governments have been too weak to complete the structural reforms which they espouse. National supervision of the banking sector has failed.

At the level of the heads of government, meeting in the European Council, the response has tended to be too little too late. Under the pressure of external shocks, the EU has managed to put in place a regulatory framework for the financial services sector which should prevent a banking meltdown. Smart action by the European Central Bank (ECB) has so far avoided a country from exiting the euro. But for all the crisis management measures, progress towards building a proper banking union has slowed and confidence has not returned. Courtesy of the EU and the IMF, fiscal discipline has been imposed in countries that could not impose it upon themselves. Yet rigid austerity is proving counterproductive, certainly in terms of youth unemployment and of escalating national debt.

In such circumstances it is hardly a surprise that 'Europe' is getting blamed, although the precise target of the blame remains unclear because the governance of the Union is diffuse and opaque. Citizens who look to Europe for more solidarity are bound to be disappointed. Despite many months of technical talks, the political debate among Europe's leaders about the possibility of sharing the burden between tax-payers at the European level has scarcely begun. The large majority of national party leaders in government and opposition maintain their rhetorical commitment to the Union, but the European Council has had to resort to ways and means outside the Union framework, such as the fiscal compact treaty, to shore up the single currency. The governance of the Union itself looks incapable of effective action and is accused of lacking deep democratic legitimacy. Nationalist opposition to the European project, masquerading as 'euroscepticism', grows.

And abroad, in a troubled world, much more is expected of the European Union in international affairs than it is able to deliver. Although the European External Action Service is operational, the reforms introduced by the Treaty of Lisbon to the direction of the EU's common foreign, security and defence policies have not succeeded as much as was hoped.

So how should a more united Europe best be governed?

In response to this crisis, federalists argue that the European Union must deepen its integration or risk falling apart. 'More of the same' is not an option. The historic mission to unite Europe's states and peoples needs to be refurbished. Reform needs to be driven not by a retreat to old nationalisms but by a fresh assertion of the values and principles on which the Union is founded, aided by modern standards of open, democratic government, with the powers and resources needed to meet contemporary challenges.

These challenges require the Union to reform fundamentally its constitutional architecture. A more federal structure would provide for more unity and cohesion between its member states and more solidarity among its citizens. By 'federal' we do not mean a centralised superstate but, rather, a constitutional union in which different levels of democratic government are coordinate, not subordinate. The federal legal framework would serve to strengthen government at the level of the Union for the exercise of those competences conferred by treaty on the Union. A more federal democratic system would bring the Union and its citizens closer together, and make the Union's institutions more responsive to the needs and aspirations of the people they serve. These reforms, building on what has been achieved so far and lessons learned during the crisis, brought together in a Fundamental Law, will bolster the European Union for the longer term at home and abroad.

Status quo no longer

Reluctance to embark on the complex and serious business of EU treaty reform is perfectly understandable. Many are intimidated by the relative failure of the last big effort to develop the Union along federal lines, a process which started in 2001 at Laeken but stumbled in the humiliation of the French and Dutch referendums in 2005, and was only to be concluded when the Treaty of Lisbon came into force in December 2009. We should do better this time: the scale and gravity of the present crisis change the context in which this round of reform is conducted as well as providing the occasion for it.

Although much has been and is being done under the Treaty of Lisbon to address the crisis, treaty revision is inescapable if the more fiscally integrated Union is to be put on a surer foundation. A new treaty is needed to mark the important fresh stage in European integration in which the eurozone is transformed into a fiscal union run by a federal economic government. To fail to make this transformation jeopardises the EU's very survival. The present treaties are being stretched close to their limits by the welter of crisis management measures, which unintentionally render the EU even more officious and technocratic than before.

Where is the democratic legitimacy of the European Council, for example, in imposing tax rises in Greece or wage cuts in Portugal? How is the European Commission to be held accountable for its work as a member of the economic troika, along with the ECB and the IMF? While such a situation might be tolerable on the grounds of expediency in the very short term, there is bound to be an adverse reaction in the markets and in the courts, to say nothing of on the streets, if nothing is done to regularise the situation by restoring in a democratic manner the scrupulous rule of law.

How to change the treaties

Article 48 of the Treaty on European Union tells us how to change the treaties. The amendment process will start with a Convention and continue with an Intergovernmental Conference. It will conclude with ratification by all 28 Member States of the Union according to their own constitutional requirements. In several countries, either those constitutional requirements or mere political expediency will involve the holding of a national referendum.

How successful and quick this constitutional exercise will be depends on the scope of its ambition and, to some extent, on the quality of its preparation. The Spinelli Group of federalist MEPs publishes this Fundamental Law as a contribution to that preparation. We draw conclusions from our experience of previous rounds of treaty change, and do not hesitate to recommend adjustments to the Treaty of Lisbon in the quest for a better governed Union.

We look forward to receiving in due course other informed contributions towards treaty change, not least from the European Commission.

We already know that the intergovernmental Treaty on Stability, Coordination and Governance (better known as the fiscal compact treaty) lays down that its substance is to be incorporated into the legal framework of the Union before the end of 2017. Likewise, some elements of the ambitious agenda for banking and fiscal union require legal bases which can only be assured through treaty change.

Pressure from the judiciary will also spur the treaty revision exercise – not least from the German Federal Constitutional Court in Karlsruhe, worried about the democratic legitimacy of the European project and the incursion of the Union into areas of law, notably on taxation, which have previously been subject to the exclusive realm of national parliaments.

We take note of the intention of the British Prime Minister, David Cameron, to renegotiate the terms of British membership of the EU. By way of a catalyst, the UK government is already conducting a unilateral review of EU competences and powers, presumably with an eye to possible repatriation. A referendum looks certain in Britain as soon as 2017, presumably on the outcome of the treaty negotiations.

So, starting in all probability in spring 2015, there will be a Convention to draft the treaty amendments. The main items on the agenda of the Convention begin already to be clear: to codify in the primary law of the Union the essential elements of reinforced economic governance; to rectify some of the weaker provisions of the Lisbon treaty; and to cater for British renegotiation.

The Convention will be made up of representatives of the European Council, the European Commission, the European Parliament and national parliaments. It will sit probably for many months to reflect on the present state of the Union, to consult widely, and to consider the various proposals for reform. It will work by consensus, and its outcome will be sent forward to member states in the hope that unanimity can be achieved. The Convention process in itself provides a high degree of democratic legitimacy combined with legal rigour, in which national governments and parliaments have equal status with the EU institutions.

New forms for new functions

For the sake of argument, let us call our new constitutional treaty *A Fundamental Law of the European Union.* Merging the current Treaty on European Union (TEU) and the Treaty on the Functioning of the European Union (TFEU) into one document allows us to shorten the whole by reducing repetition and eliminating duplication, and to rearrange the chapters in a more logical way.

We lift many prohibitions on the powers of the European Commission, European Parliament and European Court of Justice, rendering the system of governance more permissive and thus more capable. The number of different types of decision-making procedure is reduced. Most *passerelle* clauses, blocking minorities, emergency brakes, automatic accelerators are abolished – all clever devices which may or may not have been intended ever to be used, but the inclusion of which in the Lisbon treaty has led in practice to nervous disorder. Likewise, many of the 37 Protocols and 65 Declarations attached to the Treaty of Lisbon, which seek to blunt the force or bend the interpretation of original clauses, are proposed to be deleted.

In making these changes, we will unlock the potential of the Union and reduce the sense of instability. This treaty revision is meant to last: the Fundamental Law must reassure the citizen that it provides a durable settlement of the business of the governance of the Union, along with a clearer sense of things to come.

The Fundamental Law implies a renewal of the pact on which the Union is founded along overtly federal lines. Those who sign up to it will be committing to the building of a federal polity with an enhanced capacity to act in any given field. Membership of the euro is taken as given once the convergence criteria are met. Methods are proposed to closely associate the 'pre-ins' with the decisions of the eurozone. The scope for opt-outs and derogations is minimised. States will be expected to conform to the emerging common foreign, security and defence policies of the Union as well as to the development of the area of freedom, security and justice.

Mindful of the need to protect the integrity of the existing corpus of EU law, our new treaty evolves from its predecessors and builds on experience. The purpose of the Fundamental Law is to provide a robust constitutional framework inside which Europe's governors and law makers are enabled to make effective choices about the future direction of policy and the joint management of their affairs.

At the same time, the Union must be amply equipped with such competences and its institutions with such powers as are needed to meet new challenges, not least in fiscal matters and also in the energy sector where we integrate the essence of the Euratom Treaty.

Sharing the burden

The main innovation of the Fundamental Law, spelt out in Part IV, is the installation of an economic government of the fiscal union. It will become possible for the Union to develop a common economic policy in addition to coordinating national economic policies. The eurozone is deemed to operate under the provisions of enhanced cooperation which allow some states to integrate further and faster than others. The euro states, for example, will enjoy their own fiscal capacity for contra-cyclical purposes in addition to the general EU budget.

The government of the Union's financial and economic policies is based on the European Commission which will acquire a treasury facility for the borrowing and lending of funds. A new post of Treasury Minister is created with the job of stabilising the Union's economy and allocating its resources. Since economic policy reforms by the member states impact upon the rest of the Union, national plans must be discussed and coordinated *ex ante*. In order to ensure the establishment and the functioning of the internal market and to avoid distortion of competition, the Union can adopt acts in accordance with the ordinary legislative procedure to harmonise direct and indirect taxes.

The Fundamental Law provides for the European Stability Mechanism to operate in primary as well as secondary markets. While codifying the new supervisory powers of the European Central Bank as the cornerstone of the banking union, it makes provision for the subsequent creation of a possible single financial services authority. The Fundamental Law permits the progressive mutualisation of a portion of sovereign debt, and lifts the prohibition, under certain conditions, on EU deficit financing. Legal bases are created for a common resolution mechanism and a deposit guarantee scheme.

The Fundamental Law codifies in primary law the key elements of the recent Six Pack and Two Pack legislation which strengthened EU surveillance and supervision of the individual state economies. The European Parliament has extended powers in the design of the employment and macro-economic policy guidelines, and both it and national parliaments obtain powers to intervene in the application of the excessive debt and deficit procedures. A decision by the Commission declaring a state to be in excessive debt or deficit will be valid unless the Council can marshal substantial opposition to it.

In Part III of the Fundamental Law, the Union's financial system is transformed, involving the abolition of rigid *juste retour* and the phasing out of the system of direct contributions from national treasuries. Revenue based on direct and indirect taxation will accrue directly to the EU. We abolish the unanimity rule for the decisions on own resources and the multi-annual financial framework. In a change to the annual budgetary procedure, we oblige the Council to share with the Parliament the responsibility of concluding an agreement. The new financial system of the Union will be fair, transparent and buoyant.

Democratic government

The Fundamental Law makes it explicit that Parliament and Council form the legislature of the Union and that the Commission is to be regarded as its government. Many of the executive powers now held by the Council are transferred to the Commission, subject to a possible recall by the legislature. This clearer separation of powers should make it possible for each institution to be held to account for its performance.

The role of the European Council is adjusted to reduce the risk of tension and confusion between it and the Commission. The post of supernumerary 'permanent' President of the European Council is abolished in favour of the election by the heads of government of one of their number to chair their meetings for a period of two and a half years. The European Council is made more responsible than it is today for directing and coordinating the affairs of the Council of ministers: heads of government will be enabled to sit as the General Affairs Council.

Reflecting its role as a legislative chamber, the rotating presidency of the Council of ministers is replaced by the election, in and by each formation of the Council, of a chair for two and a half years. The president of the Council of finance ministers (Ecofin) will also chair the Eurogroup. These changes will surely enhance continuity and improve the quality of chairmanship.

The European Parliament, representing directly the 508 million EU citizens, plays the central role in safeguarding the legitimacy of decisions. Throughout the Fundamental Law, co-decision between Parliament and Council replaces the Council's current rights to legislate alone. That change involves, among others, the design of the European Stability Mechanism, and the formulation of employment and macro-economic guidelines.

The European Commission is made more directly accountable to the European Parliament. The President-elect of the Commission is empowered to choose the size and composition of his or her own college, subject to parliamentary hearings. We assume a smaller Commission. This important change will provide for a more efficient executive less beholden to national governments and more capable of defining and promoting the common interest of all states and citizens.

As far as the European Parliament is concerned, provision is made for a pan-European constituency from which a certain number of deputies will be elected from trans-national lists. Such electoral reform will turn the European political parties into decent campaigning organisations, providing what is now a missing link between the electorate and elected. Parliament gains the power of co-decision on the vexed question of its seat. And it will have the right to vote on the opening and closure of all international agreements, and to give its assent to the accession of a new member state.

While the Commission retains its right to initiate EU laws, Parliament and Council gain the right to launch their own legislative proposals if the Commission declines to do their bidding. Parliament is enabled to push for the sacking of an individual Commissioner. In the case where MEPs decide to censure the whole Commission, Parliament must at the same time be able to elect a successor.

Citizenship a reality

As a federal entity the legitimacy of the European Union stems from two distinct sources, its states and its citizens. Through a change in the Preamble this is made clear in the very beginning of the Fundamental Law.

We upgrade the status and content of European Union citizenship by giving rightful prominence to the Charter of Fundamental Rights, incorporated in full as Part II of the Fundamental Law. The rules to determine whether a state has breached fundamental rights are modified: Qualified majority voting (QMV) is introduced at the level of the European Council, and the European Parliament and Court of Justice get to be involved.

Access to the European Court of Justice is eased significantly for individuals directly and adversely affected by an EU act. The judicial scope of the Court is widened to embrace areas from which it is at present excluded, including the sensitive fields of internal and external security policy.

The European Ombudsman is enabled to defend the citizens' rights more effectively, especially by gaining the right to refer cases of a breach of the Charter to the Court of Justice.

The scope of the European Citizens' Initiative is considerably widened to include political agenda-setting.

A legal base is established to extend the right of every EU citizen living in EU states other than their own to vote in all elections.

Streamlined decisions

Parts V and VI see a rationalisation and streamlining of decision-making procedures, enhancing transparency and efficiency. The Fundamental Law greatly extends

QMV in the Council at the expense of unanimous decision making. Notably, this change affects the important 'flexibility clause' which allows action to be taken by the Union in certain circumstances when such action has not been expressly foreseen by the treaties.

The Fundamental Law reduces the number of main decision-making procedures to only two. The first, the ordinary decision-making procedure, stays unchanged. The second is a special legislative procedure that replaces the numerous different procedures of the current treaties, and provides for higher QMV thresholds in both Council and Parliament.

Since legislative procedures with unanimous voting requirements are almost entirely abolished throughout the Fundamental Law, the bridging clauses *(passerelles)*, which gave the European Council the possibility to apply QMV in place of unanimity lose their purpose and are deleted. The areas concerned include the multiannual financial framework, social affairs, environmental policy, justice and home affairs, as well as common foreign and security policy. Only the main *passerelle*, which allows the European Council to transfer matters decided in accordance with the special legislative procedure to the ordinary legislative procedure, as well as the *passerelle* to ease the decision-making procedures under enhanced cooperation are kept.

A specific new legal base is created for EU agencies.

Common policies refreshed

Part V reforms the chapters on the common policies of the Union and brings a sharper focus to those which need it.

While maintaining the basic free movements of goods, persons, services and capital, the Fundamental Law strengthens the defence of the European social models. Economic policy and the policies of the internal market must be conducted in accordance with the principle of an open, highly competitive social market economy. The Union gains competence to legislate on the fiscal component of free movement of labour, abetting the portability of entitlements across national frontiers.

By tightening the horizontal social clause the Union will integrate requirements linked to the promotion of a high level of employment and social protection. Under the Fundamental Law, economic freedoms may not impair the exercise of social rights and principles as provided for in Union and state law. The lifting of the prohibition for the Union to legislate on pay further strengthens the social aspect.

In addition to the new competence of the Union in the field of energy supply, aimed at creating a genuine internal market, the provisions of the Euratom treaty with respect to nuclear safety are incorporated.

Both the common agricultural policy and common fisheries policy are modernised and disentangled from each other.

A new competition authority is created at arm's length from the European Commission in recognition of the fact that a more overtly political Commission should not also exercise quasi-judicial functions.

Other policies, such as transport and R&D, are refreshed as necessary to reflect contemporary conditions. Environment policy takes on the additional task of combating climate change.

In Part VI, current prohibitions on the harmonisation of national laws in the field of justice and interior affairs are lifted, raising the prospect of a more integrated European area of freedom, security and justice, including fully-fledged common asylum and immigration policies.

Punching its weight

In Part VIII, the treatment of common foreign and security policy (CFSP) is brought to be more closely aligned with the normal decision-making procedures, not least by enhancing the roles of the Commission and the Foreign Minister. The European Parliament is given the opportunity to exercise a right of consent if it acts within a strict time-limit. The Foreign Minister, who will be assisted by two political deputies, will continue to chair the Foreign Affairs Council but will be anchored more firmly within the Commission. (She or he, with the Treasury Minister will be senior vice-presidents of the college.) The Foreign Minister will normally represent the Union in international fora. The jurisdiction of the Court of Justice is extended over CFSP, and the scope of the flexibility clause is also widened to include CFSP. The normal procedure for the use of enhanced cooperation will now also apply to CFSP. The powers and accountability of the European Defence Agency are enhanced.

The Commission and Parliament also gain powers in the negotiation and conclusion of the Union's international treaties. Parliament's approval will be needed for all international agreements, including those in CFSP. Parliament will also be consulted over operational decisions.

Taken together, these reforms should give a much-needed impulse to the external action of the Union. The Fundamental Law simplifies and clarifies who does what in relation to common foreign, security and defence policies and to the international trade policy of the Union. We assume that a growth in mutual trust within the Council will lead to a greater willingness to use QMV, as well as agreement to let clusters of states act on behalf of the Union as a whole.

Radical constitutional changes

The Fundamental Law brings back the symbols of the Union (the flag and the anthem) which were jettisoned from the Treaty of Lisbon. It also elevates into the provisions on enlargement the critical Copenhagen criteria on good governance which must apply to candidate states.

There are two further reforms of major constitutional importance which make the Fundamental Law stand out from previous efforts at treaty revision. The first concerns the method of future treaty change. Here, we keep the method of the Convention, in which decisions are reached by consensus. But we modify the procedure for the Intergovernmental Conference to allow amendments to be agreed by three quarters of the states. The European Parliament gains the right of assent to treaty changes. Any future new treaty will enter into force either once ratified by four fifths of the states representing a majority of the EU population or, if carried in a pan-EU referendum, by a simple majority. This less rigid approach to constitutional amendment will bring the EU into line with all other international organisations and federal states, and help to avoid situations in which one recalcitrant state can take the rest hostage.

The second important constitutional change flows directly from the first. EU states cannot be forced against their will to take the federal step. At the same time, such states cannot be allowed an open-ended possibility to pick and choose what they want from the EU and discard the rest. The point has been reached when yet more *à la carte* opt-outs and derogations risk fracturing the cohesion of the *acquis communautaire*. Free-riding means disintegration.

The Fundamental Law creates a new category of associate membership for any member state which chooses not to join the more federal union. Each associate state would negotiate its own arrangement with the core states. Rights and duties would have to be clear. Institutional participation would necessarily be limited. Continued allegiance to the Union's values would be required, but political engagement in the Union's objectives would be reduced.

Associate membership could cater for the needs of Norway, Iceland and Switzerland, seeking to improve on their present unsatisfactory arrangements. Other countries, notably Turkey, choosing not to join the EU but desiring and deserving a permanent, structured relationship with it, might find associate membership to be a credible lasting settlement.

Such are the main features of the Fundamental Law, a new constitutional treaty which will strengthen the governance and cohesion of the Union and bolster democratic confidence in our common endeavour to build a better Europe.

FUNDAMENTAL LAW TEXT

COMMENT ON THE PREAMBLE

This Preamble replaces the two preambles from the Treaty on European Union (TEU) and the Treaty on the Functioning of the European Union (TFEU). It draws from the Treaty of Paris of 1951 ('destiny henceforward shared') and from the Treaty of Rome of 1957 ('ever closer union'). It introduces the idea of the interdependence of member states of the EU and asserts the openly federal character of the reformed EU which is postulated by this new Fundamental Law (FL). It defines the much misrepresented concept of federalism as 'deriving legitimacy from popular sovereignty in which no one level of government is subordinate to another but each is coordinate'.

To underline the legitimacy of the new federal union the Preamble asserts itself on behalf of 'We the Peoples of Europe' in place of the heads of the old nation states. The European peoples are to be represented in the constitutional Convention which drafts the Fundamental Law by both the member states and the institutions of the European Union (in the form of representatives of the heads of government and of European Commission, and Members of the European Parliament and national parliaments).

CURRENT TREATIES	FUNDAMENTAL LAW
PREAMBLE	**PREAMBLE**
HIS MAJESTY THE KING OF THE BELGIANS, HER MAJESTY THE QUEEN OF DENMARK, THE PRESIDENT OF THE FEDERAL REPUBLIC OF GERMANY, THE PRESIDENT OF IRELAND, THE PRESIDENT OF THE HELLENIC REPUBLIC, HIS MAJESTY THE KING OF SPAIN, THE PRESIDENT OF THE FRENCH REPUBLIC, THE PRESIDENT OF THE ITALIAN REPUBLIC, HIS ROYAL HIGHNESS THE GRAND DUKE OF LUXEMBOURG, HER MAJESTY THE QUEEN OF THE NETHERLANDS, THE PRESIDENT OF THE PORTUGUESE REPUBLIC, HER MAJESTY THE QUEEN OF THE UNITED KINGDOM OF GREAT BRITAIN AND NORTHERN IRELAND,	***WE THE PEOPLES OF EUROPE, REPRESENTED BY THE INSTITUTIONS AND MEMBER STATES OF THE EUROPEAN UNION,***
RESOLVED to mark a new stage in the process of European integration undertaken with the establishment of the European Communities,	RESOLVED to ***substitute for age-old rivalries the merging of our essential interests; to create a broad and deep community among peoples long divided; and to lay the foundations for institutions which will give direction to a destiny henceforward shared,***
RECALLING the historic importance of the ending of the division of the European continent and the need to create firm bases for the construction of the future Europe,	
CONFIRMING ***their*** attachment to the principles of liberty, democracy and respect for human rights and fundamental freedoms and of the rule of law,	CONFIRMING ***our*** attachment to the principles of liberty, democracy and respect for human rights and fundamental freedoms and of the rule of law,
CONFIRMING their attachment to fundamental social rights as defined in the European Social Charter signed at Turin on 18 October 1961 and in the 1989 Community Charter of the Fundamental Social Rights of Workers,	
DESIRING to deepen the solidarity between their peoples while respecting their history, their culture and their traditions,	DESIRING to deepen the solidarity between our peoples while respecting their history, their culture and their traditions,

DESIRING to enhance further the democratic and efficient functioning of the institutions so as to enable them better to carry out, within a single institutional framework, the tasks entrusted to them,	
RESOLVED to achieve the strengthening and the convergence of their economies and to establish an economic and monetary union including, in accordance with the provisions of this Treaty and of the Treaty on the Functioning of the European Union, a single and stable currency,	
DETERMINED to promote economic and social progress for their peoples, taking into account the principle of sustainable development and within the context of the accomplishment of the internal market and of reinforced cohesion and environmental protection, and to implement policies ensuring that advances in economic integration are accompanied by parallel progress in other fields,	
RESOLVED to establish a citizenship common to nationals of their countries,	
RESOLVED to implement a common foreign and security policy including the progressive framing of a common defence policy, which might lead to a common defence in accordance with the provisions of Article 42, thereby reinforcing the European identity and its independence in order to promote peace, security and progress in Europe and in the world,	
RESOLVED to facilitate the free movement of persons, while ensuring the safety and security of their peoples, by establishing an area of freedom, security and justice, in accordance with the provisions of this Treaty and of the Treaty on the Functioning of the European Union,	
	AFFIRMING as the essential objective of our efforts the constant improvements of the living and working conditions of the people,

	***CONFIRMING** the interdependence of the Member States of the European Union,*
RESOLVED to continue the process of creating an ever closer union among the peoples of Europe, ***in which decisions are taken as closely as possible to the citizen in accordance with the principle of subsidiarity,***	RESOLVED to continue the process of creating an ever closer union among the peoples of Europe ***by building a federal union deriving legitimacy from popular sovereignty in which no one level of government is subordinate to another but each is coordinate,***
***IN VIEW** of further steps to be taken in order to advance European integration,*	
	***RESOLVED** by thus pooling their resources to preserve and strengthen peace and liberty, and calling upon the other peoples of Europe who share their ideal to join in their efforts,*
HAVE DECIDED to establish a European Union and to this end have designated as their Plenipotentiaries:	HAVE DECIDED to establish a European Union and to this end have designated as their Plenipotentiaries: .....

PART I

CONSTITUTIONAL PROVISIONS

CHAPTER ONE

This chapter sets out in 16 articles the basic precepts, values, principles and objectives of the European Union, along with the outline of its system of governance.

Article 1 establishes that the Fundamental Law is a constitutional treaty which re-founds the EU to mark the new and necessarily more federal phase of European integration. In keeping with the Preamble, the Union's competences are conferred on it by the Member States and the citizens. The Fundamental Law replaces all the current EU treaties.

Article 2 sets out the values and Article 3 the objectives of the Union. Article 4 sets out general principles of Union law, including its own, well-attested primacy. A new paragraph 4, reflecting jurisprudence of the Court of Justice (ECJ), makes explicit the need for the states to recognise their constitutional obligations to the Union. Article 5 lays down three specific principles, namely conferral of competences, subsidiarity and proportionality.

Article 6 establishes the allegiance of the Union to fundamental rights, notably those spelled out in the Charter, which is incorporated for the first time in the treaties (as Part II). We remove the nervous constraints prescribed by the Lisbon treaty on the potential of the Charter to extend the powers of the Union. This process will accelerate once the EU has acceded to the ECHR. (Note that ex-Article 7 TEU on what happens if a state breaches fundamental rights is moved to Article 133 FL.)

Articles 7 and 8 introduce the idea of EU citizenship. A new paragraph makes it clear that the Parliament and Council form the legislature, and that the Commission is the government. Article 9 broadens the scope of the European Citizens' Initiative. Article 10 sets out the role in EU affairs of national parliaments, now including the possibility to call for a hearing on the excessive debt and deficit procedure.

Article 11 introduces the EU institutions. In Article 12 we reform the electoral law of the Parliament to include a pan-European constituency electing MEPs from transnational party lists. An arithmetical formula for the apportionment of the rest of the seats is foreseen. Parliament's basic voting procedures are prescribed.

Article 13 redefines and limits the role of the European Council as taking responsibility for the direction and coordination of the business of the Council of ministers. The heads of government may meet in the formation of the General Affairs Council. The President of the European Council will be elected by his or her peers, and shall report more frequently to the Parliament. The Presidents of the Commission and Parliament will participate in meetings of the European Council.

Article 14 redefines the role of the Council of ministers in the main not as an executive authority but as a legislative chamber. The Council will have two basic, simplified voting procedures. The Foreign Minister continues to chair the Council of Foreign Affairs. Otherwise, the current rotating presidency is abolished in favour of each formation electing its own chair, coordinated by the General Affairs Council. The chair of the Council of Economic and Financial Affairs will chair the Eurogroup.

Article 15 is the cardinal provision about the Commission. Among the modifications are that: (a) the Commission's legislative duties are enlarged; (b) Parliament and Council may, as a last resort, take over the Commission's right of legislative initiative; (c) the size of the Commission is to be decided by its President-elect, who will nominate the other members of the college; (d) Commissioners-designate will be subject to Parliamentary hearings; (e) the Commission may now only be censured by the Parliament, acting by an absolute majority (rather than two thirds), in a constructive vote of no confidence. The Foreign Minister and Treasury Minister will be Commission Vice-Presidents.

Article 16 introduces the Court of Justice, and permits the proposed new category of associate states to appoint judges.

COMMON PROVISIONS	MAIN ARTICLES
Article 1	Article 1 (ex-Article 1 TEU)
By this Treaty, the HIGH CONTRACTING PARTIES establish among themselves a EUROPEAN UNION, hereinafter called 'the Union', on which the Member States confer competences to attain objectives they have in common. This Treaty marks a new stage in the process of creating ***an ever closer*** union among the peoples of Europe, in which decisions are taken as openly as possible and as closely as possible to the citizen. The Union ***shall be founded*** on the present ***Treaty and on the Treaty on the Functioning of the European Union (hereinafter referred to as 'the Treaties'). Those two Treaties shall have the same legal value. The Union shall replace and succeed the European Community.***	By this ***constitutional*** treaty, the HIGH CONTRACTING PARTIES establish among themselves a EUROPEAN UNION, hereinafter called 'the Union', on which ***its States and citizens*** confer competences to attain objectives they have in common. This Treaty marks a new stage in the process of creating ***a federal*** union among the peoples of Europe, in which decisions are taken as openly as possible and as closely as possible to the citizen. The Union ***is re-founded*** on the present ***Fundamental Law of the European Union which shall replace and succeed the Treaty on European Union, the Treaty on the Functioning of the European Union and the Treaty establishing the European Atomic Energy Community.***
Article 2	Article 2 (ex-Article 2 TEU)
The Union is founded on the values of respect for human dignity, freedom, democracy, equality, the rule of law and respect for human rights, including the rights of persons belonging to minorities. These values are common to the Member States in a society in which pluralism, non-discrimination, tolerance, justice, solidarity and equality between women and men prevail.	The Union is founded on the values of respect for human dignity, freedom, democracy, equality, the rule of law and respect for human rights, including the rights of persons belonging to minorities. These values are common to its States ***and citizens*** in a society in which pluralism, non-discrimination, tolerance, justice, solidarity and equality between women and men prevail.

Article 3	Article 3 (ex-Article 3 TEU)
1. The Union's aim is to promote peace, its values and the well-being of its peoples.	1. The Union's aim is to promote peace, its values and the well-being of its peoples.
2. The Union shall offer its citizens an area of freedom, security and justice without internal frontiers, in which the free movement of persons is ensured in conjunction with appropriate measures with respect to external border controls, asylum, immigration and the prevention and combating of crime.	2. The Union shall offer its citizens an area of freedom, security and justice without internal frontiers, in which the free movement of persons is ensured in conjunction with appropriate measures with respect to external border controls, asylum, immigration and the prevention and combating of crime.
3. The Union shall establish an internal market. It shall work for the sustainable development of Europe based on balanced economic growth and price stability, a highly competitive social market economy, aiming at full employment and social progress, and a high level of protection and improvement of the quality of the environment. It shall promote scientific and technological advance.	3. The Union shall establish an internal market. It shall work for the sustainable development of Europe based on balanced economic growth and price stability, a highly competitive social market economy, aiming at full employment and social progress, and a high level of protection and improvement of the quality of the environment. It shall promote scientific and technological advance.
It shall combat social exclusion and discrimination, and shall promote social justice and protection, equality between women and men, solidarity between generations and protection of the rights of the child.	It shall combat social exclusion and discrimination, and shall promote social justice and protection, equality between women and men, solidarity between generations and protection of the rights of the child.
It shall promote economic, social and territorial cohesion, and solidarity among Member States.	It shall promote economic, social and territorial cohesion, and solidarity among its States ***and citizens***.
It shall respect its rich cultural and linguistic diversity, and shall ensure that Europe's cultural heritage is safeguarded and enhanced.	It shall respect its rich cultural and linguistic diversity, and shall ensure that Europe's cultural heritage is safeguarded and enhanced.
4. The Union shall establish an economic and monetary union whose currency is the euro.	4. The Union shall establish an economic and monetary union whose currency is the euro.

5. In its relations with the wider world, the Union shall uphold and promote its values and interests and contribute to the protection of its citizens. It shall contribute to peace, security, the sustainable development of the Earth, solidarity and mutual respect among peoples, free and fair trade, eradication of poverty and the protection of human rights, in particular the rights of the child, as well as to the strict observance and the development of international law, including respect for the principles of the United Nations Charter.	5. In its relations with the wider world, the Union shall uphold and promote its values and interests and contribute to the protection of its citizens. It shall contribute to peace, security, the sustainable development of the Earth, solidarity and mutual respect among peoples, free and fair trade, eradication of poverty and the protection of human rights, in particular the rights of the child, as well as to the strict observance and the development of international law, including respect for the principles of the United Nations Charter.
6. The Union shall pursue its objectives by appropriate means commensurate with the competences which are conferred upon it ***in the Treaties.***	6. The Union shall pursue its objectives by appropriate means commensurate with the competences which are conferred upon it ***under this Fundamental Law.***
Article 4	Article 4 (ex-Article 4 TEU)
1. ***In accordance with Article 5, competences not conferred upon the Union in the Treaties remain with the Member States.***	1. The Union shall respect the equality of ***its States under the Fundamental Law*** as well as their national identities, inherent in their fundamental structures, political and constitutional, inclusive of regional and local self-government. It shall respect their essential state functions, including ensuring the territorial integrity of the State, maintaining law and order and safeguarding State security.
2. The Union shall respect the equality of Member States before the Treaties as well as their national identities, inherent in their fundamental structures, political and constitutional, inclusive of regional and local self-government. It shall respect their essential State functions, including ensuring the territorial integrity of the State, maintaining law and order and safeguarding national security. ***In particular, national security remains the sole responsibility of each Member State.***	***2. The Fundamental Law and the law adopted by the Union on the basis of the Fundamental Law have primacy over the law of its States.***
3. Pursuant to the principle of sincere cooperation, the Union and the Member States shall, in full mutual respect, assist each other in carrying out tasks which flow from the Treaties.	3. Pursuant to the principle of sincere cooperation, the Union and its States shall, in full mutual respect, assist each other in carrying out tasks which flow from the Fundamental Law.
The Member States shall take any appropriate measure, general or particular, to ensure fulfilment of the obligations arising out of the Treaties or resulting from the acts of the institutions of the Union.	The States shall take any appropriate measure, general or particular, to ensure fulfilment of the obligations arising out of the Fundamental Law or resulting from the acts of the institutions of the Union.

The Member States shall facilitate the achievement of the Union's tasks and refrain from any measure which could jeopardise the attainment of the Union's objectives.	The States shall facilitate the achievement of the Union's tasks and refrain from any measure which could jeopardise the attainment of the Union's objectives. ***4. When undertaking constitutional reform at the national level, the States shall comply with their obligations as a state of the Union and pay due regard to the principles on which the Union is founded.***
Article 5	Article 5 (ex-Article 5 TEU)
1. The limits of Union competences are governed by the principle of conferral. The use of Union competences is governed by the principles of subsidiarity and proportionality.	1. The limits of Union competences are governed by the principle of conferral. The use of Union competences is governed by the principles of subsidiarity and proportionality.
2. Under the principle of conferral, the Union shall act only within the limits of the competences conferred upon it by the Member States in the Treaties to attain the objectives set out therein. Competences not conferred upon the Union in the Treaties remain with the Member States.	2. Under the principle of conferral, the Union shall act only within the limits of the competences conferred upon it by its States ***and citizens under the Fundamental Law*** to attain the objectives set out therein. Competences not conferred upon the Union ***under the Fundamental Law*** remain with the States.
3. Under the principle of subsidiarity, in areas which do not fall within its exclusive competence, the Union shall act only if and in so far as the objectives of the proposed action cannot be sufficiently achieved by the Member States, either at central level or at regional and local level, but can rather, by reason of the scale or effects of the proposed action, be better achieved at Union level.	3. Under the principle of subsidiarity, in areas which do not fall within its exclusive competence, the Union shall act only if and in so far as the objectives of the proposed action cannot be sufficiently achieved by its States, either at central level or at regional and local level, but can rather, by reason of the scale or effects of the proposed action, be better achieved at Union level.
The institutions of the Union shall apply the principle of subsidiarity as laid down in the Protocol on the application of the principles of subsidiarity and proportionality. National Parliaments ensure compliance with the principle of subsidiarity in accordance with the procedure set out in that Protocol.	The institutions of the Union shall apply the principle of subsidiarity as laid down in Protocol No 2 on the application of the principles of subsidiarity and proportionality. State Parliaments ensure compliance with the principle of subsidiarity in accordance with the procedure set out in that Protocol.
4. Under the principle of proportionality, the content and form of Union action shall not exceed what is necessary to achieve the objectives of the Treaties.	4. Under the principle of proportionality, the content and form of Union action shall not exceed what is necessary to achieve the objectives of the Fundamental Law.

The institutions of the Union shall apply the principle of proportionality as laid down in the Protocol on the application of the principles of subsidiarity and proportionality.	The institutions of the Union shall apply the principle of proportionality as laid down in the Protocol on the application of the principles of subsidiarity and proportionality.
Article 6	Article 6 (ex-Article 6 TEU)
1. The Union recognises the rights, freedoms and principles set out in the Charter of Fundamental Rights of the European Union of 7 December 2000, as adapted at Strasbourg, on 12 December 2007, which shall have the same legal value as the Treaties. ***The provisions of the Charter shall not extend in any way the competences of the Union as defined in the Treaties.*** ***The rights, freedoms and principles in the Charter shall be interpreted in accordance with the general provisions in Title VII of the Charter governing its interpretation and application and with due regard to the explanations referred to in the Charter, that set out the sources of those provisions.***	1. The Union recognises ***and promotes*** the rights, freedoms and principles set out in the Charter of Fundamental Rights of the European Union ***as laid down in Part Two of the Fundamental Law.***
2. The Union shall accede to the European Convention for the Protection of Human Rights and Fundamental Freedoms. ***Such accession shall not affect the Union's competences as defined in the Treaties.***	2. The Union shall accede to the European Convention for the Protection of Human Rights and Fundamental Freedoms.
3. Fundamental rights, as guaranteed by the European Convention for the Protection of Human Rights and Fundamental Freedoms and as they result from the constitutional traditions common to the Member States, shall constitute general principles of the Union's law.	3. Fundamental rights, as guaranteed by ***the Charter of Fundamental Rights of the European Union***, the European Convention for the Protection of Human Rights and Fundamental Freedoms and as they result from the constitutional traditions common to the States, shall constitute general principles of the Union's law. ***4. The Union shall act in the case of a serious or a persistent breach of fundamental rights by a State or Associate State in accordance with the provisions of Articles 133 and 134.***
Article 7	[delete]

Article 8 ……	[delete]
PROVISIONS ON DEMOCRATIC PRINCIPLES	DEMOCRATIC PRINCIPLES
Article 9	Article 7 (ex-Article 9 TEU)
In all its activities, the Union shall observe the principle of the equality of its citizens, who shall receive equal attention from its institutions, bodies, offices and agencies. Every national of a Member State shall be a citizen of the Union. Citizenship of the Union shall be additional to and not replace national citizenship.	In all its activities, the Union shall observe the principle of the equality of its citizens, who shall receive equal attention from its institutions, bodies, offices and agencies. Every national of a State shall be a citizen of the Union. Citizenship of the Union shall be additional to and not replace State citizenship.
Article 10	Article 8 (ex-Article 10 TEU)
1. The functioning of the Union shall be founded on representative democracy.	1. The functioning of the Union shall be founded on representative democracy.
2. Citizens are directly represented at Union level in the European Parliament.	2. Citizens are directly represented at Union level in the European Parliament.
Member States are represented in the European Council by their Heads of State or Government and in the Council by their governments, themselves democratically accountable either to their national Parliaments, or to their citizens.	States are represented in the European Council by their Heads of State or Government and in the Council by their governments, themselves democratically accountable either to their State Parliaments, or to their citizens.
	3. The European Parliament and the Council form the two chambers of the Union legislature. The European Commission is the government of the Union and is appointed by and answerable to the legislature.
3. Every citizen shall have the right to participate in the democratic life of the Union. Decisions shall be taken as openly and as closely as possible to the citizen.	4. Every citizen shall have the right to participate in the democratic life of the Union. Decisions shall be taken as openly and as closely as possible to the citizen.
4. Political parties at European level contribute to forming European political awareness and to expressing the will of citizens of the Union.	5. Political parties at European level contribute to forming European political awareness and to expressing the will of citizens of the Union.

Article 11	Article 9 (ex-Article 11 TEU)
1. The institutions shall, by appropriate means, give citizens and representative associations the opportunity to make known and publicly exchange their views in all areas of Union action.	1. The institutions shall, by appropriate means, give citizens and representative associations the opportunity to make known and publicly exchange their views in all areas of Union action.
2. The institutions shall maintain an open, transparent and regular dialogue with representative associations and civil society.	2. The institutions shall maintain an open, transparent and regular dialogue with representative associations and civil society.
3. The European Commission shall carry out broad consultations with parties concerned in order to ensure that the Union's actions are coherent and transparent.	3. The European Commission shall carry out broad consultations with parties concerned in order to ensure that the Union's actions are coherent and transparent.
4. Not less than one million citizens who are nationals of a significant number of Member States may take the initiative of inviting the ***European Commission, within the framework of its powers, to submit any appropriate proposal on matters where citizens consider that a legal act of the Union is required for the purpose of implementing the Treaties.***	4. Not less than one million citizens who are nationals of a significant number of States may take the initiative of inviting the European Commission, ***the European Parliament or the Council***, within the framework of ***their*** powers ***and in accordance with the Fundamental Law, to take a legislative initiative.***
The procedures and conditions required for such a citizens' initiative shall be determined in accordance with the first paragraph of Article 24 of the Treaty on the Functioning of the European Union.	

Article 12	Article 10 (ex-Article 12 TEU)
National Parliaments contribute actively to the good functioning of the Union:	State Parliaments contribute actively to the good functioning of the Union:
(a) through being informed by the institutions of the Union and having draft legislative acts of the Union forwarded to them in accordance with the Protocol on the role of national Parliaments in the European Union;	(a) through being informed by the institutions of the Union and having draft legislative acts of the Union forwarded to them in accordance with the Protocol No 1 on the role of State Parliaments in the European Union;
(b) by seeing to it that the principle of subsidiarity is respected in accordance with the procedures provided for in the Protocol on the application of the principles of subsidiarity and proportionality;	(b) by seeing to it that the principle of subsidiarity is respected in accordance with the procedures provided for in the Protocol No 2 on the application of the principles of subsidiarity and proportionality;
(c) by taking part, within the framework of the area of freedom, security and justice, in the evaluation mechanisms for the implementation of the Union policies in that area, ***in accordance with Article 70 of the Treaty on the Functioning of the European Union, and through being involved in the political monitoring of Europol and the evaluation of Eurojust's activities in accordance with Articles 88 and 85 of that Treaty;***	(c) by taking part, within the framework of the area of freedom, security and justice, in the evaluation mechanisms for the implementation of the Union policies in that area; ***(d) by requiring the European Parliament to hold a hearing with the Council and Commission in the case of an excessive deficit procedure;***
(d) by taking part in the revision procedures of the Treaties, in accordance with Article 48 of this Treaty;	(e) by taking part in the revision procedures of the Fundamental Law, in accordance with Article 135;
(e) by being notified of applications for accession to the Union, in accordance with Article 49 of this Treaty;	(f) by being notified of applications for accession to the Union, in accordance with Article 136;
	(g) by being notified of applications for associate membership of the Union, in accordance with Article 137;
(f) by taking part in the inter parliamentary cooperation between national Parliaments and with the European Parliament, in accordance with the Protocol on the role of national Parliaments in the European Union.	(h) by taking part in the inter-parliamentary cooperation between State Parliaments and with the European Parliament, in accordance with Protocol No 1.

PROVISIONS ON THE INSTITUTIONS	THE GOVERNANCE OF THE UNION
Article 13	Article 11 (ex-Article 9 TEU)
1. The Union shall have an institutional framework which shall aim to promote its values, advance its objectives, serve its interests, those of its citizens and those of the Member States, and ensure the consistency, effectiveness and continuity of its policies and actions.	1. The Union shall have an institutional framework which shall aim to promote its values, advance its objectives, serve its interests, those of its citizens and those of the States, and ensure the consistency, effectiveness and continuity of its policies and actions.
The Union's institutions shall be:	The Union's institutions shall be:
– the European Parliament,	– the European Parliament,
– the European Council,	– the European Council,
– the Council,	– the Council,
– the European Commission (hereinafter referred to as 'the Commission'),	– the European Commission (hereinafter referred to as 'the Commission'),
– the Court of Justice of the European Union,	– the Court of Justice of the European Union,
– the European Central Bank,	– the European Central Bank,
– the Court of Auditors.	– the Court of Auditors.
2. Each institution shall act within the limits of the powers conferred on it in the Treaties, and in conformity with the procedures, conditions and objectives set out in them. The institutions shall practice mutual sincere cooperation.	2. Each institution shall act within the limits of the powers conferred on it ***by the Fundamental Law***, and in conformity with the procedures, conditions and objectives set out in ***it***. The institutions shall practice mutual sincere cooperation.
3. ***The provisions relating to the European Central Bank and the Court of Auditors and detailed provisions on the other institutions are set out in the Treaty on the Functioning of the European Union.***	

4. The European Parliament, the Council and the Commission shall be assisted by an Economic and Social Committee and a Committee of the Regions acting in an advisory capacity.	3. The European Parliament, the Council and the Commission shall be assisted by an Economic and Social Committee and a Committee of the Regions acting in an advisory capacity.
Article 14	Article 12 (ex-Article 14 TEU)
1. The European Parliament shall, jointly with the Council, exercise legislative and budgetary functions. It shall exercise functions of political control and consultation as laid down in the Treaties. It shall elect the President of the Commission.	1. The European Parliament shall, jointly with the Council, ***form the legislature of the Union. It shall*** exercise legislative and budgetary functions ***and*** functions of political control and consultation as laid down in the Fundamental Law. It shall elect the President of the Commission.
2. The European Parliament shall be composed of representatives of the Union's citizens. They shall not exceed seven hundred and fifty in number, plus the President. ***Representation of citizens shall be degressively proportional, with a minimum threshold of six members per Member State. No Member State shall be allocated more than ninety-six seats.*** ***The European Council shall adopt by unanimity,*** on the initiative of the European Parliament ***and with its consent,*** a decision establishing the ***composition*** of the European Parliament, respecting the principles referred to in ***the first subparagraph.***	2. The European Parliament shall be composed of representatives of the Union's citizens. They shall not exceed seven hundred and fifty in number, plus the President. ***3. A certain number of Members of the Parliament shall be elected in the States. That number shall be apportioned to the States according to the principle of degressive proportionality,*** with a minimum ***base*** of ***five*** Members per ***State. In addition, a certain number of Members of the Parliament shall be elected in a single constituency comprising the whole territory of the Union.*** ***4. Before the end of the fourth calendar year of each parliamentary term, the European Parliament, acting on its own initiative, and the Council may adopt, in accordance with the special legislative procedure,*** a decision establishing ***the apportionment of seats and the electoral procedure which will apply at the subsequent election of the Parliament.*** This decision shall respect the principles referred to in ***paragraphs 2 and 3 and the provisions of Protocol No 3.***
3. The members of the European Parliament shall be elected for a term of five years by direct universal suffrage in a free and secret ballot.	5. The Members of the European Parliament shall be elected for a term of five years by direct universal suffrage in a free and secret ballot.

4. The European Parliament shall elect its President and its officers from among its members.	6. The European Parliament shall elect its President and its officers from among its Members. ***7. Save as otherwise provided in the Fundamental Law, the European Parliament shall act by a majority of the votes cast.*** ***8. Under the special legislative procedure, the European Parliament shall act by a majority of its component Members.***
Article 15	Article 13 (ex-Article 15 TEU)
1. The European Council shall provide the ***Union*** with the necessary impetus ***for its development*** and shall define the general political directions and priorities thereof. ***It shall not exercise legislative functions.***	1. The European Council ***shall define the general political direction and priorities of the Council.***
2. The European Council shall consist of the Heads of State or Government of the Member States, ***together with its President and*** the President of the Commission. ***The High Representative of the Union for Foreign Affairs and Security Policy shall take part in its work.***	2. The European Council shall consist of the Heads of State or Government of the States. The President of the Commission, ***the President of the European Parliament and the President of the European Central Bank may participate in its meetings.***
3. The European Council shall meet twice every six months, convened by its President. When the agenda so requires, the members of the European Council may decide each to be assisted by a minister and, in the case of the President of the Commission, by a member of the Commission. When the situation so requires, the President shall convene a special meeting of the European Council. 4. Except where the Treaties provide otherwise, decisions of the European Council shall be taken by consensus.	3. The European Council shall meet twice every six months, convened by its President. When the situation so requires, the President shall convene a special meeting of the European Council. Except where the Fundamental Law provides otherwise, decisions of the European Council shall be taken by consensus. ***Without prejudice to the first subparagraph, the European Council may meet in the formation of the General Affairs Council.***

5. The European Council shall elect its President, by a qualified majority, for a term of two and a half years, renewable once. ***In the event of an impediment or serious misconduct, the European Council can end the President's term of office in accordance with the same procedure.***	5. The European Council shall elect its President, by a qualified majority, for a term of two and a half years, renewable once. The President shall present a report to the European Parliament ***before and*** after each of the meetings of the European Council.
6. The President of the European Council: ***(a) shall chair it and drive forward its work;*** ***(b) shall ensure the preparation and continuity of the work of the European Council in cooperation with the President of the Commission, and on the basis of the work of the General Affairs Council;*** ***(c) shall endeavour to facilitate cohesion and consensus within the European Council;*** (d) shall present a report to the European Parliament after each of the meetings of the European Council. ***The President of the European Council shall, at his level and in that capacity, ensure the external representation of the Union on issues concerning its common foreign and security policy, without prejudice to the powers of the High Representative of the Union for Foreign Affairs and Security Policy.*** ***The President of the European Council shall not hold a national office.***	
Article 16	Article 14 (ex-16 TEU & 238 TFEU)
1. The Council shall, jointly with the European Parliament, exercise legislative and budgetary functions. It shall carry out ***policy-making and coordinating functions*** as laid down in the Treaties.	1. The Council shall, jointly with the European Parliament, ***form the legislature of the Union***. It shall exercise legislative and budgetary functions. It shall carry out ***other*** functions as laid down in the Fundamental Law.

2. The Council shall consist of a representative of each Member State at ministerial level, who ***may*** commit the government of the Member State in question and cast its vote.	2. The Council shall consist of a representative of ***the government of*** each State, who ***shall*** commit the government of the State in question and cast its vote.
3. The Council shall act by a qualified majority except where the Treaties provide otherwise.	3. The Council shall act by a qualified majority except where the Fundamental Law provides otherwise. Where it is required to act by a simple majority, the Council shall act by a majority of its component members. Absence or abstentions by Members present in person or represented shall not prevent the adoption by the Council of acts which require unanimity.
4. ***As from 1 November 2014***, a qualified majority shall be defined as at least 55 % of the members of the Council, comprising at least fifteen of them and representing Member States comprising at least 65 % of the population of the Union. ***A blocking minority must include at least four Council members, failing which the qualified majority shall be deemed attained.*** ***The other arrangements governing the qualified majority are laid down in Article 238(2) of the Treaty on the Functioning of the European Union.***	***4. Under the ordinary legislative procedure, the qualified majority in the Council shall be defined as at least 55% of the members of the Council representing the participating States comprising at least 65% of the population of these States.***
5. The transitional provisions relating to the definition of the qualified majority which shall be applicable until 31 October 2014 and those which shall be applicable from 1 November 2014 to 31 March 2017 are laid down in the Protocol on transitional provisions.	***5. Under the special legislative procedure, the qualified majority in the Council shall be defined as at least two thirds of the members of the Council representing the States comprising at least 75% of the population of the Union;***

6. The Council shall meet in different configurations, ***the list of which shall be adopted in accordance with Article 236 of the Treaty on the Functioning of the European Union.***	6. The Council shall meet in different configurations.
The General Affairs Council shall ensure consistency in the work of the different Council configurations. It shall prepare and ensure the follow-up to meetings of the European Council, in liaison with the President of the ***European Council and the*** Commission.	The General Affairs Council shall ensure consistency ***and coordination*** in the work of the different Council configurations. It shall prepare and ensure the follow-up to meetings of the European Council, in liaison with ***the President of the European Parliament and*** the President of the Commission.
The Foreign Affairs Council shall elaborate the Union's external action on the basis of strategic guidelines laid down by the European Council and ensure that the Union's action is consistent.	
7. A Committee of Permanent Representatives of the Governments of the Member States shall be responsible for preparing the work of the Council.	7. A Committee of Permanent Representatives of the Governments of the Member States shall be responsible for preparing the work of the Council.
8. The Council shall meet in public when it deliberates and votes on a draft legislative act. To this end, each Council meeting shall be divided into two parts, dealing respectively with deliberations on Union legislative acts and non-legislative activities.	8. The Council shall meet in public when it deliberates and votes on a draft legislative act. To this end, each Council meeting shall be divided into two parts, dealing respectively with deliberations on Union legislative acts and non-legislative activities.
9. The ***Presidency*** of Council configurations, other than that of Foreign Affairs, shall be held ***by Member State representatives in the Council on the basis of equal rotation, in accordance with the conditions established in accordance with Article 236 of the Treaty on the Functioning of the European Union.***	9. The ***Chairs*** of the Council configurations, other than that of Foreign Affairs, shall be held ***by one of the members of each Council for a period of two and a half years. The term of the Chair shall be renewable once. The election of the Chair shall be by simple majority.***
	In the case that no decision can be reached within a reasonable time on the election of a Chair to a configuration of the Council, the matter shall be referred to the European Council, which shall take a decision by qualified majority.
	10. The chair of the Council of Foreign Affairs will be held by the Foreign Minister.
	The chair of the Council of Economic and Financial Affairs will chair the Eurogroup.

Article 17	Article 15 (ex-Article 17 TEU)
1. The Commission shall promote the general interest of the Union and take appropriate initiatives to that end. It shall ensure the application of the Treaties, and of measures adopted by the institutions pursuant to them. It shall oversee the application of Union law under the control of the Court of Justice of the European Union. It shall execute the budget and manage programmes. It shall exercise coordinating, executive and management functions, as laid down in the Treaties. With the exception of the common foreign and security policy, and other cases provided for in the Treaties, it shall ensure the Union's external representation. It shall initiate the Union's annual and multiannual programming with a view to achieving interinstitutional agreements.	1. The Commission shall promote the general interest of the Union and take appropriate initiatives to that end. It shall ensure the application of the Fundamental Law, and of measures adopted by the institutions pursuant to ***it***. It shall oversee the application of Union law under the control of the Court of Justice of the European Union. It shall execute the budget and manage programmes. It shall exercise ***the*** coordinating, executive and management functions ***of the federal government of the Union***, as laid down in the Fundamental Law. It shall ensure the Union's external representation. It shall initiate the Union's annual and multiannual programming with a view to achieving interinstitutional agreements.
2. Union legislative acts may only be adopted on the basis of a Commission proposal, except where the Treaties provide otherwise. Other acts shall be adopted on the basis of a Commission proposal where the Treaties so provide.	2. Union legislative acts may only be adopted on the basis of a Commission proposal, except where the Fundamental Law provides otherwise. ***The Commission shall undertake appropriate consultations with interested parties before taking a legislative initiative, and shall publish an impact assessment of the proposed measure.***
	3. Either the European Parliament or the Council may request the Commission to submit any appropriate proposal on matters on which they consider that a Union act is required for the purpose of implementing the Fundamental Law. If, within three months, the Commission decides not to submit a proposal, it shall inform the legislature of its reasons for not doing so.
	In that case, either the European Parliament or the Council may make a proposal for a legislative act, after having followed similar consultation and assessment procedures as those laid down in paragraph 2. The ordinary legislative procedure shall then apply in accordance with Article 87.

3. The Commission's term of office shall be five years.

The members of the Commission shall be chosen on the ground of their general competence and European commitment from persons whose independence is beyond doubt.

In carrying out its responsibilities, the Commission shall be completely independent. Without prejudice to Article 18(2), the members of the Commission shall neither seek nor take instructions from any Government or other institution, body, office or entity. They shall refrain from any action incompatible with their duties or the performance of their tasks.

4. The Commission appointed between the date of entry into force of the Treaty of Lisbon and 31 October 2014, shall consist of one national of each Member State, including its President and the High Representative of the Union for Foreign Affairs and Security Policy who shall be one of its Vice-Presidents.

5. As from 1 November 2014, the Commission shall consist of a number of members, including its President and the High Representative of the Union for Foreign Affairs and Security Policy, corresponding to two thirds of the number of Member States, unless the European Council, acting unanimously, decides to alter this number.

The members of the Commission shall be chosen from among the nationals of the Member States on the basis of a system of strictly equal rotation between the Member States, reflecting the demographic and geographical range of all the Member States. This system shall be established unanimously by the European Council in accordance with Article 244 of the Treaty on the Functioning of the European Union.

4. The Commission's term of office shall be five years.

The members of the Commission shall be chosen on the ground of their general competence and European commitment from persons whose independence is beyond doubt.

In carrying out its responsibilities, the Commission shall be completely independent. The members of the Commission shall neither seek nor take instructions from any Government or other institution, body, office or entity. They shall refrain from any action incompatible with their duties or the performance of their tasks.

5. The number of the Members of the Commission, which shall not exceed the number of States, shall be determined by its President. The Foreign Minister and the Treasury Minister shall both be Vice-Presidents.

6. The President of the Commission shall:

(a) lay down guidelines within which the Commission is to work;

(b) decide on the internal organisation of the Commission, ensuring that it acts consistently, efficiently and as a collegiate body;

(c) appoint Vice-Presidents, other than the High Representative of the Union for Foreign Affairs and Security Policy, from among the members of the Commission.

A member of the Commission shall resign if the President so requests. ***The High Representative of the Union for Foreign Affairs and Security Policy shall resign, in accordance with the procedure set out in Article 18(1), if the President so requests.***

7. Taking into account the elections to the European Parliament and after having held the appropriate consultations, the European Council, acting by a qualified majority, shall propose to the European Parliament a candidate for President of the Commission. This candidate shall be elected by the European Parliament by a majority of its component members. If he does not obtain the required majority, the European Council, acting by a qualified majority, shall within one month propose a new candidate who shall be elected by the European Parliament following the same procedure.

The Council, by common accord with the President-elect, shall adopt the list of the other persons whom it proposes for appointment as members of the Commission. ***They shall be selected, on the basis of the suggestions made by Member States, in accordance with the criteria set out in paragraph 3, second subparagraph, and paragraph 5, second subparagraph.***

6. The President of the Commission shall:

(a) ***chair the Commission and drive forward its work;***

(b) decide on the internal organisation of the Commission, ensuring that it acts consistently, efficiently and as a collegiate body;

(c) ***ensure the external representation of the Union.***

A member of the Commission shall resign if the President so requests.

7. Taking into account the elections to the European Parliament and after having held the appropriate consultations, the European Council, acting by a qualified majority, shall propose to the European Parliament a candidate for President of the Commission. This candidate shall be elected by the Parliament by a majority of its component members. If he ***or she*** does not obtain the required majority, the European Council, acting by a qualified majority, shall within one month propose a new candidate who shall be elected by the Parliament following the same procedure.

The President, ***the High Representative of the Union for Foreign Affairs and Security Policy and*** the other members of the Commission shall be subject as a body to a vote of consent by the European Parliament. On the basis of this consent the Commission shall be appointed by the European Council, acting by a qualified majority.	
8. The Commission, ***as a body***, shall be responsible to the European Parliament. ***In accordance with Article 234 of the Treaty on the Functioning of the European Union***, the European Parliament may vote *on a motion of censure of the Commission.* ***If such a motion is carried, the members of the Commission shall resign as a body and the High Representative of the Union for Foreign Affairs and Security Policy shall resign from the duties that he carries out in the Commission.***	8. The ***President-elect, after consulting the Council***, shall ***present to the European Parliament*** the list of the other persons whom ***he or she*** proposes for appointment as members of the Commission. ***9. Each Commissioner-designate shall be heard in public by the European Parliament, which shall be accorded any information relevant to its evaluation of the aptitude of the Commissioners-designate on the basis of the criteria laid down in paragraph 3.*** 10. The President and the other members of the Commission shall be subject as a body to a vote of consent by the European Parliament. On the basis of this consent the Commission shall be appointed by the ***Council***, acting by a qualified majority. 11. The Commission shall be responsible to the European Parliament. ***The Parliament, acting by a majority of its component Members, may vote a loss of confidence in an individual member of the Commission. In the case that the vote is carried, the President of the Commission shall request the resignation of that member or shall appear before the Parliament to explain why he or she has not done so.*** 12. The European Parliament, ***acting by a majority of its component Members***, may vote ***to censure the Commission only by nominating a successor President of the Commission. In that case, the European Council shall accept that candidate as the nomination for the new President of the Commission pursuant to paragraph 7.***
Article 18	[delete]

Article 19

1. The Court of Justice of the European Union shall include the Court of Justice, the General Court and specialised courts. It shall ensure that in the interpretation and application of the Treaties the law is observed.

Member States shall provide remedies sufficient to ensure effective legal protection in the fields covered by Union law.

2. The Court of Justice shall consist of one judge from each Member State. It shall be assisted by Advocates-General.

The General Court shall include at least one judge per Member State.

The Judges and the Advocates-General of the Court of Justice and the Judges of the General Court shall be chosen from persons whose independence is beyond doubt and who satisfy the conditions set out in Articles 253 and 254 of the Treaty on the Functioning of the European Union. They shall be appointed by common accord of the governments of the Member States for six years. Retiring Judges and Advocates-General may be reappointed.

Article 16
(ex-Article 19 TEU)

1. The Court of Justice of the European Union shall include the Court of Justice, the General Court and specialised courts. It shall ensure that in the interpretation and application of the Fundamental Law the law is observed.

The States shall provide remedies sufficient to ensure effective legal protection in the fields covered by Union law.

2. The Court of Justice shall consist of ***at least*** one judge from each State ***and Associate State.*** It shall be assisted by Advocates-General.

The General Court shall include at least one judge per State ***and Associate State.***

Judges from Associate States shall not sit in cases that do not relate to the law applicable to those Associate States.

The Judges and the Advocates-General of the Court of Justice and the Judges of the General Court shall be chosen from persons whose independence is beyond doubt and who satisfy the conditions set out in Articles 49 and 50. They shall be appointed by common accord of the governments of the States for six years. Retiring Judges and Advocates-General may be reappointed.

3. The Court of Justice of the European Union shall, in accordance with the Treaties:	3. The Court of Justice of the European Union shall, in accordance with the Treaties:
(a) rule on actions brought by a Member State, an institution or a natural or legal person;	(a) rule on actions brought by a State, ***an Associate State***, an institution or a natural or legal person;
(b) give preliminary rulings, at the request of courts or tribunals of the Member States, on the interpretation of Union law or the validity of acts adopted by the institutions;	(b) give preliminary rulings, at the request of courts or tribunals of the States ***or of the Associated States***, on the interpretation of Union law or the validity of acts adopted by the institutions;
(c) rule in other cases provided for in the Treaties.	(c) rule in other cases provided for in the Fundamental Law.

POWERS AND COMPETENCES

CHAPTER TWO

The six articles of Chapter Two deal in more detail with the powers of the institutions and the competences of the Union.

Article 17 lays down the three categories of competence: exclusive, shared and supplementary. It removes the blanket restriction in the area of the Union's supplementary competence that prohibits the harmonisation of national laws.

Articles 18–20 spell out which policy sector falls within each of three categories of competence. The main changes are to make nuclear safety an exclusive competence (consequent on the incorporation of the Euratom Treaty), and to promote economic, fiscal and employment policies, as well as the common foreign, security and defence policies as normal shared competences between the Union and its States.

Article 21 is the famous 'flexibility' clause which allows the EU to act within its competences when the Treaty has not provided the necessary powers. The scope of the article is widened to include common foreign and security policy. Under the present treaties, this article operates under a special law of the Council, decided by unanimity: in the Fundamental Law it becomes a normal law of the Parliament and Council subject to the special legislative procedure.

Article 22 creates a formal legal base for the setting up of Union agencies, most of which have been previously established under the flexibility clause.

CATEGORIES AND AREAS OF UNION COMPETENCE	CATEGORIES OF UNION COMPETENCE
PREAMBLE TFEU	[delete]
Article 1 TFEU	[delete]
Article 2	Article 17 (ex-Article 2 TFEU)
1. When the Treaties confer on the Union exclusive competence in a specific area, only the Union may legislate and adopt legally binding acts, the Member States being able to do so themselves only if so empowered by the Union or for the implementation of Union acts.	1. When the Fundamental Law confers on the Union exclusive competence in a specific area, only the Union may legislate and adopt legally binding acts, the States being able to do so themselves only if so empowered by the Union or for the implementation of Union acts.
2. When the Treaties confer on the Union a competence shared with the Member States in a specific area, the Union and the Member States may legislate and adopt legally binding acts in that area. The Member States shall exercise their competence to the extent that the Union has not exercised its competence. The Member States shall again exercise their competence to the extent that the Union has decided to cease exercising its competence.	2. When the Fundamental Law confers on the Union a competence shared with the States in a specific area, the Union and the States may legislate and adopt legally binding acts in that area. The States shall exercise their competence to the extent that the Union has not exercised its competence. The States shall again exercise their competence to the extent that the Union has decided to cease exercising its competence.
3. The Member States shall coordinate their economic and employment policies within arrangements as determined by this Treaty, which the Union shall have competence to provide.	3. The States shall coordinate their economic and employment policies within arrangements as determined by this Fundamental Law, which the Union shall have competence to provide.
4. The Union shall have competence, in accordance with the provisions of the Treaty on European Union, to define and implement a common foreign and security policy, including the progressive framing of a common defence policy.	

5. In certain areas and under the conditions laid down in the Treaties, the Union shall have competence to carry out actions to support, coordinate or supplement the actions of the Member States, without thereby superseding their competence in these areas. ***Legally binding acts of the Union adopted on the basis of the provisions of the Treaties relating to these areas shall not entail harmonisation of Member States' laws or regulations.***	4. In certain areas and under the conditions laid down in the Fundamental Law, the Union shall have competence to carry out actions to support, coordinate or supplement the actions of the States, without thereby superseding their competence in these areas.
6. The scope of and arrangements for exercising the Union's competences shall be determined by the provisions of the Treaties relating to each area.	5. The scope of and arrangements for exercising the Union's competences shall be determined by the provisions of the Fundamental Law relating to each area.
Article 3	Article 18 (ex-Article 3 TFEU)
1. The Union shall have exclusive competence in the following areas: (a) customs union; (b) the establishing of the competition rules necessary for the functioning of the internal market; (c) monetary policy for the Member States whose currency is the euro; (d) ***the conservation of marine biological resources under the common fisheries policy;*** (e) common commercial policy.	1. The Union shall have exclusive competence in the following areas: (a) customs union; (b) the establishing of the competition rules necessary for the functioning of the internal market; (c) monetary policy for the States whose currency is the euro; (d) common commercial policy; (e) ***nuclear safety.***
2. The Union shall also have exclusive competence for the conclusion of an international agreement when its conclusion is provided for in a legislative act of the Union or is necessary to enable the Union to exercise its internal competence, or in so far as its conclusion may affect common rules or alter their scope.	2. The Union shall also have exclusive competence for the conclusion of an international agreement when its conclusion is provided for in a legislative act of the Union or is necessary to enable the Union to exercise its internal competence, or in so far as its conclusion may affect common rules or alter their scope.

Article 4	Article 19 (ex-Article 4 TFEU)
1. The Union shall share competence with the Member States where the Treaties confer on it a competence which does not relate to the areas referred to in Articles 3 and 6.	1. The Union shall share ***a general*** competence with the States where the Fundamental Law confers on it a competence which does not relate to the areas referred to in Articles 18 and 20.
2. Shared competence between the Union and the Member States applies in the following principal areas:	2. ***The general competence of the Union and the States is shared specifically*** in the following principal areas:
(a) internal market; (b) social policy, for the aspects defined in this Treaty; (c) economic, social and territorial cohesion; (d) agriculture and fisheries, excluding the conservation of marine biological resources; (e) environment; (f) consumer protection; (g) transport; (h) trans-European networks; (i) energy; (j) area of freedom, security and justice; (k) common safety concerns in public health matters, for the aspects defined in this Treaty.	(a) ***common fiscal and economic policy;*** (b) internal market; (c) social policy; (d) ***employment policy;*** (e) ***cohesion policy;*** (f) agriculture; (g) fisheries; (h) environment ***and climate change;*** (i) consumer protection; (j) transport; (k) trans-European networks; (l) energy; (m) industrial policy; (n) ***research and development;*** (o) ***space policy;*** (p) ***digital policy;*** (q) ***borders policy, asylum and immigration;*** (r) ***judicial cooperation;*** (s) ***police cooperation;*** (t) ***public health;*** (u) ***overseas aid and development;*** (v) ***common foreign and security policy;*** (w) ***common security and defence policy.***
3. In the areas of research, technological development and space, the Union shall have competence to carry out activities, in particular to define and implement programmes; however, the exercise of that competence shall not result in Member States being prevented from exercising theirs.	3. In the areas of research, technological development and space, the Union shall have competence to carry out activities, in particular to define and implement programmes; however, the exercise of that competence shall not result in States being prevented from exercising theirs.
4. In the areas of development cooperation and humanitarian aid, the Union shall have competence to carry out activities and conduct a common policy; however, the exercise of that competence shall not result in Member States being prevented from exercising theirs.	4. In the areas of development cooperation and humanitarian aid, the Union shall have competence to carry out activities and conduct a common policy; however, the exercise of that competence shall not result in States being prevented from exercising theirs.

Article 5	[delete]
Article 6	Article 20 (ex-Article 6 TFEU)
The Union shall have competence to carry out actions to support, coordinate or supplement the actions of the Member States. The areas of such action shall, at European level, be:	The Union shall have competence to carry out actions to support, coordinate or supplement the actions of the States ***in other areas, such as:***
(a) ***protection and improvement of human health;*** (b) ***industry;*** (c) culture; (d) ***tourism;*** (e) education, vocational training, youth and sport; (f) civil protection; (g) administrative cooperation.	(a) culture; (b) education; (c) vocational training; (d) youth; (e) sport; (f) civil protection; (g) administrative cooperation.
	FLEXIBILITY PROVISION
Article 352	Article 21 (ex-Article 352 TFEU)
1. If action by the Union should prove necessary, within the framework of the policies defined in the Treaties, to attain one of the objectives set out in the Treaties, and the Treaties have not provided the necessary powers, ***the Council, acting unanimously on a proposal from the Commission and after obtaining the consent of the European Parliament,*** shall adopt the appropriate measures. ***Where the measures in question are adopted by the Council in accordance with a special legislative procedure, it shall also act unanimously on a proposal from the Commission and after obtaining the consent of the European Parliament.***	1. If action by the Union should prove necessary, within the framework of the policies defined in the Fundamental Law, to attain one of the objectives set out in the Fundamental Law, and the Fundamental Law has not provided the necessary powers, ***the European Parliament and*** the Council, acting on a proposal from the Commission ***in accordance with the special legislative procedure as laid down in Article 88***, shall adopt the appropriate measures.

2. Using the procedure for monitoring the subsidiarity principle referred to in Article 5(3) of the Treaty on European Union, the Commission shall draw national Parliaments' attention to proposals based on this Article.	2. Using the procedure for monitoring the subsidiarity principle referred to in Article 5(3), the Commission shall draw the attention of State Parliaments to proposals based on this Article.
3. Measures based on this Article shall not entail harmonisation of Member States' laws or regulations in cases where the Treaties exclude such harmonisation.	3. Measures based on this Article shall not entail harmonisation of States' laws or regulations in cases where the Fundamental Law excludes such harmonisation.
4. This Article cannot serve as a basis for attaining objectives pertaining to the common foreign and security policy and any acts adopted pursuant to this Article shall respect the limits set out in Article 40, second paragraph, of the Treaty on European Union.	
	Article 22 *1. The European Parliament and the Council, acting in accordance with the special legislative procedure as laid down in Article 88, may establish agencies to carry out specific executive and implementing functions on behalf of the Commission.* *2. The European Parliament and the Council, acting in accordance with the ordinary legislative procedure as laid down in Article 87, shall enact regulations determining the internal organisation and lines of accountability of the agencies.*

THE FUNCTIONING OF THE INSTITUTIONS

CHAPTER THREE

Articles 23–34 lay down specific provisions for the operation of the European Parliament, including in those areas where, exceptionally, Parliament has the right of initiative – namely, its electoral procedure, committees of enquiry, and the office of Ombudsman. Decision-making procedures are eased with respect to the statutes for MEPs and political parties, and to committees of enquiry.

The Ombudsman is given wider powers to advance the cause of the EU citizen, including the right to refer to the ECJ cases concerning a breach of the Charter.

The Court is given full command of its own rules of procedure. Article 58 serves to widen access to the Court of Justice in important ways a change which will serve to develop the role of the ECJ as a federal supreme court. Article 64 makes it possible to attack in the Court a decision of the Parliament taken against a state charged with a breach of fundamental rights.

In Article 76, Parliament gets the right to join in the appointment of the Board of the European Central Bank (ECB) – important in the new context of banking union. Article 77 transfers from the Council to the Commission the right to propose a policy to the ECB, the logic of which will be followed in subsequent chapters.

INSTITUTIONAL PROVISIONS	THE FUNCTIONING OF THE INSTITUTIONS
THE EUROPEAN PARLIAMENT	THE EUROPEAN PARLIAMENT
Article 223	Article 23 (ex-Article 223 TFEU)
1. The European Parliament shall draw up a proposal to lay down the provisions necessary for the election of its Members by direct universal suffrage in accordance with a uniform procedure in all Member States or in accordance with principles common to all Member States.	1. The European Parliament shall draw up a proposal to lay down the provisions necessary for the election of its Members by direct universal suffrage in accordance with a uniform procedure in all States or in accordance with principles common to all States.
The ***Council, acting unanimously*** in accordance with a special legislative procedure ***and after obtaining the consent of the European Parliament, which shall act by a majority of its component Members***, shall lay down the necessary provisions. ***These provisions shall enter into force following their approval by the Member States in accordance with their respective constitutional requirements.***	The ***European Parliament and*** Council, ***acting on the initiative of the Parliament***, in accordance with ***the*** special legislative procedure shall lay down the necessary provisions.
2. The European Parliament, acting by means of regulations on its own initiative in accordance with a special legislative procedure after seeking an opinion from the Commission ***and with the consent of the Council***, shall lay down the regulations and general conditions governing the performance of the duties of its Members. ***All rules or conditions relating to the taxation of Members or former Members shall require unanimity within the Council.***	2. The European Parliament ***and Council, acting on the initiative of the Parliament***, after seeking an opinion from the Commission, ***in accordance with the special legislative procedure***, shall lay down the regulations and general conditions governing the performance of the duties of its Members.
Article 224	Article 24 (ex-Article 224 TFEU)
The European Parliament and the Council, acting in accordance with the ordinary legislative procedure, by means of regulations, shall lay down the regulations governing political parties at European level ***referred to in Article 10(4) of the Treaty on European Union and in particular the rules regarding their funding.***	The European Parliament and the Council, acting in accordance with the ordinary legislative procedure, by means of regulations, shall lay down the regulations governing political parties at European level.

Article 225	Article 25 (ex-Article 225 TFEU)
The European Parliament may, acting by a majority of its component Members, request the Commission to submit any appropriate proposal on matters on which it considers that a Union act is required for the purpose of implementing the Treaties. If the Commission does not submit a proposal, it shall inform the European Parliament of the reasons.	The European Parliament may, acting by a majority of its component Members, request the Commission to submit any appropriate proposal on matters on which it considers that a Union act is required for the purpose of implementing the Fundamental Law. ***Pursuant to Article 15(3),*** if the Commission does not submit a proposal, it shall inform the European Parliament of the reasons.
Article 226	Article 26 (ex-Article 226 TFEU)
In the course of its duties, the European Parliament may, at the request of a quarter of its component Members, set up a temporary Committee of Inquiry to investigate, without prejudice to the powers conferred by the Treaties on other institutions or bodies, alleged contraventions or maladministration in the implementation of Union law, except where the alleged facts are being examined before a court and while the case is still subject to legal proceedings. The temporary Committee of Inquiry shall cease to exist on the submission of its report. The detailed provisions governing the exercise of the right of inquiry shall be determined by the European Parliament, acting by means of regulations on its own initiative in accordance with a special legislative procedure, after obtaining the consent of the Council and the Commission.	In the course of its duties, the European Parliament may, at the request of a quarter of its component Members, set up a temporary Committee of Inquiry to investigate, without prejudice to the powers conferred by the Fundamental Law on other institutions or bodies, alleged contraventions or maladministration in the implementation of Union law, except where the alleged facts are being examined before a court and while the case is still subject to legal proceedings. The temporary Committee of Inquiry shall cease to exist on the submission of its report. The detailed provisions governing the exercise of the right of inquiry shall be determined by the European Parliament ***and the Council, on the initiative of the European Parliament,*** acting by means of regulations in accordance with ***the*** special legislative procedure, after ***consulting*** the Commission.
Article 227	Article 27 (ex-Articles 227 TFEU) .....

Article 228

1. A European Ombudsman, elected by the European Parliament, shall be empowered to receive complaints from any ***citizen of the Union or any natural or legal*** person residing or having its registered office in a Member State concerning ***instances of*** maladministration in the activities of the Union institutions, bodies, offices or agencies, with the exception of the Court of Justice of the European Union acting in its judicial role. He or she shall examine such complaints and report on them.

In accordance with his duties, the Ombudsman shall conduct inquiries for which he finds grounds, either on his own initiative or on the basis of complaints submitted to him direct or through a Member of the European Parliament, except where the alleged facts are or have been the subject of legal proceedings. Where the Ombudsman establishes an instance of maladministration, he shall refer the matter to the institution, body, office or agency concerned, which shall have a period of three months in which to inform him of its views. The Ombudsman shall then forward a report to the European Parliament and the institution, body, office or agency concerned. The person lodging the complaint shall be informed of the outcome of such inquiries.

The Ombudsman shall submit an annual report to the European Parliament on the outcome of his inquiries.

Article 28
(ex-Article 228 TFEU)

1. A European Ombudsman, elected by the European Parliament, shall be empowered to receive complaints from any natural or legal person residing or having its registered office in a State concerning maladministration in the activities of the Union institutions, bodies, offices or agencies, with the exception of the Court of Justice of the European Union acting in its judicial role. He or she shall examine such complaints and report on them.

In accordance with his duties, the Ombudsman shall conduct inquiries for which he or she finds grounds, either on his or her own initiative or on the basis of complaints submitted to him direct or through a Member of the European Parliament, except where the alleged facts are or have been the subject of legal proceedings. Where the Ombudsman establishes an instance of maladministration, he or she shall refer the matter to the institution, body, office or agency concerned, which shall have a period of three months in which to inform him or her of its views. The Ombudsman shall then forward a report to the European Parliament and the institution, body, office or agency concerned. The person lodging the complaint shall be informed of the outcome of such inquiries.

The Ombudsman may request the Court of Justice for leave to refer to the Court, in the role of amicus curiae, a case in which his or her inquiries reveal a serious breach of the Charter of Fundamental Rights.

The Ombudsman may issue general guidance on good administration.

The Ombudsman shall submit an annual report to the European Parliament on the outcome of his or her inquiries.

2. The Ombudsman shall be elected ***after each election of the European Parliament for the duration of its term of office.*** The Ombudsman shall be eligible for reappointment.	2. The Ombudsman shall be elected ***in the third year of each mandate of the European Parliament.*** The Ombudsman shall be eligible for reappointment.
The Ombudsman may be dismissed by the Court of Justice at the request of the European Parliament if he no longer fulfils the conditions required for the performance of his duties or if he is guilty of serious misconduct.	The Ombudsman may be dismissed by the Court of Justice at the request of the European Parliament if he or she no longer fulfils the conditions required for the performance of his or her duties or if he or she is guilty of serious misconduct.
3. The Ombudsman shall be completely independent in the performance of his duties. In the performance of those duties he shall neither seek nor take instructions from any Government, institution, body, office or entity. The Ombudsman may not, during his term of office, engage in any other occupation, whether gainful or not.	3. The Ombudsman shall be completely independent in the performance of his or her duties. In the performance of those duties he or she shall neither seek nor take instructions from any government, institution, body, office or entity. The Ombudsman may not, during his or her term of office, engage in any other occupation, whether gainful or not.
4. The European Parliament acting by means of regulations on its own initiative in accordance with a special legislative procedure shall, after seeking an opinion from the Commission and with the consent of the Council, lay down the regulations and general conditions governing the performance of the Ombudsman's duties.	4. The European Parliament acting by means of regulations on its own initiative in accordance with a special legislative procedure shall, after seeking an opinion from the Commission and with the consent of the Council, lay down the regulations and general conditions governing the performance of the Ombudsman's duties.
Articles 229–230	Articles 29–30 (ex-Articles 229–230) .....
Article 231	Article 31 (ex-Article 231 TFEU)
Save as otherwise provided in the Treaties, the European Parliament shall act by a majority of the votes cast.	***The European Parliament shall vote in public.***
The Rules of Procedure shall determine the quorum.	The Rules of Procedure shall determine the quorum.
Articles 232–233	Articles 32–33 (ex-Articles 232–233 TFEU) .....

Article 234	Article 34 (ex-Article 234 TFEU)
If a motion of censure on the activities of the Commission is tabled before it, the European Parliament shall not vote thereon until at least three days after the motion has been tabled and only by open vote. If the motion of censure is carried by ***a two-thirds majority of the votes cast, representing*** a majority of the component Members of the European Parliament, the members of the Commission shall resign as a body ***and the High Representative of the Union for Foreign Affairs and Security Policy shall resign from duties that he or she carries out in the Commission.*** They shall remain in office and continue to deal with current business until they are replaced in accordance with Article 17 of the Treaty on European Union. In this case, the term of office of the members of the Commission appointed to replace them shall expire on the date on which the term of office of the members of the Commission obliged to resign as a body would have expired.	If a motion of censure on the activities of the Commission is tabled before it, the European Parliament shall not vote thereon until at least three days after the motion has been tabled and only by open vote. If the motion of censure is carried by ***a majority of the component Members*** of the European Parliament, the members of the Commission shall resign as a body. They shall remain in office and continue to deal with current business until they are replaced in accordance with Article 15. In this case, the term of office of the members of the Commission appointed to replace them shall expire on the date on which the term of office of the members of the Commission obliged to resign as a body would have expired.
THE EUROPEAN COUNCIL	THE EUROPEAN COUNCIL
Article 235	Article 35 (ex-Article 235 TFEU)
1. Where a vote is taken, any member of the European Council may also act on behalf of not more than one other member. ***Article 16(4) of the Treaty on European Union and Article 238(2) of this Treaty shall apply to the European Council when it is acting by a qualified majority. Where the European Council decides by vote, its President and the President of the Commission shall not take part in the vote.*** Abstentions by members present in person or represented shall not prevent the adoption by the European Council of acts which require unanimity.	1. Where a vote is taken, any member of the European Council may also act on behalf of not more than one other member. Abstentions by members present in person or represented shall not prevent the adoption by the European Council of acts which require unanimity.

2. The President of the European Parliament may be invited to be heard by the European Council.	
3. The European Council shall act by a simple majority for procedural questions and for the adoption of its Rules of Procedure.	2. The European Council shall act by a simple majority for procedural questions and for the adoption of its Rules of Procedure.
4. The European Council shall be assisted by the General Secretariat of the Council.	3. The European Council shall be assisted by the General Secretariat of the Council.
Article 236	[delete]
THE COUNCIL	THE COUNCIL
Article 237	Article 36 (ex-Article 237 TFEU)
The Council shall meet when convened by its President on his own initiative or at the request of one of its Members or of the Commission.	The Council shall meet when convened by its President on his ***or her*** own initiative or at the request of one of its Members or of the Commission.
Article 238	[delete]
Articles 239–240	Article 37–38 (ex-Articles 239–240 TFEU) .....
Article 241	Article 39 (ex-Article 241 TFEU)
The Council acting by a simple majority may request the Commission to undertake any studies the Council considers desirable for the attainment of the common objectives, and to submit to it any appropriate proposals. If the Commission does not submit a proposal, it shall inform the Council of the reasons.	The Council acting by a simple majority may request the Commission to undertake any studies the Council considers desirable for the attainment of the common objectives, and to submit to it any appropriate proposals. ***Pursuant to Article 15(3),*** if the Commission does not submit a proposal, it shall inform the Council of the reasons.
Article 242	[delete]

Article 243	Article 40 (ex-Article 243 TFEU)
The Council shall determine the salaries, allowances and pensions of the President of the European Council, the President of the Commission, the High Representative of the Union for Foreign Affairs and Security Policy, the Members of the Commission, the Presidents, Members and Registrars of the Court of Justice of the European Union, and the Minister-General of the Council. It shall also determine any payment to be made instead of remuneration.	***The European Parliament and the Council, acting on a proposal of the Commission,*** shall determine the salaries, allowances and pensions of the President of the Commission, the Members of the Commission, the Presidents, Members and Registrars of the Court of Justice of the European Union, and the ***Secretary-General*** of the Council. It shall also determine any payment to be made instead of remuneration.
THE COMMISSION	THE COMMISSION
Article 244	[delete]
Article 245	Article 41 (ex-Article 245 TFEU) .....
Article 246	Article 42 (ex-Article 246 TFEU)
Apart from normal replacement, or death, the duties of a Member of the Commission shall end when he resigns or is compulsorily retired. A vacancy caused by resignation, compulsory retirement or death shall be filled for the remainder of the Member's term of office by a new Member of the same nationality appointed by the Council, by common accord with the President of the Commission, after consulting the European Parliament and in accordance with the criteria set out in the second subparagraph of Article 17(3) of the Treaty on European Union. The Council may, acting unanimously on a proposal from the President of the Commission, decide that such a vacancy need not be filled, in particular when the remainder of the Member's term of office is short.	Apart from normal replacement, or death, the duties of a Member of the Commission shall end when he resigns or is compulsorily retired. A vacancy caused by resignation, compulsory retirement or death shall be filled for the remainder of the Member's term of office in accordance with the procedure laid down in Article 15(8–9). ***By way of derogation from the procedure laid down in Article 15(10), when the vote of the European Parliament concerns the appointment of a single Commissioner, the vote shall be by secret ballot.*** The Council may, acting unanimously on a proposal from the President of the Commission, decide that such a vacancy need not be filled, in particular when the remainder of the Member's term of office is short.

In the event of resignation, compulsory retirement or death, the President shall be replaced for the remainder of his term of office. The procedure laid down in the first subparagraph of Article 17(7) of the Treaty on European Union shall be applicable for the replacement of the President. In the event of resignation, compulsory retirement or death, the High Representative of the Union for Foreign Affairs and Security Policy shall be replaced, for the remainder of his or her term of office, in accordance with Article 18(1) of the Treaty on European Union. In the case of the resignation of all the Members of the Commission, they shall remain in office and continue to deal with current business until they have been replaced, for the remainder of their term of office, in accordance with Article 17 of the Treaty on European Union.	In the event of resignation, compulsory retirement or death, the President shall be replaced for the remainder of his term of office. The procedure laid down in Article 15(7) shall be applicable for the replacement of the President. In the case of the resignation of all the Members of the Commission, they shall remain in office and continue to deal with current business ***until they have been replaced in accordance with the procedures laid down in Article 15(7–10).***
Articles 247–250	Article 43–46 (ex-Articles 247–250 TFEU) .....
THE COURT OF JUSTICE	THE COURT OF JUSTICE
Articles 251–252	Articles 47–48 (ex-Articles 251–252 TFEU) .....
Article 253 The Judges and Advocates-General of the Court of Justice shall be chosen from persons whose independence is beyond doubt and who possess the qualifications required for appointment to the highest judicial offices in their respective countries or who are jurisconsults of recognised competence; they shall be appointed by common accord of the governments of the Member States for a term of six years, after consultation of the panel provided for in Article 255.	Article 49 (ex-Article 253 TFEU) The Judges and Advocates-General of the Court of Justice shall be chosen from persons whose independence is beyond doubt and who possess the qualifications required for appointment to the highest judicial offices in their respective countries or who are jurisconsults of recognised competence; they shall be appointed by common accord of the governments of the States for a term of six years, after consultation of the panel provided for in Article 51.

Every three years there shall be a partial replacement of the Judges and Advocates-General, in accordance with the conditions laid down in the Statute of the Court of Justice of the European Union. The Judges shall elect the President of the Court of Justice from among their number for a term of three years. He may be re-elected. Retiring Judges and Advocates-General may be reappointed. The Court of Justice shall appoint its Registrar and lay down the rules governing his service. The Court of Justice shall establish its Rules of Procedure. ***Those Rules shall require the approval of the Council.***	Every three years there shall be a partial replacement of the Judges and Advocates-General, in accordance with the conditions laid down in the Statute of the Court of Justice of the European Union. The Judges shall elect the President of the Court of Justice from among their number for a term of three years. He may be re-elected. Retiring Judges and Advocates-General may be reappointed. The Court of Justice shall appoint its Registrar and lay down the rules governing his service. The Court of Justice shall establish its Rules of Procedure.
Articles 254–261	Articles 50–57 (ex-Articles 254–261 TFEU) .....
Article 262	[delete]
Article 263 The Court of Justice of the European Union shall review the legality of legislative acts, of acts of the Council, of the Commission and of the European Central Bank, other than recommendations and opinions, and of acts of the European Parliament and of the European Council intended to produce legal effects vis-à-vis third parties. It shall also review the legality of acts of bodies, offices or agencies of the Union intended to produce legal effects vis-à-vis third parties.	Article 58 (ex-Article 263 TFEU) The Court of Justice of the European Union shall review the legality of legislative acts, of acts of the Council, of the Commission and of the European Central Bank, other than recommendations and opinions, and of acts of the European Parliament and of the European Council intended to produce legal effects vis-à-vis third parties. It shall also review the legality of acts of bodies, offices or agencies of the Union intended to produce legal effects vis-à-vis third parties.

It shall for this purpose have jurisdiction in actions brought by a Member State, the European Parliament, the Council or the Commission on grounds of lack of competence, infringement of an essential procedural requirement, infringement of the Treaties or of any rule of law relating to their application, or misuse of powers.	It shall for this purpose have jurisdiction in actions brought by a State, the European Parliament, the Council or the Commission on grounds of lack of competence, infringement of an essential procedural requirement, infringement of the Fundamental Law or of any rule of law relating to its application, or misuse of powers.
The Court shall have jurisdiction under the same conditions in actions brought by the Court of Auditors, by the European Central Bank and by the Committee of the Regions for the purpose of protecting their prerogatives.	The Court shall have jurisdiction under the same conditions in actions brought by the Court of Auditors, by the European Central Bank and by the Committee of the Regions for the purpose of protecting their prerogatives.
	The Court shall have jurisdiction in actions brought by the Ombudsman in cases concerning a breach of the Charter of Fundamental Rights.
Any natural or legal person may, under the conditions laid down in the first and second paragraphs, institute proceedings against an act addressed to that person or which is of direct ***and individual*** concern to them, ***and against a regulatory act which is of direct concern to them and does not entail implementing measures.***	Any natural or legal person may, under the conditions laid down in the first and second paragraphs, institute proceedings against an act addressed to that person or which is manifestly of direct concern to them.
Acts setting up bodies, offices and agencies of the Union may lay down specific conditions and arrangements concerning actions brought by natural or legal persons against acts of these bodies, offices or agencies intended to produce legal effects in relation to them.	Acts setting up bodies, offices and agencies of the Union may lay down specific conditions and arrangements concerning actions brought by natural or legal persons against acts of these bodies, offices or agencies intended to produce legal effects in relation to them.
The proceedings provided for in this Article shall be instituted within two months of the publication of the measure, or of its notification to the plaintiff, or, in the absence thereof, of the day on which it came to the knowledge of the latter, as the case may be.	The proceedings provided for in this Article shall be instituted within two months of the publication of the measure, or of its notification to the plaintiff, or, in the absence thereof, of the day on which it came to the knowledge of the latter, as the case may be.
Articles 264–268	Articles 59–63 (ex-Articles 264–268 TFEU) .....

Article 269	Article 64 (ex-Article 269 TFEU)
The Court of Justice shall have jurisdiction to decide on the legality of an act adopted by the European Council or by the Council pursuant to Article 7 of the Treaty on European Union solely at the request of the Member State concerned by a determination of the European Council or of the Council and in respect solely of the procedural stipulations contained in that Article.	The Court of Justice shall have jurisdiction to decide on the legality of an act adopted by the European Council or by the Council pursuant to Article 133 solely at the request of the State concerned by a determination of the ***European Parliament***, the European Council or the Council.
Such a request must be made within one month from the date of such determination.	Such a request must be made within one month from the date of such determination.
The Court shall rule within one month from the date of the request.	The Court shall rule within one month from the date of the request.
Articles 270–274	Article 65–69 (ex-Articles 270–274 TFEU) .....
Articles 275–276	[delete]
Articles 277–281	Articles 70–74 (ex-Articles 277–281 TFEU) .....
THE EUROPEAN CENTRAL BANK	THE EUROPEAN CENTRAL BANK
Article 282	Article 75 (ex-Article 282) .....
Article 283	Article 76 (ex-Article 283 TFEU)
1. The Governing Council of the European Central Bank shall comprise the members of the Executive Board of the European Central Bank and the Governors of the national central banks of the Member States whose currency is the euro.	1. The Governing Council of the European Central Bank shall comprise the members of the Executive Board of the European Central Bank and the Governors of the national central banks of the States whose currency is the euro.
2. The Executive Board shall comprise the President, the Vice-President and four other members.	2. The Executive Board shall comprise the President, the Vice-President and four other members.

The President, the Vice-President and the other members of the Executive Board shall be appointed by the European Council, acting by a qualified majority, from among persons of recognised standing and professional experience in monetary or banking matters, on a recommendation from the Council, after it has consulted the European Parliament and the Governing Council of the European Central Bank.	The President, the Vice-President and the other members of the Executive Board shall be appointed by the Council, acting by a qualified majority, ***and by the European Parliament*** from among persons of recognised standing and professional experience in monetary or banking matters, on a recommendation from the Commission, after it has consulted the Governing Council of the European Central Bank.
Their term of office shall be eight years and shall not be renewable.	Their term of office shall be eight years and shall not be renewable.
Only nationals of Member States may be members of the Executive Board.	
Article 284	Article 77 (ex-Article 284 TFEU)
1. The President of the Council and a ***Member of the Commission*** may participate, without having the right to vote, in meetings of the Governing Council of the European Central Bank.	1. The President of the Council and ***the Treasury Minister*** may participate, without having the right to vote, in meetings of the Governing Council of the European Central Bank.
The ***President of the Council*** may submit a motion for deliberation to the Governing Council of the European Central Bank.	The ***Commission*** may submit a motion for deliberation to the Governing Council of the European Central Bank.
2. The President of the European Central Bank shall be invited to participate in Council meetings when the Council is discussing matters relating to the objectives and tasks of the ESCB.	2. The President of the European Central Bank shall be invited to participate in Council meetings when the Council is discussing matters relating to the objectives and tasks of the ESCB.
3. The European Central Bank shall address an annual report on the activities of the ESCB and on the monetary policy of both the previous and current year to the European Parliament, the Council and the Commission, and also to the European Council. The President of the European Central Bank shall present this report to the Council and to the European Parliament, which may hold a general debate on that basis.	3. The European Central Bank shall address an annual report on the activities of the ESCB and on the monetary policy of both the previous and current year to the European Parliament, the Council and the Commission. The President of the European Central Bank shall present this report to the Council and to the European Parliament, which may hold a general debate on that basis.

The President of the European Central Bank and the other members of the Executive Board may, at the request of the European Parliament or on their own initiative, be heard by the competent committees of the European Parliament.	The President of the European Central Bank and the other members of the Executive Board may, at the request of the European Parliament or on their own initiative, be heard by the competent committees of the European Parliament.
THE COURT OF AUDITORS	THE COURT OF AUDITORS
Article 285 The Court of Auditors shall carry out the Union's audit. ***It shall consist of one national of each Member State.*** Its Members shall be completely independent in the performance of their duties, in the Union's general interest.	Article 78 (ex-Article 285 TFEU) The Court of Auditors shall carry out the Union's audit. ***The number of Members of the Court shall not exceed the number of States and Associate States.*** Its Members shall be completely independent in the performance of their duties, ***and shall act*** in the Union's general interest.
Articles 286–287	Articles 79–80 (ex-Articles 286–287 TFEU) .....

THE LEGAL ACTS OF THE UNION

CHAPTER FOUR

The chapter makes provision for the executive and legislative acts of the Union and lays down their respective decision-making procedures.

Changes to the key Article 83 on delegated acts and to Article 84 on implementing measures extend those powers to an EU agency.

The Fundamental Law streamlines the legislative procedures of the Union. The whole ordinary legislative procedure, involving co-decision between Parliament and Council, is laid down in Article 87. In one important amendment, the Council will be obliged to act at first reading within six months of having received Parliament's position.

The special legislative procedure, with higher qualified majority thresholds for both Parliament and Council, is explained in Article 88.

Articles 94–101 provide for the Economic and Social Committee and the Committee of the Regions to advise the institutions, principally the Commission, in policy areas relevant to their members. In a move which may trigger the modernisation of these advisory bodies, the European Parliament is given the power to co-decide with the Council on the mandate and organisation of these bodies. Elsewhere in the Fundamental Law, specific references to the Committees are removed, thereby enlarging their potential.

LEGAL ACTS OF THE UNION, ADOPTION PROCEDURES AND OTHER PROVISIONS	THE LEGISLATIVE PROCEDURES
Article 288	Article 81 (ex-Article 288 TFEU)
To exercise the Union's competences, the institutions shall adopt regulations, directives, decisions, recommendations and opinions.	To exercise the Union's competences, the institutions shall adopt regulations, directives, decisions, recommendations and opinions.
A regulation shall have general application. It shall be binding in its entirety and directly applicable in all Member States.	A regulation ***is a law which*** shall have general application. It shall be binding in its entirety and directly applicable in all States.
A directive shall be binding, as to the result to be achieved, upon each Member State to which it is addressed, but shall leave to the national authorities the choice of form and methods.	A directive ***is a law which*** shall be binding, as to the result to be achieved, upon each State to which it is addressed, but shall leave to the national authorities the choice of form and methods.
A decision shall be binding in its entirety. A decision which specifies those to whom it is addressed shall be binding only on them.	A decision ***is a legal act which*** shall be binding in its entirety. A decision which specifies those to whom it is addressed shall be binding only on them.
Recommendations and opinions shall have no binding force.	Recommendations and opinions shall have no binding force.
Article 289	Article 82 (ex-Article 289 TFEU)
1. The ordinary legislative procedure shall consist in the joint adoption by the European Parliament and the Council of a regulation, directive or decision on a proposal from the Commission. This procedure is defined in Article 294.	1. The ordinary legislative procedure shall consist in the joint adoption by the European Parliament and the Council of a regulation, directive or decision on a proposal from the Commission. This procedure is defined in Article 87.
2. In the specific cases provided for by the Treaties, the adoption of a regulation, directive or decision by the European Parliament with the participation of the Council, or by the latter with the participation of the European Parliament, shall constitute a special legislative procedure.	2. In the specific cases provided for by the Fundamental Law, the adoption of a regulation, directive or decision by the European Parliament with the participation of the Council, or by the latter with the participation of the European Parliament, shall constitute a special legislative procedure.
3. Legal acts adopted by legislative procedure shall constitute legislative acts.	3. Legal acts adopted by legislative procedure shall constitute legislative acts.

4. In the specific cases provided for by the Treaties, legislative acts may be adopted on the initiative of a group of Member States or of the European Parliament, on a recommendation from the European Central Bank or at the request of the Court of Justice or the European Investment Bank.	4. In the specific cases provided for by the Fundamental Law, legislative acts may be adopted on the initiative of a group of States or of the European Parliament, on a recommendation from the European Central Bank or at the request of the Court of Justice or the European Investment Bank.
Article 290	Article 83 (ex-Article 290 TFEU)
1. A legislative act may delegate to the Commission the power to adopt non-legislative acts of general application to supplement or amend certain non-essential elements of the legislative act.	1. A legislative act may delegate to the Commission ***or to a Union agency*** the power to adopt non-legislative acts of general application to supplement or amend certain non-essential elements of the legislative act.
The objectives, content, scope and duration of the delegation of power shall be explicitly defined in the legislative acts. The essential elements of an area shall be reserved for the legislative act and accordingly shall not be the subject of a delegation of power.	The objectives, content, scope and duration of the delegation of power shall be explicitly defined in the legislative acts. The essential elements of an area shall be reserved for the legislative act and accordingly shall not be the subject of a delegation of power.
2. Legislative acts shall explicitly lay down the conditions to which the delegation is subject; these conditions may be as follows:	2. Legislative acts shall explicitly lay down the conditions to which the delegation is subject; these conditions may be as follows:
(a) the European Parliament or the Council may decide to revoke the delegation;	(a) the European Parliament or the Council may decide to revoke the delegation;
(b) the delegated act may enter into force only if no objection has been expressed by the European Parliament or the Council within a period set by the legislative act.	(b) the delegated act may enter into force only if no objection has been expressed by the European Parliament or the Council within a period set by the legislative act.
For the purposes of (a) and (b), the European Parliament shall act by a majority of its component members, and the Council by a qualified majority.	For the purposes of (a) and (b), the European Parliament shall act by a majority of its component members, and the Council by a qualified majority.
3. The adjective 'delegated' shall be inserted in the title of delegated acts.	3. The adjective 'delegated' shall be inserted in the title of delegated acts.

Article 291	Article 84 (ex-Article 291)
1. Member States shall adopt all measures of national law necessary to implement legally binding Union acts.	1. The States shall adopt all measures of State law necessary to implement legally binding Union acts.
2. Where uniform conditions for implementing legally binding Union acts are needed, those acts shall confer implementing powers on the Commission, or, in duly justified specific cases and in the cases provided for in Articles 24 and 26 of the Treaty on European Union, on the Council.	2. Where uniform conditions for implementing legally binding Union acts are needed, those acts shall confer implementing powers on the Commission ***or on a Union agency.***
3. For the purposes of paragraph 2, the European Parliament and the Council, acting by means of regulations in accordance with the ordinary legislative procedure, shall lay down in advance the rules and general principles concerning mechanisms for control by Member States of the Commission's exercise of implementing powers.	3. For the purposes of paragraph 2, the European Parliament and the Council, acting by means of regulations in accordance with the ordinary legislative procedure, shall lay down in advance the rules and general principles concerning mechanisms for control of the implementing powers ***of the Commission and the agencies.***
4. The word 'implementing' shall be inserted in the title of implementing acts.	4. The word 'implementing' shall be inserted in the title of implementing acts.
Article 292	Article 85 (ex-Article 292 TFEU)
The Council shall adopt recommendations. It shall act on a proposal from the Commission in all cases where the Treaties provide that it shall adopt acts on a proposal from the Commission. It shall act unanimously in those areas in which unanimity is required for the adoption of a Union act. The Commission, and the European Central Bank in the specific cases provided for in the Treaties, shall adopt recommendations.	The Council shall adopt recommendations. It shall act on a proposal from the Commission in all cases where the Fundamental Law provides that it shall adopt acts on a proposal from the Commission. It shall act unanimously in those areas in which unanimity is required for the adoption of a Union act. The Commission, and the European Central Bank in the specific cases provided for in the Fundamental Law, shall adopt recommendations.

Article 293	Article 86 (ex-Article 293 TFEU)
1. Where, pursuant to the Treaties, the Council acts on a proposal from the Commission, it may amend that proposal only by acting unanimously, except in the cases referred to in paragraphs 10 and 13 of Article 294, in Articles 310, 312 and 314 and in the second paragraph of Article 315.	1. Where, pursuant to the Fundamental Law, the Council acts on a proposal from the Commission, it may amend that proposal only by acting unanimously, except in the cases referred to in paragraphs 10 and 13 of Article 87, in Article 199 and in the second paragraph of Article 207.
2. As long as the Council has not acted, the Commission may alter its proposal at any time during the procedures leading to the adoption of a Union act.	2. As long as the Council has not acted, the Commission may alter its proposal at any time during the procedures leading to the adoption of a Union act.
Article 294	Article 87 (ex-Article 294 TFEU)
1. Where reference is made in the Treaties to the ordinary legislative procedure for the adoption of an act, the following procedure shall apply.	1. Where reference is made in the Fundamental Law to the ordinary legislative procedure for the adoption of an act, the following procedure shall apply.
2. The Commission shall submit a proposal to the European Parliament and the Council.	2. The Commission shall submit a proposal to the European Parliament and the Council, ***except where otherwise provided in the Fundamental Law.***
First reading	*First reading*
3. The European Parliament shall adopt its position at first reading and communicate it to the Council.	3. The European Parliament shall adopt its position at first reading, ***or, as provided by the Fundamental Law, its proposal for an own initiative,*** and communicate it to the Council.
4. If the Council approves the European Parliament's position, the act concerned shall be adopted in the wording which corresponds to the position of the European Parliament.	4. If, ***within six months of receiving the Parliament's position***, the Council ***either*** approves the European Parliament's position ***or does not take a decision***, the act concerned shall be adopted in the wording which corresponds to the position of the European Parliament.

5. If the Council does not approve the European Parliament's position, it shall adopt its position at first reading and communicate it to the European Parliament.

6. The Council shall inform the European Parliament fully of the reasons which led it to adopt its position at first reading. The Commission shall inform the European Parliament fully of its position.

Second reading

7. If, within three months of such communication, the European Parliament:

(a) approves the Council's position at first reading or has not taken a decision, the act concerned shall be deemed to have been adopted in the wording which corresponds to the position of the Council;

(b) rejects, by a majority of its component members, the Council's position at first reading, the proposed act shall be deemed not to have been adopted;

(c) proposes, by a majority of its component members, amendments to the Council's position at first reading, the text thus amended shall be forwarded to the Council and to the Commission, which shall deliver an opinion on those amendments.

8. If, within three months of receiving the European Parliament's amendments, the Council, acting by a qualified majority:

(a) approves all those amendments, the act in question shall be deemed to have been adopted;

(b) does not approve all the amendments, the President of the Council, in agreement with the President of the European Parliament, shall within six weeks convene a meeting of the Conciliation Committee.

5. If the Council does not approve the European Parliament's position, it shall adopt its position at first reading and communicate it to the European Parliament.

6. The Council shall inform the European Parliament fully of the reasons which led it to adopt its position at first reading. The Commission shall inform the European Parliament fully of its position.

Second reading

7. If, within three months of such communication, the European Parliament:

(a) approves the Council's position at first reading or has not taken a decision, the act concerned shall be deemed to have been adopted in the wording which corresponds to the position of the Council;

(b) rejects, by a majority of its component members, the Council's position at first reading, the proposed act shall be deemed not to have been adopted;

(c) proposes, by a majority of its component members, amendments to the Council's position at first reading, the text thus amended shall be forwarded to the Council and to the Commission, which shall deliver an opinion on those amendments.

8. If, within three months of receiving the European Parliament's amendments, the Council, acting by a qualified majority:

(a) approves all those amendments, the act in question shall be deemed to have been adopted;

(b) does not approve all the amendments, the President of the Council, in agreement with the President of the European Parliament, shall within six weeks convene a meeting of the Conciliation Committee.

9. The Council shall act unanimously on the amendments on which the Commission has delivered a negative opinion.

Conciliation

10. The Conciliation Committee, which shall be composed of the members of the Council or their representatives and an equal number of members representing the European Parliament, shall have the task of reaching agreement on a joint text, by a qualified majority of the members of the Council or their representatives and by a majority of the members representing the European Parliament within six weeks of its being convened, on the basis of the positions of the European Parliament and the Council at second reading.

11. The Commission shall take part in the Conciliation Committee's proceedings and shall take all necessary initiatives with a view to reconciling the positions of the European Parliament and the Council.

12. If, within six weeks of its being convened, the Conciliation Committee does not approve the joint text, the proposed act shall be deemed not to have been adopted.

Third reading

13. If, within that period, the Conciliation Committee approves a joint text, the European Parliament, acting by a majority of the votes cast, and the Council, acting by a qualified majority, shall each have a period of six weeks from that approval in which to adopt the act in question in accordance with the joint text. If they fail to do so, the proposed act shall be deemed not to have been adopted.

9. The Council shall act unanimously on the amendments on which the Commission has delivered a negative opinion.

Conciliation

10. The Conciliation Committee, which shall be composed of the members of the Council or their representatives and an equal number of members representing the European Parliament, shall have the task of reaching agreement on a joint text, by a qualified majority of the members of the Council or their representatives and by a majority of the members representing the European Parliament within six weeks of its being convened, on the basis of the positions of the European Parliament and the Council at second reading.

11. The Commission shall take part in the Conciliation Committee's proceedings and shall take all necessary initiatives with a view to reconciling the positions of the European Parliament and the Council.

12. If, within six weeks of its being convened, the Conciliation Committee does not approve the joint text, the proposed act shall be deemed not to have been adopted.

Third reading

13. If, within that period, the Conciliation Committee approves a joint text, the European Parliament, acting by a majority of the votes cast, and the Council, acting by a qualified majority, shall each have a period of six weeks from that approval in which to adopt the act in question in accordance with the joint text. If they fail to do so, the proposed act shall be deemed not to have been adopted.

14. The periods of three months and six weeks referred to in this Article shall be extended by a maximum of one month and two weeks respectively at the initiative of the European Parliament or the Council. *Special provisions* 15. Where, in the cases provided for in the Treaties, a legislative act is submitted to the ordinary legislative procedure on the initiative of a group of Member States, on a recommendation by the European Central Bank, or at the request of the Court of Justice, paragraph 2, the second sentence of paragraph 6, and paragraph 9 shall not apply. In such cases, the European Parliament and the Council shall communicate the proposed act to the Commission with their positions at first and second readings. The European Parliament or the Council may request the opinion of the Commission throughout the procedure, which the Commission may also deliver on its own initiative. It may also, if it deems it necessary, take part in the Conciliation Committee in accordance with paragraph 11.	14. The periods of three months and six weeks referred to in this Article shall be extended by a maximum of one month and two weeks respectively at the initiative of the European Parliament or the Council. *Special provisions* 15. Where, in the cases provided for in the Fundamental Law, a legislative act is submitted to the ordinary legislative procedure on a recommendation by the European Central Bank, or at the request of the Court of Justice, paragraph 2, the second sentence of paragraph 6, and paragraph 9 shall not apply. In such cases, the European Parliament and the Council shall communicate the proposed act to the Commission with their positions at first and second readings. The European Parliament or the Council may request the opinion of the Commission throughout the procedure, which the Commission may also deliver on its own initiative. It may also, if it deems it necessary, take part in the Conciliation Committee in accordance with paragraph 11.
	Article 88 ***Where reference is made in the Fundamental Law to the special legislative procedure, the procedures laid down in Article 87 shall apply except that:*** ***(a) the qualified majority in the European Parliament shall be as defined in Article 12(8);*** ***(b) the qualified majority in the Council shall be as defined by Article 14(5).***
Articles 295–299	Articles 89–93 (ex-Articles 295–299 TFEU) .....

THE UNION'S ADVISORY BODIES	ADVISORY BODIES
Article 300	Article 94 (ex-Article 300 TFEU)
1. The European Parliament, the Council and the Commission shall be assisted by an Economic and Social Committee and a Committee of the Regions, exercising advisory functions. 2. The Economic and Social Committee shall consist of representatives of organisations of employers, of the employed, and of other parties representative of civil society, notably in socio economic, civic, professional and cultural areas. 3. The Committee of the Regions shall consist of representatives of regional and local bodies who either hold a regional or local authority electoral mandate or are politically accountable to an elected assembly. 4. The members of the Economic and Social Committee and of the Committee of the Regions shall not be bound by any mandatory instructions. They shall be completely independent in the performance of their duties, in the Union's general interest. 5. The rules referred to in paragraphs 2 and 3 governing the nature ***of the composition*** of the Committees shall be reviewed at regular intervals ***by the Council to take account of economic, social and demographic developments within the Union. The Council, on a proposal from the Commission,*** shall adopt decisions to that end.	1. The European Parliament, the Council and the Commission shall be assisted by an Economic and Social Committee and a Committee of the Regions, exercising advisory functions. 2. The Economic and Social Committee shall consist of representatives of organisations of employers, of the employed, and of other parties representative of civil society, notably in socio-economic, civic, professional and cultural areas. 3. The Committee of the Regions shall consist of representatives of regional and local bodies who either hold a regional or local authority electoral mandate or are politically accountable to an elected assembly. 4. The members of the Economic and Social Committee and of the Committee of the Regions shall not be bound by any mandatory instructions. They shall be completely independent in the performance of their duties, in the Union's general interest. 5. The rules referred to in paragraphs 2 and 3 governing the nature of the Committees shall be reviewed at regular intervals. ***The European Parliament and the Council, in accordance with the ordinary legislative procedure,*** shall adopt decisions ***on their composition, terms and conditions of membership.***
Articles 301–307	Articles 95–101 (ex-Articles 301–307 TFEU) .....
Articles 308–309	Articles 102–103 (ex-Articles 308–309 TFEU) .....

ENHANCED COOPERATION

CHAPTER FIVE

The Treaty of Lisbon went some way to facilitate enhanced cooperation by a group of states which chooses to integrate further and faster in any field of shared competence. The Fundamental Law takes further steps towards rationalising and simplifying the procedures by and through which the variable geometry of the larger Union can be expressed in terms of governance.

Importantly, in the key Article 104, we remove the constraint that enhanced cooperation can only be deployed as a matter of last resort.

In particular, in Article 105, we place the workings of the eurozone expressly within the context of enhanced cooperation.

The special arrangements for the use of enhanced cooperation in the field of common foreign and security policy are ended. Normal institutional procedures will now apply.

In Article 111, we have the first of several references to the special fiscal capacity of the eurozone.

PROVISIONS ON ENHANCED COOPERATION	ENHANCED COOPERATION
Article 20 TEU	Article 104 (ex-Article 20 TEU)
1. Member States which wish to establish enhanced cooperation between themselves within the framework of the Union's non-exclusive competences may make use of its institutions and exercise those competences ***by applying the relevant provisions of the Treaties, subject to the limits and in accordance with the detailed arrangements laid down in this Article and in Articles 326 to 334 of the Treaty on the Functioning of the European Union.***	1. States which wish to establish enhanced cooperation between themselves within the framework of the Union's non-exclusive competences may make use of its institutions and exercise those competences.
Enhanced cooperation shall aim to further the objectives of the Union, protect its interests and reinforce its integration process. Such cooperation shall be open at any time to all Member States, ***in accordance with Article 328 of the Treaty on the Functioning of the European Union.***	Enhanced cooperation shall aim to further the objectives of the Union, protect its interests and reinforce its integration process. Such cooperation shall be open at any time to all States.
2. The decision authorising enhanced cooperation shall be adopted by the Council ***as a last resort***, when it has established that the objectives of such cooperation cannot be attained within a reasonable period by the Union as a whole, and provided that at least nine Member States participate in it. ***The Council shall act in accordance with the procedure laid down in Article 329 of the Treaty on the Functioning of the European Union.***	2. The decision authorising enhanced cooperation shall be adopted by the Council when it has established that the objectives of such cooperation cannot be attained within a reasonable period by the Union as a whole, and provided that at least nine States participate in it.
3. All members of the Council may participate in its deliberations, but only members of the Council representing the Member States participating in enhanced cooperation shall take part in the vote. ***The voting rules are set out in Article 330 of the Treaty on the Functioning of the European Union.***	3. All members of the Council may participate in its deliberations, but only members of the Council representing the States participating in enhanced cooperation shall take part in the vote.

4. Acts adopted in the framework of enhanced cooperation shall bind only participating Member States. They shall not be regarded as part of the acquis which has to be accepted by candidate States for accession to the Union.	4. Acts adopted in the framework of enhanced cooperation shall bind only participating States. They shall not be regarded as part of the acquis which has to be accepted by candidate states for accession to the Union.
Article 326	Article 105 (ex-Article 326 TFEU)
Any enhanced cooperation shall comply with the Treaties and Union law. Such cooperation shall not undermine the internal market or economic, social and territorial cohesion. It shall not constitute a barrier to or discrimination in trade between Member States, nor shall it distort competition between them.	1. Any enhanced cooperation shall comply with the Treaties and Union law. Such cooperation shall not undermine the internal market or economic, social and territorial cohesion. It shall not constitute a barrier to or discrimination in trade between Member States, nor shall it distort competition between them. ***2. States whose currency is the euro are deemed to have established enhanced cooperation between themselves and shall act in accordance with these provisions save where the Fundamental Law otherwise provides.***
Articles 327–328	Articles 106–107 (ex-Articles 327–328 TFEU) .....
Article 329	Article 108 (ex-Article 329 TFEU)
1. Member States which wish to establish enhanced cooperation between themselves in one of the areas covered by the Treaties, ***with the exception of fields of exclusive competence and the common foreign and security policy***, shall address a request to the Commission, specifying the scope and objectives of the enhanced cooperation proposed. The Commission may submit a proposal to the Council to that effect. In the event of the Commission not submitting a proposal, it shall inform the Member States concerned of the reasons for not doing so.	States which wish to establish enhanced cooperation between themselves in one of the areas covered by the Fundamental Law shall address a request to the Commission, specifying the scope and objectives of the enhanced cooperation proposed. The Commission may submit a proposal to the Council to that effect. In the event of the Commission not submitting a proposal, it shall inform the States concerned of the reasons for not doing so.

Authorisation to proceed with the enhanced cooperation referred to in the first subparagraph shall be granted by the Council, on a proposal from the Commission and after obtaining the consent of the European Parliament. ***2. The request of the Member States which wish to establish enhanced cooperation between themselves within the framework of the common foreign and security policy shall be addressed to the Council. It shall be forwarded to the High Representative of the Union for Foreign Affairs and Security Policy, who shall give an opinion on whether the enhanced cooperation proposed is consistent with the Union's common foreign and security policy, and to the Commission, which shall give its opinion in particular on whether the enhanced cooperation proposed is consistent with other Union policies. It shall also be forwarded to the European Parliament for information.*** ***Authorisation to proceed with enhanced cooperation shall be granted by a decision of the Council acting unanimously.***	Authorisation to proceed with the enhanced cooperation referred to in the first subparagraph shall be granted by the Council, on a proposal from the Commission and after obtaining the consent of the European Parliament.
Article 330 All members of the Council may participate in its deliberations, but only members of the Council representing the Member States participating in enhanced cooperation shall take part in the vote. Unanimity shall be constituted by the votes of the representatives of the participating Member States only. A qualified majority shall be defined in accordance with Article 238(3).	Article 109 (ex-Article 330 TFEU) All members of the Council may participate in its deliberations, but only members of the Council representing the States participating in enhanced cooperation shall take part in the vote. Unanimity shall be constituted by the votes of the representatives of the participating States only. A qualified majority shall be defined in accordance with Article 14(4).
Article 331 1. Any Member State which wishes to participate in enhanced cooperation in progress in one of the areas referred to in Article 329(1) shall notify its intention to the Council and the Commission.	Article 110 (ex-Article 331 TFEU) Any State which wishes to participate in enhanced cooperation in progress shall notify its intention to the Council and the Commission.

The Commission shall, within four months of the date of receipt of the notification, confirm the participation of the Member State concerned. It shall note where necessary that the conditions of participation have been fulfilled and shall adopt any transitional measures necessary with regard to the application of the acts already adopted within the framework of enhanced cooperation.

However, if the Commission considers that the conditions of participation have not been fulfilled, it shall indicate the arrangements to be adopted to fulfil those conditions and shall set a deadline for re-examining the request. On the expiry of that deadline, it shall re-examine the request, in accordance with the procedure set out in the second subparagraph. If the Commission considers that the conditions of participation have still not been met, the Member State concerned may refer the matter to the Council, which shall decide on the request. The Council shall act in accordance with Article 330. It may also adopt the transitional measures referred to in the second subparagraph on a proposal from the Commission.

The Commission shall, within four months of the date of receipt of the notification, confirm the participation of the State concerned. It shall note where necessary that the conditions of participation have been fulfilled and shall adopt any transitional measures necessary with regard to the application of the acts already adopted within the framework of enhanced cooperation.

However, if the Commission considers that the conditions of participation have not been fulfilled, it shall indicate the arrangements to be adopted to fulfil those conditions and shall set a deadline for re-examining the request. On the expiry of that deadline, it shall re-examine the request, in accordance with the procedure set out in the second subparagraph. If the Commission considers that the conditions of participation have still not been met, the State concerned may refer the matter to the Council, which shall decide on the request. The Council shall act in accordance with Article 109. It may also adopt the transitional measures referred to in the second subparagraph on a proposal from the Commission.

2. Any Member State which wishes to participate in enhanced cooperation in progress in the framework of the common foreign and security policy shall notify its intention to the Council, the High Representative of the Union for Foreign Affairs and Security Policy and the Commission. *The Council shall confirm the participation of the Member State concerned, after consulting the High Representative of the Union for Foreign Affairs and Security Policy and after noting, where necessary, that the conditions of participation have been fulfilled. The Council, on a proposal from the High Representative, may also adopt any transitional measures necessary with regard to the application of the acts already adopted within the framework of enhanced cooperation. However, if the Council considers that the conditions of participation have not been fulfilled, it shall indicate the arrangements to be adopted to fulfil those conditions and shall set a deadline for re-examining the request for participation.* *For the purposes of this paragraph, the Council shall act unanimously and in accordance with Article 330.*	
Article 332 Expenditure resulting from implementation of enhanced cooperation, other than administrative costs entailed for the institutions, shall be borne by the participating Member States, unless all members of the Council, acting unanimously after consulting the European Parliament, decide otherwise.	Article 111 (ex-Article 332 TFEU) ***In accordance with the provisions of Part III,*** expenditure resulting from implementation of enhanced cooperation, other than administrative costs entailed for the institutions, shall be borne by the participating States, unless ***the European Parliament and the Council, acting in accordance with the special legislative procedure,*** decide otherwise. ***This provision shall be without prejudice to expenditure resulting from the fiscal capacity of the States whose currency is the euro, as established in accordance with Article 236(3).***
Articles 333–334	Articles 112–113 (ex-Articles 333–334) .....

GENERAL PROVISIONS

CHAPTER SIX

Articles 114–132 contain provisions of a general constitutional nature.

Notable innovations are, in Article 120, a liberalisation of the rules to decide on the controversial question of the location of the seats of the institutions and of EU bodies. Unanimity in the Council is replaced by the special legislative procedure.

As far as the controversial question of the seat of Parliament is concerned, we propose that, in a reciprocal arrangement with the Council, the Parliament may decide where it is to work but must first obtain the consent of the Council to its choice – acting, in the normal way, by qualified majority.

GENERAL AND FINAL PROVISIONS	GENERAL PROVISIONS
Article 335	Article 114 (ex-Articles 47 TEU & 335 TFEU)
	1. ***The Union shall have legal personality.***
In each of the Member States, the Union shall enjoy the most extensive legal capacity accorded to legal persons under their laws; it may, in particular, acquire or dispose of movable and immovable property and may be a party to legal proceedings. To this end, the Union shall be represented by the Commission. However, the Union shall be represented by each of the institutions, by virtue of their administrative autonomy, in matters relating to their respective operation.	2. In each of the States, the Union shall enjoy the most extensive legal capacity accorded to legal persons under their laws; it may, in particular, acquire or dispose of movable and immovable property and may be a party to legal proceedings. To this end, the Union shall be represented by the Commission. However, the Union shall be represented by each of the institutions, by virtue of their administrative autonomy, in matters relating to their respective operation.
Articles 336–340	Articles 115–119 (ex-Articles 336–340 TFEU) .....

Article 341 The seat of the institutions of the Union shall be determined by common accord of the governments of the Member States.	Article 120 (ex-Article 341 TFEU) 1. The seat of the institutions, ***agencies and bodies of the Union shall be determined by the European Parliament and the Council, on a proposal of the Commission, acting in accordance with the special legislative procedure.*** ***2. By way of derogation from paragraph 1, the European Parliament and the Council shall each decide the location of their own seat, after having obtained the consent of the other.***
Article 342 The rules governing the languages of the institutions of the Union shall, without prejudice to the provisions contained in the Statute of the Court of Justice of the European Union, be determined by the Council, ***acting unanimously*** by means of regulations.	Article 121 (ex-Article 342 TFEU) The rules governing the languages of the institutions of the Union shall, without prejudice to the provisions contained in the Statute of the Court of Justice of the European Union, be determined by ***means of regulations by the European Parliament, which shall act by a majority of its component Members, and by the Council, which shall act unanimously.***
Articles 343–345	Articles 122–124 (ex-Articles 343–345 TFEU) .....
Article 346 1. The provisions of the Treaties shall not preclude the application of the following rules: (a) no Member State shall be obliged to supply information the disclosure of which it considers contrary to the essential interests of its security;	Article 125 (ex-Article 346 TFEU) 1. The provisions of the Fundamental Law shall not preclude the application of the following rules: (a) no State shall be obliged to supply information the disclosure of which it considers contrary to the essential interests of its ***own state*** security;

(b) any Member State may take such measures as it considers necessary for the protection of the essential interests of its security which are connected with the production of or trade in arms, munitions and war material; such measures shall not adversely affect the conditions of competition in the internal market regarding products which are not intended for specifically military purposes.	(b) any State may take such measures as it considers necessary for the protection of the essential interests of its ***own state*** security which are connected with the production of or trade in arms, munitions and war material. ***However,*** such measures shall not adversely affect the conditions of competition in the internal market.
2. The Council may, ***acting unanimously*** on a proposal from the Commission, make changes to the list, which it drew up on 15 April 1958, of the products to which the provisions of paragraph 1(b) apply.	2. ***The European Parliament and the Council,*** on a proposal from the Commission ***and acting in accordance with the special legislative procedure,*** may make changes to the list, which the Council drew up on 15 April 1958, of the products to which the provisions of paragraph 1(b) apply.
Articles 347–351	Articles 126–130 (ex-Articles 347–351 TFEU) .....
Article 353	[delete]
Articles 355–356	Articles 131–132 (ex-Articles 355–356 TFEU) .....
Articles 357–358	[delete]

FINAL PROVISIONS

CHAPTER SEVEN

This Chapter closes Part I with key constitutional provisions.

Articles 133–134 concern the procedures to adopt if a state is suspected and/or found to be in breach of fundamental rights. These amendments will: (a) widen the scope of the ties which have to be respected to include the primacy of EU law, the principles of sincere cooperation and the constitutional interdependence of EU states, as well as explicit respect for the Charter; (b) increase the powers of the Parliament (consent procedure) and the Court (consultation) in the process of dealing with a breach; and (c) allow the European Council to take decisions by a super-qualified majority (in place of unanimity). Significantly, the new category of associate states will also be subject to these rules.

Article 135 deals with the procedures that will apply to amend the Fundamental Law in future. Several important changes are made to the current rigid system in which every treaty change has always to be agreed by everyone, namely: (a) the intergovernmental conference (IGC) will decide on amendments to the treaty by a special qualified majority of three quarters of the states; (b) the European Parliament, acting by a two-thirds majority, gains the right of consent to the amended draft of the IGC.

Entry into force of the revised Fundamental Law will take place either once four fifths of the states, representing a majority of the population, complete their national ratification processes or after an affirmative vote (simple majority) in an EU-wide simultaneous referendum. In the same vein, the general *passerelle* clause (Article 135(7)), which allows the European Council to shift special legislative procedure to the ordinary legislative procedure is lightened.

These changes taken together not only simplify the current procedures for treaty revision but also bring the Union into line with all other federal states or international organisations.

In Article 136, concerning the accession of a new member state, we insert and entrench the 'Copenhagen criteria' which have governed the enlargement process since 1993. The Commission is given the right to make a proposal about whether to open accession negotiations. And the European Parliament obtains the right of consent to enlargement.

Article 137 establishes an important new category of associate state. This new form of membership is designed to be suitable (a) for existing member states which choose not to accept in full the federal Fundamental Law; (b) for states, such as Norway, currently in variously unsatisfactory association agreements with the EU and which wish to upgrade their relationship; and (c) for third countries which decide they are either unable or unwilling to meet the demands of full EU membership. Further details about associate membership appear in Protocol No 3.

Article 138 concerns the right of secession.

Article 139 resuscitates the symbols of the Union first inscribed into the thwarted Constitutional Treaty of 2004.

	BREACH OF FUNDAMENTAL RIGHTS
Article 7 TEU	Article 133 (ex-Article 7 TEU)
1. On a reasoned proposal by one third of the Member States, by the European Parliament or by the European Commission, the Council, acting by a majority of four fifths of its members after obtaining the consent of the European Parliament, may determine that there is a clear risk of a serious breach by a Member State of the values referred to in Article 2. Before making such a determination, the Council shall hear the Member State in question and may address recommendations to it, acting in accordance with the same procedure. ***The Council shall regularly verify that the grounds on which such a determination was made continue to apply.***	1. On a reasoned proposal by one third of the States, by the European Parliament or by the European Commission, the Council, acting by a majority of four fifths of its members after obtaining the consent of the European Parliament, may determine that there is a clear risk of a serious breach by a State ***or an Associate State*** of the values referred to in Article 2, ***or of the rights and principles referred to in Articles 4 and 6.*** Before making such a determination, the Council shall hear the State in question and may address recommendations to it, acting in accordance with the same procedure.

2. The European Council, acting by ***unanimity*** on a proposal by one third of the Member States or by the Commission and after obtaining the consent of the European Parliament, may determine the existence of a serious and persistent breach by a Member State of the values referred to in Article 2, after inviting the Member State in question to submit its observations.	2. The European Council, acting by ***a majority of four fifths*** on a proposal by one third of the States or by the Commission and after obtaining the consent of the European Parliament, may determine the existence of a serious and persistent breach by a State or ***Associate State*** of the ***provisions of*** Articles 2, ***4 and 6***, after inviting the State in question to submit its observations.
3. Where a determination under paragraph 2 has been made, the Council, acting by a qualified majority, may decide to suspend certain of the rights deriving from the application of the Treaties to the Member State in question, including the voting rights of the representative of the government of that Member State in the Council. In doing so, the Council shall take into account the possible consequences of such a suspension on the rights and obligations of natural and legal persons.	3. Where a determination under paragraph 2 has been made, the Council, acting by a qualified majority, ***after having consulted the Court of Justice and after having obtained the consent of the European Parliament***, may decide to suspend certain of the rights deriving from the application of the Fundamental Law to the State ***or Associate State*** in question, including the voting rights of the representative of the government of that State in the Council. In doing so, the Council ***and Parliament*** shall take into account the possible consequences of such a suspension on the rights and obligations of natural and legal persons.
The obligations of the Member State in question under this Treaty shall in any case continue to be binding on that State.	The obligations of the State ***or Associate State*** in question under this Fundamental Law shall in any case continue to be binding on that State.
4. The Council, acting by a qualified majority, may decide subsequently to vary or revoke measures taken under paragraph 3 in response to changes in the situation which led to their being imposed.	4. The Council, acting by a qualified majority ***after having obtained the consent of the European Parliament***, may decide subsequently to vary or revoke measures taken under paragraph 3 in response to changes in the situation which led to their being imposed.
5. The voting arrangements applying to the European Parliament, the European Council and the Council for the purposes of this Article are laid down in Article 354 of the Treaty on the Functioning of the European Union.	

Article 354 TFEU	Article 134 (ex-Article 354 TFEU)
For the purposes of Article 7 of the Treaty on European Union on the suspension of certain rights resulting from Union membership, the member of the European Council or of the Council representing the Member State in question shall not take part in the vote and the Member State in question shall not be counted in the calculation of the one third or four fifths of Member States referred to in paragraphs 1 and 2 of that Article. Abstentions by members present in person or represented shall not prevent the adoption of decisions referred to in paragraph 2 of that Article.	For the purposes of Article 133 on the suspension of certain rights resulting from Union membership ***or associate membership***, the member of the European Council or of the Council representing the State in question shall not take part in the vote and the State in question shall not be counted in the calculation of the one third or four fifths of States referred to in paragraphs 1 and 2 of that Article. Abstentions by members present in person or represented shall not prevent the adoption of decisions referred to in paragraph 2 of that Article.
For the adoption of the decisions referred to in paragraphs 3 and 4 of Article 7 of the Treaty on European Union, a qualified majority shall be defined in accordance with Article 238(3)(b) of this Treaty.	For the adoption of the decisions referred to in paragraphs 3 and 4 of Article 133, a qualified majority shall be defined in accordance with Article 14(5).
Where, following a decision to suspend voting rights adopted pursuant to paragraph 3 of Article 7 of the Treaty on European Union, the Council acts by a qualified majority on the basis of a provision of the Treaties, that qualified majority shall be defined in accordance with Article 238(3)(b) of this Treaty, or, where the Council acts on a proposal from the Commission or from the High Representative of the Union for Foreign Affairs and Security Policy, in accordance with Article 238(3)(a).	Where, following a decision to suspend voting rights adopted pursuant to paragraph 3 of Article 133, the Council acts by a qualified majority on the basis of a provision of the Fundamental Law, that qualified majority shall be defined in accordance with Article 14(5), or, where the Council acts on a proposal from the Commission, in accordance with Article 14(4). ***Where these procedures relate to an Associate State, that State shall be consulted before the European Council or the Council shall take their decisions.***
For the purposes of Article 7 of the Treaty on European Union, the European Parliament shall act by a two-thirds majority of the votes cast, representing the majority of its component Members.	For the purposes of Article 133 (2) and (3), the European Parliament shall act by a two-thirds majority of the votes cast, representing the majority of its component Members.

	REVISION OF THE FUNDAMENTAL LAW
Article 48 TEU	Article 135 (ex-Article 48 TEU)
1. The Treaties may be amended in accordance with an ordinary revision procedure. They may also be amended in accordance ***with*** simplified revision procedures.	1. The Fundamental Law may be amended in accordance with ***this*** revision procedure.
Ordinary revision procedure	
2. The Government of any Member State, the European Parliament or the Commission may submit to the Council proposals for the amendment of the Treaties. These proposals may, inter alia, serve either to increase or to reduce the competences conferred on the Union in the Treaties. These proposals shall be submitted to the European Council by the Council and the national Parliaments shall be notified.	2. The Government of any State, the European Parliament or the Commission may submit to the European Council proposals for the amendment of the Fundamental Law. These proposals may, inter alia, serve either to increase or to reduce the competences conferred on the Union. The State Parliaments shall be notified.
3. If the European Council, after consulting the European Parliament and the Commission, adopts by a simple majority a decision in favour of examining the proposed amendments, the President of the European ***Council*** shall convene a Convention composed of representatives of the national Parliaments, of the Heads of State or Government of the Member States, of the European Parliament and of the Commission. The European Central Bank shall also be consulted in the case of institutional changes in the monetary area. The Convention shall examine the proposals for amendments and shall adopt by consensus a ***recommendation to a conference of representatives of the governments of the Member States as provided for in paragraph 4.***	3. If the European Council, after consulting the European Parliament and the Commission, adopts by a simple majority a decision in favour of examining the proposed amendments, the President of the European ***Commission*** shall convene a Convention composed of representatives of the State Parliaments, of the Heads of State or Government of the States, of the European Parliament and of the Commission. The European Central Bank shall also be consulted in the case of institutional changes in the monetary area. The Convention shall examine the proposals for amendments and shall adopt by consensus a ***draft amended Fundamental Law.***

The European Council may decide by a simple majority, after obtaining the consent of the European Parliament, not to convene a Convention should this not be justified by the extent of the proposed amendments. In the latter case, the European Council shall define the terms of reference for a conference of representatives of the governments of the Member States.

4. A conference of representatives of the governments of the Member States shall be convened by the President of the ***Council*** for the purpose of determining ***by common accord*** the amendments to be made to the Treaties.

The amendments shall enter into force ***after being ratified by all the Member States*** in accordance with their respective constitutional requirements.

5. If, two years after the signature of a treaty amending the Treaties, four fifths of the Member States have ratified it and one or more Member States have encountered difficulties in proceeding with ratification, the matter shall be referred to the European Council.

Simplified revision procedures

6. The Government of any Member State, the European Parliament or the Commission may submit to the European Council proposals for revising all or part of the provisions of Part Three of the Treaty on the Functioning of the European Union relating to the internal policies and action of the Union.

The European Council may adopt a decision amending all or part of the provisions of Part Three of the Treaty on the Functioning of the European Union. The European Council shall act by unanimity after consulting the European Parliament and the Commission, and the European Central Bank in the case of institutional changes in the monetary area. That decision shall not enter into force until it is approved by the Member States in accordance with their respective constitutional requirements.

The European Council may decide by a simple majority, after obtaining the consent of the European Parliament, not to convene a Convention should this not be justified by the extent of the proposed amendments. In the latter case, the European Council shall define the terms of reference for a conference of representatives of the State governments.

4. A conference of representatives of the State governments shall be convened by the President of the ***European Council*** for the purpose of determining the amendments to be made to the Fundamental Law ***on the basis of the recommendations of the Convention.***

The conference shall act by a majority of three quarters of the governments.

5. The European Parliament shall, by a two-thirds majority, vote its consent to the Fundamental Law as amended by the conference.

6. The amendments shall enter into force ***throughout the Union either*** after being ratified by ***four fifths of the States, representing a majority of the population of the Union,*** in accordance with their respective constitutional requirements, ***or after having obtained a majority in a referendum held at the same time in all States of the Union.***

The decision referred to in the second subparagraph shall not increase the competences conferred on the Union in the Treaties.

7. Where the Treaty on the Functioning of the European Union or Title V of this Treaty provides for the Council to act by unanimity in a given area or case, the European Council may adopt a decision authorising the Council to act by a qualified majority in that area or in that case. This subparagraph shall not apply to decisions with military implications or those in the area of defence.

Where the Treaty on the Functioning of the European Union provides for legislative acts to be adopted by the Council in accordance with a special legislative procedure, the European Council may adopt a decision allowing for the adoption of such acts in accordance with the ordinary legislative procedure.

Any initiative taken by the European Council on the basis of the first or the second subparagraph shall be notified to the national Parliaments. If a national Parliament makes known its opposition within six months of the date of such notification, the decision referred to in the first or the second subparagraph shall not be adopted. In the absence of opposition, the European Council may adopt the decision.

For the adoption of the decisions referred to in the first and second subparagraphs, the European Council shall act by unanimity after obtaining the consent of the European Parliament, which shall be given by a majority of its component members.

7. Where the Fundamental Law provides for legislative acts to be adopted in accordance with ***the*** special legislative procedure, the European Council may adopt a decision allowing for the adoption of such acts in accordance with the ordinary legislative procedure.

	ACCESSION TO MEMBERSHIP
Article 49	Article 136 (ex-Article 49 TEU)
Any European State which respects the values referred to in Article 2 and is committed to promoting them may apply to become a member of the Union. The European Parliament and national Parliaments shall be notified of this application. The applicant State shall address its application to the Council, which shall act unanimously after consulting the Commission and after receiving the consent of the European Parliament, which shall act by a majority of its component members. The conditions of eligibility agreed upon by the European Council shall be taken into account.	1. Any European State which respects the values referred to in Article 2 and is committed to promoting them may apply to become a member of the Union. The European Parliament and State Parliaments shall be notified of this application. The applicant State shall address its application to the Council, which shall act unanimously ***on a proposal*** of the Commission and after receiving the consent of the European Parliament, which shall act by a majority of its component members. ***2. In order to be accepted as eligible for the opening of accession negotiations, an applicant state must have stable institutions which guarantee democracy, the rule of law, human rights and respect for and protection of minorities; a functioning market economy and proven capacity to cope with competitive pressure and market forces within the Union; and the ability to take on the obligations of Union membership, including adherence to the aims of political, economic and monetary union.***
The conditions of admission and the adjustments to the Treaties on which the Union is founded, which such admission entails, shall be the subject of an agreement between the Member States and the applicant State. This agreement shall be submitted for ratification by all the contracting States in accordance with their respective constitutional requirements.	3. The conditions of admission and the adjustments to the Fundamental Law on which the Union is founded, which such admission entails, shall be the subject of an agreement between the States and the applicant State. This agreement shall be submitted for ratification by the European Parliament, which shall act ***by a majority of its component Members, and by all the contracting States in*** accordance with their respective constitutional requirements.

	ASSOCIATE MEMBERSHIP
	Article 137 *1. Any State of the Union may apply to the European Council to become an Associate State of the Union. The European Parliament and State Parliaments shall be notified of this application.* *2. Any other European state which respects the values referred to in Article 2 and is committed to promoting them may apply to the European Council to become an Associate State of the Union. The European Parliament and State Parliaments shall be notified of this application.* *3. The Commission shall negotiate an agreement with the applicant Associate State in accordance with Article 433, and with due regard to the light of guidelines laid down in Protocol No 9. The agreement will set out the terms and conditions of associate membership and the adjustments to the Fundamental Law which such association entails. The agreement may be of limited duration.* *4. The agreement shall be concluded on behalf of the Union by the Council, acting in accordance with the procedure laid down in Article 14(5). It shall be submitted for the consent of the European Parliament, which shall act by a majority of its component Members, and by all the contracting States in accordance with their respective constitutional requirements.* *The agreement shall enter into force once approved by the European Parliament and by four fifths of the State parliaments and by the applicant Associate State.*

	SECESSION FROM THE UNION
Article 50	Article 138 (ex-Article 50 TEU)
1. Any Member State may decide to withdraw from the Union in accordance with its own constitutional requirements.	1. Any State may decide to withdraw from the Union in accordance with its own constitutional requirements.
2. A Member State which decides to withdraw shall notify the European Council of its intention. In the light of the guidelines provided by the European Council, the Union shall negotiate and conclude an agreement with that State, setting out the arrangements for its withdrawal, taking account of the framework for its future relationship with the Union. That agreement shall be negotiated in accordance with Article 218(3) of the Treaty on the Functioning of the European Union. It shall be concluded on behalf of the Union by the Council, acting by a qualified majority, after obtaining the consent of the European Parliament.	2. A State which decides to withdraw shall notify the European Council of its intention. In the light of the guidelines provided by the European Council, the Union shall negotiate and conclude an agreement with that State, setting out the arrangements for its withdrawal, taking account of the framework for its future relationship with the Union. That agreement shall be negotiated in accordance with Article 433(3). It shall be concluded on behalf of the Union by the Council, acting by a qualified majority, after obtaining the consent of the European Parliament.
3. The Treaties shall cease to apply to the State in question from the date of entry into force of the withdrawal agreement or, failing that, two years after the notification referred to in paragraph 2, unless the European Council, in agreement with the Member State concerned, unanimously decides to extend this period.	3. The Fundamental Law of the Union shall cease to apply to the State in question from the date of entry into force of the withdrawal agreement or, failing that, two years after the notification referred to in paragraph 2, unless the European Council, in agreement with the State concerned, unanimously decides to extend this period.
4. For the purposes of paragraphs 2 and 3, the member of the European Council or of the Council representing the withdrawing Member State shall not participate in the discussions of the European Council or Council or in decisions concerning it.	4. For the purposes of paragraphs 2 and 3, the member of the European Council or of the Council representing the withdrawing State shall not participate in the discussions of the European Council or Council or in decisions concerning it.
A qualified majority shall be defined in accordance with Article 238(3)(b) of the Treaty on the Functioning of the European Union.	A qualified majority shall be defined in accordance with Article 14(5).
5. If a State which has withdrawn from the Union asks to rejoin, its request shall be subject to the procedure referred to in Article 49.	5. If a State which has withdrawn from the Union asks to rejoin, its request shall be subject to the procedure referred to in Article 136.

	SYMBOLS
	Article 139 ***The flag of the Union shall be a circle of twelve golden stars on a blue background.*** ***The anthem of the Union shall be based on the Ode to Joy from the Ninth Symphony by Ludwig van Beethoven.*** ***The motto of the Union shall be 'United in diversity'.*** ***Europe Day shall be celebrated on 9 May throughout the Union.***
	PROTOCOLS
Article 51	Article 140 (ex-Article 51 TEU) .....
	SIGNATORIES
Article 52	Article 141 (ex-Article 52 TEU) .....
	DURATION
Article 53	Article 142 (ex-Article 53 TEU) .....

	ENTRY INTO FORCE
Article 54	Article 143 (ex-Article 54 TEU)
1. This Treaty shall be ratified by the High Contracting Parties in accordance with their respective constitutional requirements. The instruments of ratification shall be deposited with the Government of the Italian Republic.	1. This Treaty ***establishing the Fundamental Law*** shall be ratified by the High Contracting Parties in accordance with their respective constitutional requirements. The instruments of ratification shall be deposited with the Government of the Italian Republic.
2. This Treaty shall enter into force on 1 January 1993, provided that all the Instruments of ratification have been deposited, or, failing that, on the first day of the month following the deposit of the Instrument of ratification by the last signatory State to take this step.	***2. This Fundamental Law shall enter into force on the first day of the month following the deposit of the Instrument of ratification by the governments of four fifths of the States or following the official verification by the Commission of the results of a referendum held in all States, the requisite majority having been obtained.***
	LANGUAGE VERSIONS
Article 55	Article 144 (ex-Article 55 TEU) .....

PART II

THE CHARTER OF FUNDAMENTAL RIGHTS OF THE EUROPEAN UNION

The Charter of Fundamental Rights of the European Union was drafted by the first constitutional Convention which met in 1999–2000. The Charter was signed at the IGC in Nice in December 2000 but was granted the status only of a code of conduct. Nevertheless, the Convention had famously decided to work on the text 'as if' the Charter would become binding one day. Under the Treaty of Lisbon, indeed, the Charter was given the status of primary law although it was not included in the treaty text.

Here the Charter, with only minimal changes, is fully incorporated into the Fundamental Law, which will give the Charter the visibility and prominence which it deserves.

The Charter reaffirms, with due regard for the powers and tasks of the Union and for the principle of subsidiarity, the rights as they result, in particular, from the constitutional traditions and international obligations common to the States, the European Convention for the Protection of Human Rights and Fundamental Freedoms (ECHR), the Social Charters adopted by the Union and by the Council of Europe and the case law of the ECJ in Luxembourg and of the European Court of Human Rights in Strasbourg.

We drop the Preamble to the Charter as being superfluous to requirements as well as rather unsatisfactory. The description of the field of application of the Charter is brought into line with ECJ case law (Article 195). We amend Article 196 to drop an explicit reference to the Charter's explanatory memorandum – a reference inserted at the time of the drafting of the Lisbon treaty to assuage states reluctant to embrace the development by the Union of its own federal rights regime. The ECJ, which already refers to the Charter in its case-law, will in any event not be instructed as to its interpretative sources.

PREAMBLE	[delete]
TITLE I DIGNITY	DIGNITY
Article 1 Human dignity Human dignity is inviolable. It must be respected and protected.	Article 145 (ex-Article 1 CFR) Human dignity Human dignity is inviolable. It must be respected and protected.
Article 2 Right to life 1. Everyone has the right to life. 2. No one shall be condemned to the death penalty, or executed.	Article 146 (ex-Article 2 CFR) Right to life 1. Everyone has the right to life. 2. No one shall be condemned to the death penalty, or executed.
Article 3 Right to the integrity of the person 1. Everyone has the right to respect for his or her physical and mental integrity. 2. In the fields of medicine and biology, the following must be respected in particular: (a) the free and informed consent of the person concerned, according to the procedures laid down by law; (b) the prohibition of eugenic practices, in particular those aiming at the selection of persons; (c) the prohibition on making the human body and its parts as such a source of financial gain; (d) the prohibition of the reproductive cloning of human beings.	Article 147 (ex-Article 3 CFR) Right to the integrity of the person 1. Everyone has the right to respect for his or her physical and mental integrity. 2. In the fields of medicine and biology, the following must be respected in particular: (a) the free and informed consent of the person concerned, according to the procedures laid down by law; (b) the prohibition of eugenic practices, in particular those aiming at the selection of persons; (c) the prohibition on making the human body and its parts as such a source of financial gain; (d) the prohibition of the reproductive cloning of human beings.

Article 4 Prohibition of torture and inhuman or degrading treatment or punishment No one shall be subjected to torture or to inhuman or degrading treatment or punishment.	Article 148 (ex-Article 4 CFR) Prohibition of torture and inhuman or degrading treatment or punishment No one shall be subjected to torture or to inhuman or degrading treatment or punishment.
Article 5 Prohibition of slavery and forced labour 1. No one shall be held in slavery or servitude. 2. No one shall be required to perform forced or compulsory labour. 3. Trafficking in human beings is prohibited.	Article 149 (ex-Article 5 CFR) Prohibition of slavery and forced labour 1. No one shall be held in slavery or servitude. 2. No one shall be required to perform forced or compulsory labour. 3. Trafficking in human beings is prohibited.
TITLE II FREEDOMS	FREEDOMS
Article 6 Right to liberty and security Everyone has the right to liberty and security of person.	Article 150 (ex-Article 6 CFR) Right to liberty and security Everyone has the right to liberty and security of person.
Article 7 Respect for private and family life Everyone has the right to respect for his or her private and family life, home and communications.	Article 151 (ex-Article 7 CFR) Respect for private and family life Everyone has the right to respect for his or her private and family life, home and communications.

Article 8	Article 152 (ex-Article 8 CFR)
Protection of personal data	Protection of personal data
1. Everyone has the right to the protection of personal data concerning him or her.	1. Everyone has the right to the protection of personal data concerning him or her.
2. Such data must be processed fairly for specified purposes and on the basis of the consent of the person concerned or some other legitimate basis laid down by law. Everyone has the right of access to data which has been collected concerning him or her, and the right to have it rectified.	2. Such data must be processed fairly for specified purposes and on the basis of the consent of the person concerned or some other legitimate basis laid down by law. Everyone has the right of access to data which has been collected concerning him or her, and the right to have it rectified.
3. Compliance with these rules shall be subject to control by an independent authority.	3. Compliance with these rules shall be subject to control by an independent authority.
Article 9	Article 153 (ex-Article 9 CFR)
Right to marry and right to found a family	Right to marry and right to found a family
The right to marry and the right to found a family shall be guaranteed in accordance with the national laws governing the exercise of these rights.	The right to marry and the right to found a family shall be guaranteed in accordance with the national laws governing the exercise of these rights.
Article 10	Article 154 (ex-Article 10 CFR)
Freedom of thought, conscience and religion	Freedom of thought, conscience and religion
1. Everyone has the right to freedom of thought, conscience and religion. This right includes freedom to change religion or belief and freedom, either alone or in community with others and in public or in private, to manifest religion or belief, in worship, teaching, practice and observance.	1. Everyone has the right to freedom of thought, conscience and religion. This right includes freedom to change religion or belief and freedom, either alone or in community with others and in public or in private, to manifest religion or belief, in worship, teaching, practice and observance.
2. The right to conscientious objection is recognised, in accordance with the national laws governing the exercise of this right.	2. The right to conscientious objection is recognised, in accordance with the national laws governing the exercise of this right.

Article 11 Freedom of expression and information 1. Everyone has the right to freedom of expression. This right shall include freedom to hold opinions and to receive and impart information and ideas without interference by public authority and regardless of frontiers. 2. The freedom and pluralism of the media shall be respected.	Article 155 (ex-Article 11 CFR) Freedom of expression and information 1. Everyone has the right to freedom of expression. This right shall include freedom to hold opinions and to receive and impart information and ideas without interference by public authority and regardless of frontiers. 2. The freedom and pluralism of the media shall be respected.
Article 12 Freedom of assembly and of association 1. Everyone has the right to freedom of peaceful assembly and to freedom of association at all levels, in particular in political, trade union and civic matters, which implies the right of everyone to form and to join trade unions for the protection of his or her interests. 2. Political parties at Union level contribute to expressing the political will of the citizens of the Union.	Article 156 (ex-Article 12 CFR) Freedom of assembly and of association 1. Everyone has the right to freedom of peaceful assembly and to freedom of association at all levels, in particular in political, trade union and civic matters, which implies the right of everyone to form and to join trade unions for the protection of his or her interests. 2. Political parties at Union level contribute to expressing the political will of the citizens of the Union.
Article 13 Freedom of the arts and sciences The arts and scientific research shall be free of constraint. Academic freedom shall be respected.	Article 157 (ex-Article 13 CFR) Freedom of the arts and sciences The arts and scientific research shall be free of constraint. Academic freedom shall be respected.

Article 14	Article 158 (ex-Article 14 CFR)
Right to education	Right to education
1. Everyone has the right to education and to have access to vocational and continuing training.	1. Everyone has the right to education and to have access to vocational and continuing training.
2. This right includes the possibility to receive free compulsory education.	2. This right includes the possibility to receive free compulsory education.
3. The freedom to found educational establishments with due respect for democratic principles and the right of parents to ensure the education and teaching of their children in conformity with their religious, philosophical and pedagogical convictions shall be respected, in accordance with the national laws governing the exercise of such freedom and right.	3. The freedom to found educational establishments with due respect for democratic principles and the right of parents to ensure the education and teaching of their children in conformity with their religious, philosophical and pedagogical convictions shall be respected, in accordance with the national laws governing the exercise of such freedom and right.
Article 15	Article 159 (ex-Article 15 CFR)
Freedom to choose an occupation and right to engage in work	Freedom to choose an occupation and right to engage in work
1. Everyone has the right to engage in work and to pursue a freely chosen or accepted occupation.	1. Everyone has the right to engage in work and to pursue a freely chosen or accepted occupation.
2. Every citizen of the Union has the freedom to seek employment, to work, to exercise the right of establishment and to provide services in any Member State.	2. Every citizen of the Union has the freedom to seek employment, to work, to exercise the right of establishment and to provide services in any State.
3. Nationals of third countries who are authorised to work in the territories of the Member States are entitled to working conditions equivalent to those of citizens of the Union.	3. Nationals of third countries who are authorised to work in the territories of the States are entitled to working conditions equivalent to those of citizens of the Union.

Article 16 Freedom to conduct a business The freedom to conduct a business in accordance with Union law and national laws and practices is recognised.	Article 160 (ex-Article 16 CFR) Freedom to conduct a business The freedom to conduct a business in accordance with Union law and national laws and practices is recognised.
Article 17 Right to property 1. Everyone has the right to own, use, dispose of and bequeath his or her lawfully acquired possessions. No one may be deprived of his or her possessions, except in the public interest and in the cases and under the conditions provided for by law, subject to fair compensation being paid in good time for their loss. The use of property may be regulated by law in so far as is necessary for the general interest. 2. Intellectual property shall be protected.	Article 161 (ex-Article 17 CFR) Right to property 1. Everyone has the right to own, use, dispose of and bequeath his or her lawfully acquired possessions. No one may be deprived of his or her possessions, except in the public interest and in the cases and under the conditions provided for by law, subject to fair compensation being paid in good time for their loss. The use of property may be regulated by law in so far as is necessary for the general interest. 2. Intellectual property shall be protected.
Article 18 Right to asylum The right to asylum shall be guaranteed with due respect for the rules of the Geneva Convention of 28 July 1951 and the Protocol of 31 January 1967 relating to the status of refugees and in accordance with the Treaty on European Union and the Treaty on the Functioning of the European Union (hereinafter referred to as 'the Treaties').	Article 162 (ex-Article 18 CFR) Right to asylum The right to asylum shall be guaranteed with due respect for the rules of the Geneva Convention of 28 July 1951 and the Protocol of 31 January 1967 relating to the status of refugees and in accordance with the Fundamental Law.

Article 19 Protection in the event of removal, expulsion or extradition 1. Collective expulsions are prohibited. 2. No one may be removed, expelled or extradited to a State where there is a serious risk that he or she would be subjected to the death penalty, torture or other inhuman or degrading treatment or punishment.	Article 163 (ex-Article 19 CFR) Protection in the event of removal, expulsion or extradition 1. Collective expulsions are prohibited. 2. No one may be removed, expelled or extradited to a state where there is a serious risk that he or she would be subjected to the death penalty, torture or other inhuman or degrading treatment or punishment.
TITLE III EQUALITY	EQUALITY
Article 20 Equality before the law Everyone is equal before the law.	Article 164 (ex-Article 20 CFR) Equality before the law Everyone is equal before the law.
Article 21 Non-discrimination 1. Any discrimination based on any ground such as sex, race, colour, ethnic or social origin, genetic features, language, religion or belief, political or any other opinion, membership of a national minority, property, birth, disability, age or sexual orientation shall be prohibited. 2. Within the scope of application of the Treaties and without prejudice to any of their specific provisions, any discrimination on grounds of nationality shall be prohibited.	Article 165 (ex-Article 21 CFR) Non-discrimination 1. Any discrimination based on any ground such as sex, race, colour, ethnic or social origin, genetic features, language, religion or belief, political or any other opinion, membership of a national minority, property, birth, disability, age or sexual orientation shall be prohibited. 2. Within the scope of application of the Fundamental Law and without prejudice to any of their specific provisions, any discrimination on grounds of nationality shall be prohibited.
Article 22 Cultural, religious and linguistic diversity The Union shall respect cultural, religious and linguistic diversity.	Article 166 (ex-Article 22 CFR) Cultural, religious and linguistic diversity The Union shall respect cultural, religious and linguistic diversity.

Article 23	Article 167 (ex-Article 23 CFR)
Equality between women and men	Equality between women and men
Equality between women and men must be ensured in all areas, including employment, work and pay.	Equality between women and men must be ensured in all areas, including employment, work and pay.
The principle of equality shall not prevent the maintenance or adoption of measures providing for specific advantages in favour of the under-represented sex.	The principle of equality shall not prevent the maintenance or adoption of measures providing for specific advantages in favour of the under-represented sex.
Article 24	Article 168 (ex-Article 24 CFR)
The rights of the child	The rights of the child
1. Children shall have the right to such protection and care as is necessary for their well-being. They may express their views freely. Such views shall be taken into consideration on matters which concern them in accordance with their age and maturity.	1. Children shall have the right to such protection and care as is necessary for their well-being. They may express their views freely. Such views shall be taken into consideration on matters which concern them in accordance with their age and maturity.
2. In all actions relating to children, whether taken by public authorities or private institutions, the child's best interests must be a primary consideration.	2. In all actions relating to children, whether taken by public authorities or private institutions, the child's best interests must be a primary consideration.
3. Every child shall have the right to maintain on a regular basis a personal relationship and direct contact with both his or her parents, unless that is contrary to his or her interests	3. Every child shall have the right to maintain on a regular basis a personal relationship and direct contact with both his or her parents, unless that is contrary to his or her interests.
Article 25	Article 169 (ex-Article 25 CFR)
The rights of the elderly	The rights of the elderly
The Union recognises and respects the rights of the elderly to lead a life of dignity and independence and to participate in social and cultural life.	The Union recognises and respects the rights of the elderly to lead a life of dignity and independence and to participate in social and cultural life.

Article 26	Article 170 (ex-Article 26 CFR)
Integration of persons with disabilities	Integration of persons with disabilities
The Union recognises and respects the right of persons with disabilities to benefit from measures designed to ensure their independence, social and occupational integration and participation in the life of the community.	The Union recognises and respects the right of persons with disabilities to benefit from measures designed to ensure their independence, social and occupational integration and participation in the life of the community.
TITLE IV SOLIDARITY	SOLIDARITY
Article 27	Article 171 (ex-Article 27 CFR)
Workers' right to information and consultation within the undertaking	Workers' right to information and consultation within the undertaking
Workers or their representatives must, at the appropriate levels, be guaranteed information and consultation in good time in the cases and under the conditions provided for by Union law and national laws and practices.	Workers or their representatives must, at the appropriate levels, be guaranteed information and consultation in good time in the cases and under the conditions provided for by Union law and national laws and practices.
Article 28	Article 172 (ex-Article 28 CFR)
Right of collective bargaining and action	Right of collective bargaining and action
Workers and employers, or their respective organisations, have, in accordance with Union law and national laws and practices, the right to negotiate and conclude collective agreements at the appropriate levels and, in cases of conflicts of interest, to take collective action to defend their interests, including strike action.	Workers and employers, or their respective organisations, have, in accordance with Union law and national laws and practices, the right to negotiate and conclude collective agreements at the appropriate levels and, in cases of conflicts of interest, to take collective action to defend their interests, including strike action.
Article 29	Article 173 (ex-Article 29 CFR)
Right of access to placement services	Right of access to placement services
Everyone has the right of access to a free placement service.	Everyone has the right of access to a free placement service.

Article 30 Protection in the event of unjustified dismissal Every worker has the right to protection against unjustified dismissal, in accordance with Union law and national laws and practices.	Article 174 (ex-Article 30 CFR) Protection in the event of unjustified dismissal Every worker has the right to protection against unjustified dismissal, in accordance with Union law and national laws and practices.
Article 31 Fair and just working conditions 1. Every worker has the right to working conditions which respect his or her health, safety and dignity. 2. Every worker has the right to limitation of maximum working hours, to daily and weekly rest periods and to an annual period of paid leave.	Article 175 (ex-Article 31 CFR) Fair and just working conditions 1. Every worker has the right to working conditions which respect his or her health, safety and dignity. 2. Every worker has the right to limitation of maximum working hours, to daily and weekly rest periods and to an annual period of paid leave.
Article 32 Prohibition of child labour and protection of young people at work The employment of children is prohibited. The minimum age of admission to employment may not be lower than the minimum school-leaving age, without prejudice to such rules as may be more favourable to young people and except for limited derogations. Young people admitted to work must have working conditions appropriate to their age and be protected against economic exploitation and any work likely to harm their safety, health or physical, mental, moral or social development or to interfere with their education.	Article 176 (ex-Article 32 CFR) Prohibition of child labour and protection of young people at work The employment of children is prohibited. The minimum age of admission to employment may not be lower than the minimum school-leaving age, without prejudice to such rules as may be more favourable to young people and except for limited derogations. Young people admitted to work must have working conditions appropriate to their age and be protected against economic exploitation and any work likely to harm their safety, health or physical, mental, moral or social development or to interfere with their education.

Article 33	Article 177 (ex-Article 33 CFR)
Family and professional life	Family and professional life
1. The family shall enjoy legal, economic and social protection.	1. The family shall enjoy legal, economic and social protection.
2. To reconcile family and professional life, everyone shall have the right to protection from dismissal for a reason connected with maternity and the right to paid maternity leave and to parental leave following the birth or adoption of a child.	2. To reconcile family and professional life, everyone shall have the right to protection from dismissal for a reason connected with maternity and the right to paid maternity leave and to parental leave following the birth or adoption of a child.
Article 34	Article 178 (ex-Article 34 CFR)
Social security and social assistance	Social security and social assistance
1. The Union recognises and respects the entitlement to social security benefits and social services providing protection in cases such as maternity, illness, industrial accidents, dependency or old age, and in the case of loss of employment, in accordance with the rules laid down by Union law and national laws and practices.	1. The Union recognises and respects the entitlement to social security benefits and social services providing protection in cases such as maternity, illness, industrial accidents, dependency or old age, and in the case of loss of employment, in accordance with the rules laid down by Union law and national laws and practices.
2. Everyone residing and moving legally within the European Union is entitled to social security benefits and social advantages in accordance with Union law and national laws and practices.	2. Everyone residing and moving legally within the European Union is entitled to social security benefits and social advantages in accordance with Union law and national laws and practices.
3. In order to combat social exclusion and poverty, the Union recognises and respects the right to social and housing assistance so as to ensure a decent existence for all those who lack sufficient resources, in accordance with the rules laid down by Union law and national laws and practices.	3. In order to combat social exclusion and poverty, the Union recognises and respects the right to social and housing assistance so as to ensure a decent existence for all those who lack sufficient resources, in accordance with the rules laid down by Union law and national laws and practices.

Article 35 Health care Everyone has the right of access to preventive health care and the right to benefit from medical treatment under the conditions established by national laws and practices. A high level of human health protection shall be ensured in the definition and implementation of all the Union's policies and activities.	Article 179 (ex-Article 35 CFR) Health care Everyone has the right of access to preventive health care and the right to benefit from medical treatment under the conditions established by national laws and practices. A high level of human health protection shall be ensured in the definition and implementation of all the Union's policies and activities.
Article 36 Access to services of general economic interest The Union recognises and respects access to services of general economic interest as provided for in national laws and practices, in accordance with the Treaties, in order to promote the social and territorial cohesion of the Union.	Article 180 (ex-Article 36 CFR) Access to services of general economic interest The Union recognises and respects access to services of general economic interest as provided for in national laws and practices, in accordance with the Fundamental Law, in order to promote the social and territorial cohesion of the Union.
Article 37 Environmental protection A high level of environmental protection and the improvement of the quality of the environment must be integrated into the policies of the Union and ensured in accordance with the principle of sustainable development.	Article 181 (ex-Article 37 CFR) Environmental protection A high level of environmental protection and the improvement of the quality of the environment must be integrated into the policies of the Union and ensured in accordance with the principle of sustainable development.
Article 38 Consumer protection Union policies shall ensure a high level of consumer protection.	Article 182 (ex-Article 38 CFR) Consumer protection Union policies shall ensure a high level of consumer protection.

TITLE V CITIZENS' RIGHTS	CITIZENS' RIGHTS
Article 39	Article 183 (ex-Article 39 CFR)
Right to vote and to stand as a candidate at elections to the European Parliament	Right to vote and to stand as a candidate at elections to the European Parliament
1. Every citizen of the Union has the right to vote and to stand as a candidate at elections to the European Parliament in the Member State in which he or she resides, under the same conditions as nationals of that State.	1. Every citizen of the Union has the right to vote and to stand as a candidate at elections to the European Parliament in the State in which he or she resides, under the same conditions as nationals of that State.
2. Members of the European Parliament shall be elected by direct universal suffrage in a free and secret ballot.	2. Members of the European Parliament shall be elected by direct universal suffrage in a free and secret ballot.
Article 40	Article 184 (ex-Article 40 CFR)
Right to vote and to stand as a candidate at municipal elections	Right to vote and to stand as a candidate at municipal elections
Every citizen of the Union has the right to vote and to stand as a candidate at municipal elections in the Member State in which he or she resides under the same conditions as nationals of that State.	Every citizen of the Union has the right to vote and to stand as a candidate at municipal elections in the State in which he or she resides under the same conditions as nationals of that State.
Article 41	Article 185 (ex-Article 41 CFR)
Right to good administration	Right to good administration
1. Every person has the right to have his or her affairs handled impartially, fairly and within a reasonable time by the institutions, bodies, offices and agencies of the Union.	1. Every person has the right to have his or her affairs handled impartially, fairly and within a reasonable time by the institutions, bodies, offices and agencies of the Union.
2. This right includes: (a) the right of every person to be heard, before any individual measure which would affect him or her adversely is taken; (b) the right of every person to have access to his or her file, while respecting the legitimate interests of confidentiality and of professional and business secrecy; (c) the obligation of the administration to give reasons for its decisions.	2. This right includes: (a) the right of every person to be heard, before any individual measure which would affect him or her adversely is taken; (b) the right of every person to have access to his or her file, while respecting the legitimate interests of confidentiality and of professional and business secrecy; (c) the obligation of the administration to give reasons for its decisions.

3. Every person has the right to have the Union make good any damage caused by its institutions or by its servants in the performance of their duties, in accordance with the general principles common to the laws of the Member States. 4. Every person may write to the institutions of the Union in one of the languages of the Treaties and must have an answer in the same language.	3. Every person has the right to have the Union make good any damage caused by its institutions or by its servants in the performance of their duties, in accordance with the general principles common to the laws of the States. 4. Every person may write to the institutions of the Union in one of the languages of the Fundamental Law and must have an answer in the same language.
Article 42 Right of access to documents Any citizen of the Union, and any natural or legal person residing or having its registered office in a Member State, has a right of access to documents of the institutions, bodies, offices and agencies of the Union, whatever their medium.	Article 186 (ex-Article 42 CFR) Right of access to documents Any citizen of the Union, and any natural or legal person residing or having its registered office in a State, has a right of access to documents of the institutions, bodies, offices and agencies of the Union, whatever their medium.
Article 43 European Ombudsman Any citizen of the Union and any natural or legal person residing or having its registered office in a Member State has the right to refer to the European Ombudsman cases of maladministration in the activities of the institutions, bodies, offices or agencies of the Union, with the exception of the Court of Justice of the European Union acting in its judicial role.	Article 187 (ex-Article 43 CFR) European Ombudsman Any citizen of the Union and any natural or legal person residing or having its registered office in a State has the right to refer to the European Ombudsman cases of maladministration in the activities of the institutions, bodies, offices or agencies of the Union, with the exception of the Court of Justice of the European Union acting in its judicial role.
Article 44 Right to petition Any citizen of the Union and any natural or legal person residing or having its registered office in a Member State has the right to petition the European Parliament.	Article 188 (ex-Article 44 CFR) Right to petition Any citizen of the Union and any natural or legal person residing or having its registered office in a State has the right to petition the European Parliament.

Article 45	Article 189 (ex-Article 45 CFR)
Freedom of movement and of residence	Freedom of movement and of residence
1. Every citizen of the Union has the right to move and reside freely within the territory of the Member States.	1. Every citizen of the Union has the right to move and reside freely within the territory of the States.
2. Freedom of movement and residence may be granted, in accordance with the Treaties, to nationals of third countries legally resident in the territory of a Member State.	2. Freedom of movement and residence may be granted, in accordance with the Fundamental Law, to nationals of third countries legally resident in the territory of a State.
Article 46	Article 190 (ex-Article 46 CFR)
Diplomatic and consular protection	Diplomatic and consular protection
Every citizen of the Union shall, in the territory of a third country in which the Member State of which he or she is a national is not represented, be entitled to protection by the diplomatic or consular authorities of any Member State, on the same conditions as the nationals of that Member State.	Every citizen of the Union shall, in the territory of a third country in which the State of which he or she is a national is not represented, be entitled to protection by the diplomatic or consular authorities of any State, on the same conditions as the nationals of that State.
TITLE VI JUSTICE	JUSTICE
Article 47	Article 191 (ex-Article 47 CFR)
Right to an effective remedy and to a fair trial	Right to an effective remedy and to a fair trial
Everyone whose rights and freedoms guaranteed by the law of the Union are violated has the right to an effective remedy before a tribunal in compliance with the conditions laid down in this Article.	Everyone whose rights and freedoms guaranteed by the law of the Union are violated has the right to an effective remedy before a tribunal in compliance with the conditions laid down in this Article.
Everyone is entitled to a fair and public hearing within a reasonable time by an independent and impartial tribunal previously established by law. Everyone shall have the possibility of being advised, defended and represented.	Everyone is entitled to a fair and public hearing within a reasonable time by an independent and impartial tribunal previously established by law. Everyone shall have the possibility of being advised, defended and represented.

Legal aid shall be made available to those who lack sufficient resources in so far as such aid is necessary to ensure effective access to justice.	Legal aid shall be made available to those who lack sufficient resources in so far as such aid is necessary to ensure effective access to justice.
Article 48 Presumption of innocence and right of defence 1. Everyone who has been charged shall be presumed innocent until proved guilty according to law. 2. Respect for the rights of the defence of anyone who has been charged shall be guaranteed.	Article 192 (ex-Article 48 CFR) Presumption of innocence and right of defence 1. Everyone who has been charged shall be presumed innocent until proved guilty according to law. 2. Respect for the rights of the defence of anyone who has been charged shall be guaranteed.
Article 49 Principles of legality and proportionality of criminal offences and penalties 1. No one shall be held guilty of any criminal offence on account of any act or omission which did not constitute a criminal offence under national law or international law at the time when it was committed. Nor shall a heavier penalty be imposed than the one that was applicable at the time the criminal offence was committed. If, subsequent to the commission of a criminal offence, the law provides for a lighter penalty, that penalty shall be applicable. 2. This Article shall not prejudice the trial and punishment of any person for any act or omission which, at the time when it was committed, was criminal according to the general principles recognised by the community of nations. 3. The severity of penalties must not be disproportionate to the criminal offence.	Article 193 (ex-Article 49 CFR) Principles of legality and proportionality of criminal offences and penalties 1. No one shall be held guilty of any criminal offence on account of any act or omission which did not constitute a criminal offence under national law or international law at the time when it was committed. Nor shall a heavier penalty be imposed than the one that was applicable at the time the criminal offence was committed. If, subsequent to the commission of a criminal offence, the law provides for a lighter penalty, that penalty shall be applicable. 2. This Article shall not prejudice the trial and punishment of any person for any act or omission which, at the time when it was committed, was criminal according to the general principles recognised by the community of nations. 3. The severity of penalties must not be disproportionate to the criminal offence.

Article 50	Article 194 (ex-Article 50 CFR)
Right not to be tried or punished twice in criminal proceedings for the same criminal offence	Right not to be tried or punished twice in criminal proceedings for the same criminal offence
No one shall be liable to be tried or punished again in criminal proceedings for an offence for which he or she has already been finally acquitted or convicted within the Union in accordance with the law.	No one shall be liable to be tried or punished again in criminal proceedings for an offence for which he or she has already been finally acquitted or convicted within the Union in accordance with the law.
TITLE VII GENERAL PROVISIONS GOVERNING THE INTERPRETATION AND APPLICATION OF THE CHARTER	GENERAL PROVISIONS
Article 51	Article 195 (ex-Article 51 CFR)
Field of application	Field of application
1. The provisions of this Charter are addressed to the institutions, bodies, offices and agencies of the Union with due regard for the principle of subsidiarity and to the Member States ***only when they are implementing*** Union law. They shall therefore respect the rights, observe the principles and promote the application thereof in accordance with their respective powers and respecting the limits of the powers of the Union as conferred on it in the Treaties.	1. The provisions of this Charter are addressed to the institutions, bodies, offices and agencies of the Union with due regard for the principle of subsidiarity and to the States ***when they act within the scope of*** Union law. They shall therefore respect the rights, observe the principles and promote the application thereof in accordance with their respective powers and respecting the limits of the powers of the Union as conferred on it in the Fundamental Law.
2. The Charter does not extend the field of application of Union law beyond the powers of the Union or establish any new power or task for the Union, or modify powers and tasks as defined in the Treaties.	2. The Charter does not extend the field of application of Union law beyond the powers of the Union or establish any new power or task for the Union, or modify powers and tasks as defined in the Fundamental Law.

Article 52

Scope and interpretation of rights and principles

1. Any limitation on the exercise of the rights and freedoms recognised by this Charter must be provided for by law and respect the essence of those rights and freedoms. Subject to the principle of proportionality, limitations may be made only if they are necessary and genuinely meet objectives of general interest recognised by the Union or the need to protect the rights and freedoms of others.

2. Rights recognised by this Charter ***for which provision is made in the Treaties*** shall be exercised under the conditions and within the limits defined by those Treaties.

3. In so far as this Charter contains rights which correspond to rights guaranteed by the Convention for the Protection of Human Rights and Fundamental Freedoms, the meaning and scope of those rights shall be the same as those laid down by the said Convention. This provision shall not prevent Union law providing more extensive protection.

4. In so far as this Charter recognises fundamental rights as they result from the constitutional traditions common to the Member States, those rights shall be interpreted in harmony with those traditions.

5. The provisions of this Charter which contain principles may be implemented by legislative and executive acts taken by institutions, bodies, offices and agencies of the Union, and by acts of Member States when they are implementing Union law, in the exercise of their respective powers. They shall be judicially cognisable only in the interpretation of such acts and in the ruling on their legality.

Article 196
(ex-Article 52 CFR)

Scope and interpretation of rights and principles

1. Any limitation on the exercise of the rights and freedoms recognised by this Charter must be provided for by law and respect the essence of those rights and freedoms. Subject to the principle of proportionality, limitations may be made only if they are necessary and genuinely meet objectives of general interest recognised by the Union or the need to protect the rights and freedoms of others.

2. Rights recognised by this Charter shall be exercised under the conditions and within the limits defined by the Fundamental Law.

3. In so far as this Charter contains rights which correspond to rights guaranteed by the Convention for the Protection of Human Rights and Fundamental Freedoms, the meaning and scope of those rights shall be the same as those laid down by the said Convention. This provision shall not prevent Union law providing more extensive protection.

4. In so far as this Charter recognises fundamental rights as they result from the constitutional traditions common to the States, those rights shall be interpreted in harmony with those traditions.

5. The provisions of this Charter which contain principles may be implemented by legislative and executive acts taken by institutions, bodies, offices and agencies of the Union, and by acts of the States when they are implementing Union law, in the exercise of their respective powers. They shall be judicially cognisable only in the interpretation of such acts and in the ruling on their legality.

6. Full account shall be taken of national laws and practices as specified in this Charter. ***7. The explanations drawn up as a way of providing guidance in the interpretation of this Charter shall be given due regard by the courts of the Union and of the Member States.***	6. Full account shall be taken of national laws and practices as specified in this Charter.
Article 53 Level of protection Nothing in this Charter shall be interpreted as restricting or adversely affecting human rights and fundamental freedoms as recognised, in their respective fields of application, by Union law and international law and by international agreements to which the Union or all the Member States are party, including the European Convention for the Protection of Human Rights and Fundamental Freedoms, and by the Member States' constitutions.	Article 197 (ex-Article 53 CFR) Level of protection Nothing in this Charter shall be interpreted as restricting or adversely affecting human rights and fundamental freedoms as recognised, in their respective fields of application, by Union law and international law and by international agreements to which the Union or all the States are party, including the European Convention for the Protection of Human Rights and Fundamental Freedoms, and by the States' constitutions.
Article 54 Prohibition of abuse of rights Nothing in this Charter shall be interpreted as implying any right to engage in any activity or to perform any act aimed at the destruction of any of the rights and freedoms recognised in this Charter or at their limitation to a greater extent than is provided for herein.	Article 198 (ex-Article 54 CFR) Prohibition of abuse of rights Nothing in this Charter shall be interpreted as implying any right to engage in any activity or to perform any act aimed at the destruction of any of the rights and freedoms recognised in this Charter or at their limitation to a greater extent than is provided for herein.

PART III

THE FINANCES OF THE UNION

The Fundamental Law makes some major changes to the Union's financial system, notably with the aim to give the Union the resources it needs to match the scale of its political ambition.

Under the revised system, the EU will be able to budget for a deficit under the same excessive debt and deficit procedures which already apply to its states. It is proposed to lighten the decision-making procedure for the agreement on the Union's revenue system of own resources (Article 200). A comparable modification is made for the decision on the multiannual financial framework (MFF) (Article 203) whose minimum duration is lowered to three years. In case there is no agreement on a new MFF, the previous framework will be carried forward, but adjusted for inflation.

EU agencies are expressly to be included in the general budget of the Union.

Article 202 gives the Union the powers to levy direct and indirect taxation as the instrument to raise its own revenue.

As far as the annual budget making procedure is concerned, we propose to return to the pre-Lisbon formula whereby both the Parliament and the Council have to take political responsibility for the passage or rejection of the budget in the event that no conciliation between them proves possible (Article 206(8)). This will serve to make an eventual budget agreement more likely than not.

The special provisions for the fiscal capacity of the eurozone feature in Article 201 (own resources), Article 204 (multiannual framework) and Article 206(11) (annual budget).

FINANCIAL PROVISIONS	THE FINANCES OF THE UNION
Article 310	Article 199 (ex-Article 310 TFEU)
1. All items of revenue and expenditure of the Union shall be included in estimates to be drawn up for each financial year and shall be shown in the budget.	1. All items of revenue and expenditure of the Union ***and of Union agencies*** shall be included in estimates to be drawn up for each financial year and shall be shown in the budget.
The Union's annual budget shall be established by the European Parliament and the Council in accordance with Article 314.	The Union's annual budget shall be established by the European Parliament and the Council in accordance with Article 206.
The revenue and expenditure shown in the budget shall be in balance.	
2. The expenditure shown in the budget shall be authorised for the annual budgetary period in accordance with the regulation referred to in Article 322.	2. The ***revenue and*** expenditure shown in the budget shall be authorised for the annual budgetary period in accordance with the regulation referred to in Article 214.
3. The implementation of expenditure shown in the budget shall require the prior adoption of a legally binding Union act providing a legal basis for its action and for the implementation of the corresponding expenditure in accordance with the regulation referred to in Article 322, except in cases for which that law provides.	3. The implementation of expenditure shown in the budget shall require the prior adoption of a legally binding Union act providing a legal basis for its action and for the implementation of the corresponding expenditure in accordance with the regulation referred to in Article 214, except in cases for which that law provides.
4. With a view to maintaining budgetary discipline, the Union shall not adopt any act which is likely to have appreciable implications for the budget without providing an assurance that the expenditure arising from such an act is capable of being financed within the limit of the Union's own resources and in compliance with the multiannual financial framework referred to in Article 312.	4. With a view to maintaining budgetary discipline, the Union shall not adopt any act which is likely to have appreciable implications for the budget without providing an assurance that the expenditure arising from such an act is capable of being financed within the limit of the Union's own resources and in compliance with ***a*** multiannual financial framework ***if such a framework has been agreed pursuant to*** Article 203.
5. The budget shall be implemented in accordance with the principle of sound financial management. Member States shall cooperate with the Union to ensure that the appropriations entered in the budget are used in accordance with this principle.	5. The budget shall be implemented in accordance with the principle of sound financial management. States shall cooperate with the Union to ensure that the appropriations entered in the budget are used in accordance with this principle.

6. The Union and the Member States, in accordance with Article 325, shall counter fraud and any other illegal activities affecting the financial interests of the Union.	6. The Union and the States, in accordance with Article 217, shall counter fraud and any other illegal activities affecting the financial interests of the Union.
THE UNION'S OWN RESOURCES	THE UNION'S OWN RESOURCES
Article 311	Article 200 (ex-Article 311 TFEU)
The Union shall provide itself with the means necessary to attain its objectives and carry through its policies.	1. The Union shall provide itself with the means necessary to attain its objectives and carry through its policies.
Without prejudice to other revenue, the budget shall be financed wholly from own resources.	Without prejudice to other revenue, the budget shall be financed wholly from own resources.
	The Union shall avoid excessive debt or deficits. The ratios of the Union's debt and deficit to gross domestic product shall not exceed the respective reference values as specified in Protocol No 10.
The Council, acting in accordance with a special legislative procedure, shall ***unanimously and after consulting the European Parliament*** adopt a decision laying down the provisions relating to the system of own resources of the Union. In this context it may establish new categories of own resources or abolish an existing category. That decision shall not enter into force until it is approved by the Member States in accordance with their respective constitutional requirements.	2. ***The European Parliament and*** the Council, acting in accordance with ***the*** special legislative procedure, shall adopt a decision laying down the provisions relating to the system of own resources of the Union. In this context ***they*** may establish new categories of own resources or abolish an existing category. That decision shall not enter into force until it is approved by ***four fifths of*** the States in accordance with their respective constitutional requirements.
The Council, acting by means of regulations in accordance with a special legislative procedure, shall lay down implementing measures for the Union's own resources system in so far as this is provided for in the decision adopted on the basis of the third paragraph. The Council shall act after obtaining the consent of the European Parliament.	3. ***The European Parliament and*** the Council, acting by means of regulations in accordance with ***the ordinary legislative procedure***, shall lay down implementing measures for the Union's own resources system in so far as this is provided for in the decision adopted on the basis of ***paragraph 2***.

	Article 201 ***Without prejudice to Article 200, and pursuant to Article 239, the European Parliament and the Council shall adopt a decision laying down the provisions relating to a system of own resources specific to those States whose currency is the euro.*** ***This revenue shall be assigned to the Union budget as the fiscal capacity referred to in Article 236(3) specific to those States.***
	Article 202 ***The European Parliament and Council, acting in accordance with the ordinary legislative procedure, may adopt measures concerning the taxation of turnover, excise duties and other forms of indirect taxation, as well as the taxation of companies, natural persons and other forms of direct taxation for the benefit of the Union.*** ***Revenue from such indirect and direct taxation shall comprise own resources pursuant to Article 200 and shall accrue to the Union budget.*** ***The collection of Union taxes shall be transparent.***
THE MULTIANNUAL FINANCIAL FRAMEWORK	THE MULTIANNUAL FINANCIAL FRAMEWORK
Article 312	Article 203 (ex-Article 312 TFEU)
1. The multiannual financial framework shall ensure that Union expenditure develops in an orderly manner and within the limits of its own resources.	1. ***The Union shall establish a*** multiannual financial framework ***in order to*** ensure that Union expenditure develops in an orderly manner and within the limits of its own resources, ***federal debt and deficits.***
It shall be established for a period of at least five years.	***In the case that a multi-annual financial framework is agreed,*** it shall be established for a period of at least ***three*** years.
The annual budget of the Union shall comply with the multiannual financial framework.	The annual budget of the Union shall comply with ***such a*** multiannual financial framework.

2. The Council, acting in accordance with a special legislative procedure, shall adopt a regulation laying down the multiannual financial framework. ***The Council shall act unanimously after obtaining the consent of the European Parliament***, which shall be given by a majority of its component members. ***The European Council may, unanimously, adopt a decision authorising the Council to act by a qualified majority when adopting the regulation referred to in the first subparagraph.***	2. ***The European Parliament and*** the Council, acting in accordance with ***the*** special legislative procedure, shall adopt a regulation laying down the multiannual financial framework.
3. The financial framework shall determine the amounts of the annual ceilings on commitment appropriations by category of expenditure and of the annual ceiling on payment appropriations. The categories of expenditure, limited in number, shall correspond to the Union's major sectors of activity. The financial framework shall lay down any other provisions required for the annual budgetary procedure to run smoothly.	3. The financial framework shall determine the amounts of the annual ceilings on commitment appropriations by category of expenditure and of the annual ceiling on payment appropriations. The categories of expenditure, limited in number, shall correspond to the Union's major sectors of activity. The financial framework shall lay down any other provisions required for the annual budgetary procedure to run smoothly.
4. Where no ***Council*** regulation determining a new financial framework has been adopted by the end of the previous financial framework, the ceilings and other provisions corresponding to the last year of that framework shall be extended until such time as that act is adopted.	4. Where no regulation determining a new financial framework has been adopted by the end of the previous financial framework, the ceilings ***as adjusted for inflation***, and other provisions corresponding to the last year of that framework shall be extended until such time as that act is adopted.
5. Throughout the procedure leading to the adoption of the financial framework, the European Parliament, the Council and the Commission shall take any measure necessary to facilitate its adoption.	5. Throughout the procedure leading to the adoption of the financial framework, the European Parliament, the Council and the Commission shall take any measure necessary to facilitate its adoption.
	Article 204 ***Without prejudice to Article 203, and pursuant to Article 239, the European Parliament and the Council may adopt a regulation laying down the multiannual financial framework for the fiscal capacity of the States whose currency is the euro.***

THE ANNUAL BUDGET	THE ANNUAL BUDGET
Article 313	Article 205 (ex-Article 313 TFEU) .....
Article 314	Article 206 (ex-Article 314 TFEU)
The European Parliament and the Council, acting in accordance with a special legislative procedure, shall establish the Union's annual budget in accordance with the following provisions.	The European Parliament and the Council ***shall establish the Union's annual budget in accordance with the following provisions:***
1. With the exception of the European Central Bank, each institution shall, before 1 July, draw up estimates of its expenditure for the following financial year. The Commission shall consolidate these estimates in a draft budget, which may contain different estimates.	1. With the exception of the European Central Bank, each institution shall, before 1 July, draw up estimates of its expenditure for the following financial year. The Commission shall consolidate these estimates in a draft budget, which may contain different estimates.
The draft budget shall contain an estimate of revenue and an estimate of expenditure.	The draft budget shall contain an estimate of revenue and an estimate of expenditure.
2. The Commission shall submit a proposal containing the draft budget to the European Parliament and to the Council not later than 1 September of the year preceding that in which the budget is to be implemented.	2. The Commission shall submit a proposal containing the draft budget to the European Parliament and to the Council not later than 1 September of the year preceding that in which the budget is to be implemented.
The Commission may amend the draft budget during the procedure until such time as the Conciliation Committee, referred to in paragraph 5, is convened.	The Commission may amend the draft budget during the procedure until such time as the Conciliation Committee, referred to in paragraph 5, is convened.
3. The Council shall adopt its position on the draft budget and forward it to the European Parliament not later than 1 October of the year preceding that in which the budget is to be implemented. The Council shall inform the European Parliament in full of the reasons which led it to adopt its position.	3. The Council shall adopt its position on the draft budget and forward it to the European Parliament not later than 1 October of the year preceding that in which the budget is to be implemented. The Council shall inform the European Parliament in full of the reasons which led it to adopt its position.

4. If, within forty-two days of such communication, the European Parliament:

(a) approves the position of the Council, the budget shall be adopted;

(b) has not taken a decision, the budget shall be deemed to have been adopted;

(c) adopts amendments by a majority of its component members, the amended draft shall be forwarded to the Council and to the Commission. The President of the European Parliament, in agreement with the President of the Council, shall immediately convene a meeting of the Conciliation Committee. However, if within ten days of the draft being forwarded the Council informs the European Parliament that it has approved all its amendments, the Conciliation Committee shall not meet.

5. The Conciliation Committee, which shall be composed of the members of the Council or their representatives and an equal number of members representing the European Parliament, shall have the task of reaching agreement on a joint text, by a qualified majority of the members of the Council or their representatives and by a majority of the representatives of the European Parliament within twenty-one days of its being convened, on the basis of the positions of the European Parliament and the Council.

The Commission shall take part in the Conciliation Committee's proceedings and shall take all the necessary initiatives with a view to reconciling the positions of the European Parliament and the Council.

6. If, within the twenty-one days referred to in paragraph 5, the Conciliation Committee agrees on a joint text, the European Parliament and the Council shall each have a period of fourteen days from the date of that agreement in which to approve the joint text.

4. If, within forty-two days of such communication, the European Parliament:

(a) approves the position of the Council, the budget shall be adopted;

(b) has not taken a decision, the budget shall be deemed to have been adopted;

(c) adopts amendments by a majority of its component members, the amended draft shall be forwarded to the Council and to the Commission. The President of the European Parliament, in agreement with the President of the Council, shall immediately convene a meeting of the Conciliation Committee. However, if within ten days of the draft being forwarded the Council informs the European Parliament that it has approved all its amendments, the Conciliation Committee shall not meet.

5. The Conciliation Committee, which shall be composed of the members of the Council and an equal number of Members of the European Parliament, shall have the task of reaching agreement on a joint text, by a qualified majority of the members of the Council and by a majority of the Members of the European Parliament within twenty-one days of its being convened, on the basis of the positions of the European Parliament and the Council.

The Commission shall take part in the Conciliation Committee's proceedings and shall take all the necessary initiatives with a view to reconciling the positions of the European Parliament and the Council.

6. If, within the twenty-one days referred to in paragraph 5, the Conciliation Committee agrees on a joint text, the European Parliament, ***acting by a majority of its component Members,*** and the Council, ***acting by qualified majority***, shall each have a period of fourteen days from the date of that agreement in which to approve the joint text.

7. If, within the period of fourteen days referred to in paragraph 6:

(a) the European Parliament and the Council both approve the joint text or fail to take a decision, or if one of these institutions approves the joint text while the other one fails to take a decision, the budget shall be deemed to be definitively adopted in accordance with the joint text; or

(b) the European Parliament, acting by a majority of its component members, and the Council both reject the joint text, or if one of these institutions rejects the joint text while the other one fails to take a decision, a new draft budget shall be submitted by the Commission; or

(c) the European Parliament, acting by a majority of its component members, rejects the joint text while the Council approves it, a new draft budget shall be submitted by the Commission; or

(d) the European Parliament approves the joint text whilst the Council rejects it, the European Parliament may, within fourteen days from the date of the rejection by the Council and acting by a majority of its component members and three-fifths of the votes cast, decide to confirm all or some of the amendments referred to in paragraph 4(c). Where a European Parliament amendment is not confirmed, the position agreed in the Conciliation Committee on the budget heading which is the subject of the amendment shall be retained. The budget shall be deemed to be definitively adopted on this basis.

7. If, within the period of fourteen days referred to in paragraph 6:

(a) the European Parliament and the Council both approve the joint text or fail to take a decision, or if one of these institutions approves the joint text while the other one fails to take a decision, the budget shall be deemed to be definitively adopted in accordance with the joint text; or

(b) the European Parliament, acting by a majority of its component members, and the Council both reject the joint text, or if one of these institutions rejects the joint text while the other one fails to take a decision, a new draft budget shall be submitted by the Commission; or

(c) the European Parliament, acting by a majority of its component members, rejects the joint text while the Council approves it, a new draft budget shall be submitted by the Commission; or

(d) the European Parliament approves the joint text whilst the Council rejects it, the European Parliament may, within fourteen days from the date of the rejection by the Council and acting by a majority of its component members and three-fifths of the votes cast, decide to confirm all or some of the amendments referred to in paragraph 4(c). Where a European Parliament amendment is not confirmed, the position agreed in the Conciliation Committee on the budget heading which is the subject of the amendment shall be retained. The budget shall be deemed to be definitively adopted on this basis.

8. If, within the twenty-one days referred to in paragraph 5, the Conciliation Committee does not agree on a joint text, a new draft budget shall be submitted by the Commission.	8. If, within the twenty-one days referred to in paragraph 5, the Conciliation Committee does not agree on a joint text, ***the European Parliament may, within fourteen days, confirm its amendments by an absolute majority of its Members and by three fifths of the votes cast. In this case the budget shall be deemed adopted as such, unless the Council, within fourteen days, expresses its opposition. In that case,*** a new draft budget shall be submitted by the Commission.
9. When the procedure provided for in this Article has been completed, the President of the European Parliament shall declare that the budget has been definitively adopted.	9. When the procedure provided for in this Article has been completed, the President of the European Parliament shall declare that the budget has been definitively adopted.
10. Each institution shall exercise the powers conferred upon it under this Article in compliance with the Treaties and the acts adopted thereunder, with particular regard to the Union's own resources and the balance between revenue and expenditure.	10. Each institution shall exercise the powers conferred upon it under this Article in compliance with the Fundamental Law and the acts adopted thereunder, with particular regard to the Union's own resources.
	11. Without prejudice to this Article, and pursuant to Article 239, the European Parliament and the Council shall adopt a regulation laying down the annual budget for the expenditure of the fiscal capacity of the States whose currency is the euro.
Article 315	Article 207 (ex-Article 315 TFEU)
If, at the beginning of a financial year, the budget has not yet been definitively adopted, a sum equivalent to not more than one twelfth of the budget appropriations for the preceding financial year may be spent each month in respect of any chapter of the budget in accordance with the provisions of the Regulations made pursuant to Article 322; that sum shall not, however, exceed one twelfth of the appropriations provided for in the same chapter of the draft budget.	If, at the beginning of a financial year, the budget has not yet been definitively adopted, a sum equivalent to not more than one twelfth of the budget appropriations for the preceding financial year, ***adjusted for inflation,*** may be spent each month in respect of any chapter of the budget in accordance with the provisions of the Regulations made pursuant to Article 214; that sum shall not, however, exceed one twelfth of the appropriations provided for in the same chapter of the draft budget ***as adjusted for inflation.***

The Council on a proposal by the Commission, may, provided that the other conditions laid down in the first paragraph are observed, authorise expenditure in excess of one twelfth in accordance with the regulations made pursuant to Article 322. The Council shall forward the decision immediately to the European Parliament. The decision referred to in the second paragraph shall lay down the necessary measures relating to resources to ensure application of this Article, in accordance with the acts referred to in Article 311. It shall enter into force thirty days following its adoption if the European Parliament, acting by a majority of its component Members, has not decided to reduce this expenditure within that time limit.	The Council on a proposal by the Commission, may, provided that the other conditions laid down in the first paragraph are observed, authorise expenditure in excess of one twelfth in accordance with the regulations made pursuant to Article 214. The Council shall forward the decision immediately to the European Parliament. The decision referred to in the second paragraph shall lay down the necessary measures relating to resources to ensure application of this Article, in accordance with the acts referred to in Article 200. It shall enter into force thirty days following its adoption if the European Parliament, acting by a majority of its component Members, has not decided to reduce this expenditure within that time limit.
Article 316	Article 208 (ex-Article 316 TFEU) .....
IMPLEMENTATION OF THE BUDGET AND DISCHARGE	IMPLEMENTATION OF THE BUDGET AND DISCHARGE
Articles 317–319	Articles 209–211 (ex-Articles 317–319 TFEU) .....
COMMON PROVISIONS	COMMON PROVISIONS
Articles 320–321	Articles 212–213 (ex-Articles 320–321 TFEU) .....
Article 322 1. The European Parliament and the Council, acting in accordance with the ordinary legislative procedure, and after consulting the Court of Auditors, shall adopt by means of regulations: (a) the financial rules which determine in particular the procedure to be adopted for establishing and implementing the budget and for presenting and auditing accounts;	Article 214 (ex-Article 322 TFEU) 1. The European Parliament and the Council, acting in accordance with the ordinary legislative procedure, and after consulting the Court of Auditors, shall adopt by means of regulations: (a) the financial rules which determine in particular the procedure to be adopted for establishing and implementing the budget and for presenting and auditing accounts;

(b) rules providing for checks on the responsibility of financial actors, in particular authorising officers and accounting officers.	(b) rules providing for checks on the responsibility of financial actors, in particular authorising officers and accounting officers.
2. The Council, ***acting on a proposal from the Commission and after consulting the European Parliament*** and the Court of Auditors, shall determine the methods and procedure whereby the budget revenue provided under the arrangements relating to the Union's own resources shall be made available to the Commission, and determine the measures to be applied, if need be, to meet cash requirements.	2. The ***European Parliament and the*** Council, ***acting in accordance with the special legislative procedure***, and after consulting the Court of Auditors, shall determine the methods and procedure whereby the budget revenue provided under the arrangements relating to the Union's own resources shall be made available to the Commission, and determine the measures to be applied, if need be, to meet cash requirements.
Articles 323–324	Articles 215–216 (ex-Articles 323–324 TFEU) .....
COMBATTING FRAUD	COMBATTING FRAUD
Article 325	Article 217 (ex-Article 325 TFEU) .....

PART IV

ECONOMIC AND MONETARY UNION

CHAPTER ONE

In this chapter we propose a radical reform of the arrangements for Economic and Monetary Union as first prescribed by the Treaty of Maastricht. In summary, a common economic policy of the EU, with the aim of achieving a 'highly competitive social market economy', will supersede the mere coordination of national economic policies. This process will be driven by the Commission, in which a powerful new Treasury Minister will be a Vice-President. The powers of Parliament are considerably enhanced.

In accordance with the Fiscal Compact Treaty (2012) and the laws recently put in place to manage the financial crisis – colloquially, the 'Six Pack' and the 'Two Pack' – the states are required to observe much stronger fiscal discipline according to jointly agreed rules. The powers of the Commission to scrutinise national performance and, accordingly, to make proposals to the Council and the states about their own economic policies are much enhanced.

The broad macro-economic policy guidelines (Article 220) become subject to co-decision by the Parliament and Council, within the context of an annual European semester. Parliament will also be consulted before necessary corrective recommendations are made to an errant state, and may seek to amend the Commission's proposals before their adoption by the Council.

The ECB is empowered to buy sovereign bonds of states under the European Stability Mechanism in the primary as well as the secondary markets (Article 222). The famous 'no bail out' clause is revised to allow for the eurozone states to establish a system for the common management of sovereign debt, subject to strict conditionality (Article 224).

The revised excessive debt or deficit procedure is fully laid out in Article 225, as follows: (a) Parliament is consulted on a decision to declare an excessive deficit; (b) Commission proposals stand unless the Council opposes them by QMV without the participation of the errant state; (c) in that case, the Commission can ask Parliament to trigger the excessive deficit procedure; (d) in the event of an excessive deficit, the Commission publishes its recommendations to the state concerned; (e) where the state does not accept the recommendations made to it, the Council may propose tougher measures, on a proposal of the Commission; (f) where the Council refuses to act, Parliament may do so; (g) where the state still refuses to take the remedial action prescribed, penalties may be imposed by the Council. The national parliament of the state concerned can demand a hearing, and the European Parliament may amend the Commission's position unless both Commission and Council agree to reject the amendments.

Importantly, the prohibition on the right of the Commission or a state to bring an action in the Court of Justice, in the context of the excessive deficit procedure, is lifted (deletion of ex-Article 126(10) TEFU). Lastly, states' direct contributions to the EU budget will not be taken into account in assessing an excessive deficit. Such direct payments will in any event be phased out (Article 225(14)).

Article 227 sets out the new role of the European Central Bank in respect of the prudential supervision of the financial sector, allowing for the creation of a single financial authority for the whole banking union. In respect of the banking union, the ECB is made accountable to the Parliament.

ECONOMIC AND MONETARY POLICY	ECONOMIC AND MONETARY POLICY
Article 119	Article 218 (ex-Article 119 TFEU)
1. For the purposes set out in Article 3 of the Treaty on European Union, ***the activities of the Member States and the Union shall include, as provided in the Treaties, the adoption of an economic policy*** which is based on the close coordination of Member States' economic policies, on the internal market and on the definition of common objectives, and conducted in accordance with the principle of an open market economy ***with free competition.***	1. For the purposes set out in Article 3, the Union shall ***adopt common fiscal, economic and monetary policies*** which are based on the close coordination of States' economic policies, on the ***establishment of the euro***, on the internal market and on the definition of common objectives, and conducted in accordance with the principle of an open, ***highly competitive social*** market economy.
2. ***Concurrently with the foregoing, and as provided in the Treaties and in accordance with the procedures set out therein, these activities shall include a single currency, the euro, and the definition and conduct of a single monetary policy and exchange-rate policy the primary objective of both of which*** shall be to maintain price stability and, without prejudice to this objective, to support the general economic policies in the Union, in accordance with the principle of an open market economy with free competition.	2. ***The common economic policy of the Union shall promote job creation, investment, economic stability, social cohesion and sustainable development. The Commission shall be responsible for driving forward the common economic policy and, in particular, through a treasury facility, for the borrowing and lending of funds, the operation and maintenance of the financial system, the collection of revenues, the management of accounts, the enforcement of tax laws and the imposition of penalties.***
	3. ***The common monetary policy of the Union*** shall be to maintain price stability and, without prejudice to the objective of price stability, to support the ***common economic policy. The European Central Bank shall be responsible for the common monetary policy.***
3. These activities of the Member States and the Union shall entail compliance with the following guiding principles: stable prices, sound public finances and monetary conditions and a sustainable balance of payments.	4. These activities of the States and the Union shall entail compliance with the following guiding principles: stable prices, sound public finances and monetary conditions and a sustainable ***European*** balance of payments.

Article 120	Article 219 (ex-Article 120 TFEU)
Member States shall conduct their economic policies with a view to contributing to the achievement of the objectives of the Union, as defined in Article 3 of the Treaty on European Union, and in the context of the broad guidelines referred to in Article 121(2). The Member States and the Union shall act in accordance with the principle of an open market economy ***with free competition***, favouring an efficient allocation of resources, and in compliance with the principles set out in Article 119.	1. States shall conduct their economic policies with a view to contributing to the achievement of the objectives of the Union, as defined in Article 3 and in the context of the broad guidelines referred to in Article 220(2). The States and the Union shall act in accordance with the principle of an open, ***highly competitive social*** market economy, favouring an efficient allocation of resources, and in compliance with the principles set out in Article 218. 2. ***The Union shall take all necessary actions and measures in all the areas which are essential to the proper functioning of the economic and monetary union in pursuit of the objectives of fostering enhanced convergence and competitiveness, of promoting employment and social cohesion, of environmental sustainability, of contributing further to the sustainability of public finances and of reinforcing financial stability.*** 3. ***The States shall ensure that all major economic policy reforms that they plan to undertake will be discussed ex-ante and, where appropriate, coordinated among themselves and with the Commission.***
Article 121	Article 220 (ex-Article 121 TFEU)
1. Member States shall regard their economic policies as a matter of common concern and shall coordinate them within the Council, in accordance with the provisions of Article 120.	1. States shall regard their economic policies as a matter of common concern and shall coordinate them within the Council, in accordance with the provisions of Article 219. ***In particular, the coordination of the budgetary policies of the States and of the Union will take place within the context of a European semester.***
2. The Council shall, ***on a recommendation from the Commission***, formulate a draft for the broad guidelines of the economic policies of the Member States and of the Union, and shall ***report its findings*** to the European Council.	2. ***The Commission*** shall, ***after consulting the European Parliament and the Council,*** formulate a draft for the broad guidelines of the economic policies of the Union and the States, and shall ***make a proposal*** to the European Council.

The European Council shall, acting on the basis of the ***report from the Council***, discuss a conclusion on the broad guidelines of the economic policies of the Member States and of the Union.

On the basis of this conclusion, the Council shall adopt a recommendation setting out these broad guidelines. ***The Council shall inform the European Parliament of its recommendation.***

3. In order to ensure closer coordination of economic policies and sustained convergence of the economic performances of the Member States, the ***Council*** shall, ***on the basis of reports submitted by the Commission,*** monitor economic developments in each of the Member States and in the Union as well as the consistency of economic policies with the broad guidelines referred to in paragraph 2, and regularly carry out an overall assessment.

For the purpose of this multilateral surveillance, Member States shall forward information to the Commission about important measures taken by them in the field of their economic policy and such other information as they deem necessary.

4. Where it is established, under the procedure referred to in paragraph 3, that the economic policies of a Member State are not consistent with the broad guidelines referred to in paragraph 2 or that they risk jeopardising the proper functioning of economic and monetary union, the Commission ***may*** address a warning to the Member State concerned. The Council, on a ***recommendation*** from the Commission, may address the necessary recommendations to the Member State concerned. The Council may, on a proposal from the Commission, decide to make its recommendations public.

The European Council shall, acting on the basis of the ***Commission's proposal***, discuss a conclusion on the broad guidelines of the economic policies of the Union and the States.

Having considered this conclusion, ***the European Parliament and Council, acting in accordance with the ordinary legislative procedure,*** shall adopt a recommendation setting out these broad guidelines.

3. In order to ensure closer coordination of economic policies and sustained convergence of the economic performances of the States, the ***Commission shall monitor*** economic developments in each of the States and in the Union, ***including macroeconomic imbalances***, as well as the consistency of economic policies with the broad guidelines referred to in paragraph 2, and regularly carry out an overall assessment.

For the purpose of this multilateral surveillance, States shall forward information to the Commission about important measures taken by them in the field of their economic policy and such other information as they deem necessary ***or as the Commission so requires.***

4. Where it is established, under the procedure referred to in paragraph 3, that the economic policies of a State are not consistent with the broad guidelines referred to in paragraph 2 or that they risk jeopardising the proper functioning of economic and monetary union, the Commission ***shall*** address a warning to the State concerned.

The Council may, on a ***proposal*** from the Commission, ***and after consulting the European Parliament***, address the necessary recommendations to the State concerned. The recommendations ***shall be made*** public.

Within the scope of this paragraph, the Council shall act without taking into account the vote of the member of the Council representing the Member State concerned. A qualified majority of the other members of the Council shall be defined in accordance with Article 238(3)(a).	***In the case that a State fails to follow the recommendations, the Council may decide, on a proposal of the Commission, to take more intensive action.***
5. The President of the Council and the Commission shall report to the European Parliament on the results of multilateral surveillance. The President of the Council may be invited to appear before the competent committee of the European Parliament ***if the Council has made its recommendations public.***	***5. At any stage of the procedure, the European Parliament may request the right to be heard and may propose amendments to the Commission's proposal for recommendations. The Council may reject those amendments if the Commission delivers a negative opinion. Otherwise the Commission's proposal shall be deemed to have been adopted by the Council in its amended version.*** 6. Within the scope of ***paragraphs 4 and 5***, the Council shall act without taking into account the vote of the member of the Council representing the State concerned. A qualified majority of the other members of the Council shall be defined in accordance with Article 109. 7. ***The Commission shall report regularly to the European Parliament and Council on the results of multilateral surveillance, and in particular on risks to financial stability.*** The President of the Council may be invited to appear before the competent committee of the European Parliament.
6. The European Parliament and the Council, acting by means of regulations in accordance with the ordinary legislative procedure, ***may*** adopt detailed rules for the multilateral surveillance procedure ***referred to in paragraphs 3 and 4.***	8. The European Parliament and the Council, acting by means of regulations in accordance with the ordinary legislative procedure, ***shall*** adopt detailed rules for the ***conduct of*** the multilateral surveillance procedure ***during the European semester.***

Article 122	Article 221 (ex-Article 122 TFEU)
1. Without prejudice to any other procedures provided for in the Treaties, the ***Council, on a proposal from the Commission,*** may decide, in a spirit of solidarity ***between Member States***, upon the measures appropriate to the economic situation, in particular if severe difficulties arise in the supply of certain products, notably in the area of energy.	1. Without prejudice to any other procedures provided for in the Fundamental Law, ***the Commission, after having consulted the Council***, may decide, in a spirit of ***Union solidarity***, upon the measures appropriate to the economic situation, in particular if severe difficulties arise in the supply of certain products, notably in the area of energy.
2. Where a Member State is in difficulties or is seriously threatened with severe difficulties caused by natural disasters or exceptional occurrences beyond its control, the ***Council, on a proposal from the Commission***, may grant, under certain conditions, Union financial assistance to the Member State concerned. ***The President of the Council shall inform the European Parliament of the decision taken.***	2. Where a State is in difficulties or is seriously threatened with severe difficulties caused by natural disasters or exceptional occurrences beyond its control, ***the Commission, after obtaining the consent of the Council***, may grant, under certain conditions, Union financial assistance to the State concerned. ***The Commission shall keep the European Parliament fully informed at all stages of the process.***
Article 123	Article 222 (ex-Article 123 TFEU)
1. Overdraft facilities or any other type of credit facility with the European Central Bank or with the central banks of the Member States (hereinafter referred to as 'national central banks') in favour of Union institutions, bodies, offices or agencies, central governments, regional, local or other public authorities, other bodies governed by public law, or public undertakings of Member States shall be prohibited, as shall the purchase directly from them by the European Central Bank or national central banks of debt instruments.	1. Overdraft facilities or any other type of credit facility with the European Central Bank or with the central banks of the States (hereinafter referred to as 'national central banks') in favour of Union institutions, bodies, offices or agencies, central governments, regional, local or other public authorities, other bodies governed by public law, or public undertakings of States shall be prohibited, as shall the purchase directly from them by the European Central Bank or national central banks of debt instruments. ***2. By way of derogation from paragraph 1, the European Central Bank may purchase government bonds in the primary and secondary markets issued by States whose currency is the euro and which are subject to a programme of the European Stability Mechanism.***

2. Paragraph 1 shall not apply to publicly owned credit institutions which, in the context of the supply of reserves by central banks, shall be given the same treatment by national central banks and the European Central Bank as private credit institutions.	3. Paragraph 1 shall not apply to publicly owned credit institutions which, in the context of the supply of reserves by central banks, shall be given the same treatment by national central banks and the European Central Bank as private credit institutions.
Article 124	Article 223 (ex-Article 124 TFEU)
Any measure, not based on prudential considerations, establishing privileged access by Union institutions, bodies, offices or agencies, central governments, regional, local or other public authorities, other bodies governed by public law, or public undertakings of Member States to financial institutions, shall be prohibited.	Any measure, not based on prudential considerations, establishing privileged access by Union institutions, bodies, offices or agencies, central governments, regional, local or other public authorities, other bodies governed by public law, or public undertakings of States to financial institutions, shall be prohibited.
Article 125	Article 224 (ex-Article 125 TFEU)
1. The Union shall not be liable for or assume the commitments of central governments, regional, local or other public authorities, other bodies governed by public law, or public undertakings of any Member State, without prejudice to mutual financial guarantees for the joint execution of a specific project. A Member State shall not be liable for or assume the commitments of central governments, regional, local or other public authorities, other bodies governed by public law, or public undertakings of another Member State, without prejudice to mutual financial guarantees for the joint execution of a specific project. *2. The Council, on a proposal from the Commission and after consulting the European Parliament, may, as required, specify definitions for the application of the prohibitions referred to in Articles 123 and 124 and in this Article.*	*The European Parliament and the Council, acting accordance with the special legislative procedure, and after having consulted the European Central Bank, may establish for the States whose currency is the euro a system for the common management of sovereign debt. Participation in such a system shall be subject to strict conditionality.*

Article 126

1. Member States shall avoid excessive government deficits.

2. The Commission shall monitor the development of the budgetary situation and of the stock of government debt in the Member States with a view to identifying gross errors. In particular it shall examine compliance with budgetary discipline on the basis of the following two criteria:

(a) whether the ratio of the planned or actual government deficit to gross domestic product exceeds a reference value, unless:

– either the ratio has declined substantially and continuously and reached a level that comes close to the reference value,

– or, alternatively, the excess over the reference value is only exceptional and temporary and the ratio remains close to the reference value;

(b) whether the ratio of government debt to gross domestic product exceeds a reference value, unless the ratio is sufficiently diminishing and approaching the reference value at a satisfactory pace.

The reference values are specified in the Protocol on the excessive deficit procedure annexed to the Treaties.

3. If a Member State does not fulfil the requirements under one or both of these criteria, the Commission shall prepare a report. The report of the Commission shall also take into account whether the government deficit exceeds government investment expenditure and take into account all other relevant factors, including the medium-term economic and budgetary position of the Member State.

Article 225
(ex-Article 126 TFEU)

1. The States shall avoid excessive government ***debt or*** deficits.

2. The Commission shall monitor the development of the budgetary situation and of the stock of government debt in the States with a view to identifying gross errors. In particular it shall examine compliance with budgetary discipline on the basis of the following two criteria:

(a) whether the ratio of the planned or actual government deficit to gross domestic product exceeds a reference value, unless:

– either the ratio has declined substantially and continuously and reached a level that comes close to the reference value,

– or, alternatively, the excess over the reference value is only exceptional and temporary and the ratio remains close to the reference value;

(b) whether the ratio of government debt to gross domestic product exceeds a reference value, unless the ratio is sufficiently diminishing and approaching the reference value at a satisfactory pace.

The reference values are specified in the Protocol on the excessive deficit procedure.

3. If a State does not fulfil the requirements under one or both of these criteria, the Commission shall prepare a report. The report of the Commission shall also take into account whether the government deficit exceeds government investment expenditure and take into account all other relevant factors, including the medium-term economic and budgetary position of the State.

The Commission may also prepare a report if, notwithstanding the fulfilment of the requirements under the criteria, it is of the opinion that there is a risk of an excessive deficit in a Member State.

4. The Economic and Financial Committee shall formulate an opinion on the report of the Commission.

5. If the Commission considers that an excessive deficit in a Member State exists or may occur, it shall address an opinion to the Member State concerned and shall inform the Council accordingly.

6. The Council shall, on a proposal from the Commission, and having considered any observations which the Member State concerned may wish to make, decide after an overall assessment whether an excessive deficit exists.

7. Where the Council decides, in accordance with paragraph 6, that an excessive deficit exists, ***it*** shall adopt, without undue delay, on a recommendation from the Commission, recommendations addressed to the Member State concerned with a view to bringing that situation to an end within a given period. ***Subject to the provisions of paragraph 8***, these recommendations shall ***not*** be made public.

The Commission may also prepare a report if, notwithstanding the fulfilment of the requirements under the criteria, it is of the opinion that there is a risk of an excessive ***debt or*** deficit in a State.

4. The Economic and Financial Committee shall formulate an opinion on the report of the Commission.

5. If the Commission considers that an excessive ***debt or*** deficit in a State exists or may occur, it shall address an opinion to the State concerned and shall inform ***the European Parliament and*** the Council accordingly.

6. The Council shall, on a proposal from the Commission, ***after having consulted the European Parliament***, and having considered any observations which the State concerned may wish to make, decide after an overall assessment whether an excessive ***debt or*** deficit exists.

In the case that the Council opposes the Commission's proposal, the European Parliament, at the request of the Commission, may decide that an excessive debt or deficit exists. The Parliament shall decide by a majority of its component Members, acting within four weeks of the Council's decision to oppose the Commission's proposal.

7. Where ***either*** the Council ***or the European Parliament*** decides, in accordance with paragraph 6, that an excessive ***debt or*** deficit exists, ***the Council*** shall adopt, without undue delay, on a recommendation of the Commission, recommendations addressed to the State concerned with a view to bringing that situation to an end within a given period. ***These recommendations shall be made public.***

8. Where it establishes that there has been no effective action in response to its recommendations within the period laid down, the Council may make its recommendations public.

9. If a Member State persists in failing to put into practice the recommendations of the Council, the Council may decide to give notice to the Member State to take, within a specified time limit, measures for the deficit reduction which is judged necessary by the Council in order to remedy the situation.

In such a case, the Council may request the Member State concerned to submit reports in accordance with a specific timetable in order to examine the adjustment efforts of that Member State.

10. The rights to bring actions provided for in Articles 258 and 259 may not be exercised within the framework of paragraphs 1 to 9 of this Article.

11. As long as a Member State fails to comply with a decision taken in accordance with paragraph 9, the Council may decide to apply or, as the case may be, intensify one or more of the following measures:

– to require the Member State concerned to publish additional information, to be specified by the Council, before issuing bonds and securities,

– to invite the European Investment Bank to reconsider its lending policy towards the Member State concerned,

– to require the Member State concerned to make a non-interest-bearing deposit of an appropriate size with the Union until the excessive deficit has, in the view of the Council, been corrected,

8. If a State persists in failing to put into practice the recommendations of the Council, the Council may decide, ***on a proposal of the Commission***, to give notice to the State to take, within a specified time limit, measures for the reduction ***of the debt or deficit*** in order to remedy the situation.

In the case that the Council opposes the Commission's proposal, the European Parliament, at the request of the Commission, may adopt the decision. The Parliament shall decide by a majority of its component Members, acting within four weeks of the Council's decision to oppose the Commission's proposal.

The ***Commission*** may request the State concerned to submit reports in accordance with a specific timetable in order to examine the adjustment efforts of that State.

9. As long as a State fails to comply with a decision taken in accordance with paragraph 8, the Council, ***on a proposal of the Commission***, may decide to apply or, as the case may be, intensify one or more of the following measures:

– to require the State concerned to publish additional information before issuing bonds and securities,

– to invite the European Investment Bank to reconsider its lending policy towards the State concerned,

– to require the State concerned to make a non-interest-bearing deposit of an appropriate size with the Union until the excessive deficit has been corrected,

– to impose fines of an appropriate size.

The President of the Council shall inform the European Parliament of the decisions taken.

12. The Council shall abrogate some or all of ***its*** decisions or recommendations referred to in paragraphs 6 to 9 and 11 to the extent that the excessive deficit in the Member State concerned has, in the view of the ***Council***, been corrected. ***If the Council has previously made public recommendations, it shall, as soon as the decision under paragraph 8 has been abrogated, make a public statement that an excessive deficit in the Member State concerned no longer exists.***

13. When taking the decisions or recommendations referred to in paragraphs 8, 9, 11 and 12, the Council shall act on a recommendation from the Commission.

When the Council adopts the measures referred to in paragraphs 6 to 9, 11 and 12, it shall act without taking into account the vote of the member of the Council representing the Member State concerned.

A qualified majority of the other members of the Council shall be defined in accordance with Article 238(3)(a).

14. Further provisions relating to the implementation of the procedure described in this Article are set out in the Protocol on the excessive deficit procedure annexed to the Treaties.

– to impose fines of an appropriate size.

10. The ***Commission*** and the Council shall abrogate some or all of their decisions or recommendations referred to in paragraphs 6 to 9 to the extent that the excessive deficit in the State concerned has, in the view of the ***Commission***, been corrected.

11. At any stage of the proceedings in paragraphs 6 to 10, the parliament of the State concerned may require the European Parliament to hold an urgent hearing of the Commission and the Council.

12. At any stage of the proceedings in paragraphs 6 to 10, ***the European Parliament may propose amendments to the Commission's recommendations or proposals. The Council may reject those amendments if the Commission delivers a negative opinion. Otherwise the recommendations or proposals shall be deemed to have been adopted by the Commission in their amended version.***

The Commission's recommendations or proposals shall be deemed to be adopted unless opposed by the Council, which shall act without the participation in the vote of the State concerned. A qualified majority shall be defined in accordance with Article 109.

13. The Council and Commission shall keep the European Parliament fully informed of the proposed recommendations, proposals and decisions throughout the procedures laid down in paragraphs 6 to 10. The President of the Council and the Commission may be invited to appear before the responsible committee of the Parliament.

14. Further provisions relating to the implementation of the procedure described in this Article are set out in the Protocol No 10 on the excessive deficit procedure.

The Council shall, ***acting unanimously in accordance with a special legislative procedure*** and after consulting ***the European Parliament and*** the European Central Bank, adopt the appropriate provisions which shall then replace the said Protocol. Subject to the other provisions of this paragraph, the Council shall, ***on a proposal from the Commission and after consulting the European Parliament***, lay down detailed rules and definitions for the application of the provisions of the said Protocol.	***The European Parliament and the Council shall, acting in accordance with the special legislative procedure*** and after consulting the European Central Bank, adopt the appropriate provisions which shall then replace the said Protocol. Subject to the other provisions of this paragraph, ***the European Parliament and the Council shall, in accordance with the ordinary legislative procedure***, lay down detailed rules and definitions for the application of the provisions of the said Protocol. ***15. Without prejudice to Article 200, in the case that the States make direct contributions to the financing of the Union budget, those contributions shall not be taken into account for the purposes of the excessive debt or deficit procedure as laid down in this article. In any case, such direct contributions shall cease to be made five years after the entry into force of the Fundamental Law.***
Article 127	Article 226 (ex-Article 127 TFEU)
1. The primary objective of the European System of Central Banks (hereinafter referred to as 'the ESCB') shall be to maintain price stability. Without prejudice to the objective of price stability, the ESCB shall support the general economic policies in the Union with a view to contributing to the achievement of the objectives of the Union as laid down in Article 3 of the Treaty on European Union. The ESCB shall act in accordance with the principle of an open market economy ***with free competition***, favouring an efficient allocation of resources, and in compliance with the principles set out in Article 119.	1. The primary objective of the European System of Central Banks (hereinafter referred to as 'the ESCB') shall be to maintain price stability. Without prejudice to the objective of price stability, the ESCB shall support the general economic policies in the Union with a view to contributing to the achievement of the objectives of the Union as laid down in Article 3. The ESCB shall act in accordance with the principle of an open, ***highly competitive social*** market economy, favouring an efficient allocation of resources, and in compliance with the principles set out in Article 218.

2. The basic tasks to be carried out through the ESCB shall be:

– to define and implement the monetary policy of the Union,

– to conduct foreign-exchange operations consistent with the provisions of Article 219,

– to hold and manage the official foreign reserves of the Member States,

– to promote the smooth operation of payment systems.

3. The third indent of paragraph 2 shall be without prejudice to the holding and management by the governments of Member States of foreign-exchange working balances.

4. The European Central Bank shall be consulted:

– on any proposed Union act in its fields of competence,

– by national authorities regarding any draft legislative provision in its fields of competence, but within the limits and under the conditions set out by the Council in accordance with the procedure laid down in Article 129(4).

The European Central Bank may submit opinions to the appropriate Union institutions, bodies, offices or agencies or to national authorities on matters in its fields of competence.

5. The ESCB shall contribute to the smooth conduct of policies pursued by the competent authorities relating to the prudential supervision of credit institutions and the stability of the financial system.

2. The basic tasks to be carried out through the ESCB shall be:

– to define and implement the monetary policy of the Union,

– to conduct foreign-exchange operations consistent with the provisions of Article 441,

– to hold and manage the official foreign reserves of the States,

– to promote the smooth operation of payment systems.

3. The third indent of paragraph 2 shall be without prejudice to the holding and management by the State governments of foreign-exchange working balances.

4. The European Central Bank shall be consulted:

– on any proposed Union act in its fields of competence,

– by State authorities regarding any draft legislative provision in its fields of competence, but within the limits and under the conditions set out by the Council in accordance with the procedure laid down in Article 229(4).

The European Central Bank may submit opinions to the appropriate Union institutions, bodies, offices or agencies or to national authorities on matters in its fields of competence.

5. The ESCB shall contribute to the smooth conduct of policies pursued by the competent authorities relating to the prudential supervision of credit institutions and the stability of the financial system.

6. The Council, acting by means of regulations in accordance with a special legislative procedure, may unanimously, and after consulting the European Parliament and the European Central Bank, confer specific tasks upon the European Central Bank concerning policies relating to the prudential supervision of credit institutions and other financial institutions with the exception of insurance undertakings.

Article 227

1. The Union shall undertake prudential oversight of credit institutions and other financial institutions. For these purposes, it shall establish within a banking union an integrated financial framework open to all States on a non-discriminatory basis.

The European Parliament and the Council, acting in accordance with the ordinary legislative procedure, and after having consulted the European Central Bank, shall lay down the provisions governing a single supervisory mechanism and the establishment of an appropriate regulatory framework for the banking union as a whole, including a common resolution mechanism and deposit guarantee insurance. The prudential supervision of credit institutions and other financial institutions may be conferred upon the European Central Bank.

2. For carrying out its functions, the single supervisory mechanism shall be accountable to the European Parliament and the Council. State Parliaments shall be kept informed as to the decisions taken under the single supervisory mechanism relevant to that State.

Without prejudice to Article 26, the European Parliament shall have the power to investigate the conduct of the single supervisory mechanism at all levels. State authorities and State parliaments are expected to cooperate with the European Parliament in ensuring effective parliamentary control of the exercise by the Union of prudential supervision.

	3. Without prejudice to Article 230, the functions of the European Central Bank in the field of surveillance and supervision of credit institutions shall not affect its independence in the area of monetary policy. *4. In respect of the banking union, the Commission shall assure the integrity of the internal market in financial services.*
Articles 128–135	Articles 228–235 (ex-Articles 128–135 TFEU) .....

THE EUROZONE

CHAPTER TWO

This chapter deals with the arrangements for those states whose currency is the euro – soon to be, with Latvia, 18 out of 28 states. It incorporates at the level of primary law the relevant aspects of the measures taken by the EU since the onset of the financial crisis in 2007–08.

Article 236, the key provision, widens the scope for action of the eurozone states to develop a common economic policy, including the setting of minimum standards, within the context of enhanced cooperation. The European Stability Mechanism is brought within the proper Union framework. Formal provision is made for the creation by the euro states of the special fiscal capacity for the eventual purpose of macro-economic stabilisation. This will be supplementary to the ordinary EU budget, whose primary purpose will continue to be the maintenance of support for the cohesion and competitiveness of the single market. Reform 'budgetary and economic partnership' programmes for eurozone states under the excessive deficit procedure shall be subject to a normal Union law. The national parliament of that state is enabled to call for a hearing in the European Parliament, and to formally address the Commission.

Provision is made for those states which are on track to joining the euro to participate to the maximum possible extent in meetings of the Eurogroup and Euro Summits (Article 237). The President of the Commission will chair the Euro Summits, and report to Parliament.

The Commission will represent the eurozone in international financial negotiations (Article 238).

Article 239 establishes that only those ministers coming from eurozone states will participate in decisions on those legal acts which concern exclusively the eurozone, including those on the fiscal capacity. However, 'pre-in' states near to joining the euro will get automatic admission under the enhanced cooperation rules to the inner workings of the eurozone (Article 241).

MEASURES SPECIFIC TO THE EURO STATES	THE EUROZONE
Article 136	Article 236 (ex-Article 136 TFEU)
1. In order to ensure the proper functioning of economic and monetary union, and in accordance with the relevant provisions of the Treaties, the Council shall, in accordance with the relevant procedure from among those referred to in Articles 121 and 126, with the exception of the procedure set out in Article 126(14), adopt measures specific to those Member States whose currency is the euro:	1. In order to ensure the proper functioning of economic and monetary union, ***and without prejudice to Articles 104, 105 and 113, the European Parliament and the Council shall, in accordance with the ordinary legislative procedure***, adopt ***enhanced cooperation*** measures specific to those States whose currency is the euro:
(a) to strengthen the coordination and surveillance of their budgetary discipline;	(a) to strengthen the coordination and surveillance of their budgetary discipline;
(b) to set out economic policy guidelines for them, while ensuring that they are compatible with those adopted for the whole of the Union and are kept under surveillance.	(b) to ***develop a common*** economic policy for them, while ensuring that ***it is*** compatible with ***the economic policy guidelines*** adopted for the whole of the Union. ***These measures may include the setting of minimum standards.***
2. For those measures set out in paragraph 1, only members of the Council representing Member States whose currency is the euro shall take part in the vote. ***A qualified majority of the said members shall be defined in accordance with Article 238(3)(a).***	
3. The Member States whose currency is the euro may establish a stability mechanism to be activated if indispensable to safeguard the stability of the euro area as a whole. The granting of any required financial assistance under the mechanism will be made subject to strict conditionality.	2. ***The European Parliament and the Council, acting in accordance with the ordinary legislative procedure***, may establish for the States whose currency is the euro a European stability mechanism to be activated if indispensable to safeguard the stability of the euro area as a whole. The granting of any required financial assistance under the mechanism will be made subject to strict conditionality. ***3. The European Parliament and the Council, acting pursuant to Article 239, shall establish within the Union budget a specific fiscal capacity of the States whose currency is the euro.***

	4. A State whose currency is the euro that is subject to an excessive deficit procedure pursuant to Article 225 shall put in place a budgetary and economic partnership programme including a detailed description of the structural reforms which must be put in place and implemented to ensure an effective and durable correction of its excessive deficit. The content and format of such programmes shall be defined in a Union law which shall be enacted under the ordinary legislative procedure. *The implementation of the budgetary and economic partnership programme, and the yearly budgetary plans consistent with it, will be monitored and applied by the Commission.* *The Parliament of the State concerned may require the European Parliament to hold an urgent hearing of the Commission and the Council. At the conclusion of the hearing, that Parliament, acting either alone or jointly with the European Parliament, may address to the Commission a resolution. The Commission shall respond to the parliamentary resolution by way of a reasoned opinion within ten days.* *5. With a view to the planning of debt issuance, the States shall report ex-ante on their public debt issuance plans to the Commission. The Commission shall inform the European Parliament and the Council.*
Article 137	Article 237 (ex-Article 137 TFEU)
Arrangements for meetings between ministers of those Member States whose currency is the euro are laid down by the Protocol on the Euro Group.	1. Arrangements for meetings ***between Heads of State or Government and*** between ministers of those States whose currency is the euro are laid down by the Protocol No 12 on the ***Eurogroup. The Euro Summits will be chaired by the President of the Commission.*** *2. Meetings of the Eurogroup will be chaired by the chair of the Council of Economic and Financial Affairs who shall be drawn from the government of a State whose currency is the euro.*

	3. Notwithstanding the provisions on enhanced cooperation, States with a derogation shall participate in Euro Summit and Eurogroup meetings when those meetings concern the implementation of the rules for fiscal discipline, the modification of the global architecture of the euro area and the fundamental rules which apply to it. *4. The President of the European Parliament shall participate at meetings of the Eurogroup Summit. The President of the Commission shall present a report to the Parliament after each Euro Summit meeting.*
Article 138 1. In order to secure the euro's place in the international monetary system, the Council, on a proposal from the Commission, shall adopt a decision establishing common positions on matters of particular interest for economic and monetary union within the competent international financial institutions and conferences. The Council shall act after consulting the European Central Bank. 2. The *Council, on a proposal from the Commission, may adopt appropriate measures to ensure unified representation* within the international financial institutions and conferences. The Council shall act after consulting the European Central Bank. *3. For the measures referred to in paragraphs 1 and 2, only members of the Council representing Member States whose currency is the euro shall take part in the vote.* *A qualified majority of the said members shall be defined in accordance with Article 238(3)(a).*	Article 238 (ex-Article 138 TFEU) 1. In order to secure the euro's place in the international monetary system, the Council, on a proposal from the Commission, shall adopt a decision establishing common positions on matters of particular interest for economic and monetary union within the competent international financial institutions and conferences. The Council shall act after consulting the European Central Bank. 2. *The Commission, in close cooperation with the European Central Bank, shall represent the Union* within the international financial institutions and conferences.
	Article 239 *For the adoption of measures set out in Articles 201, 204, 206(11), 236, 237 and 238, only members of the Council representing States whose currency is the euro shall take part in the vote, in accordance with Article 109.*

Article 139	Article 240 (ex-Article 139 TFEU) .....
	Article 241 ***In accordance with the procedure laid down in Article 110, a State with a derogation may apply to join the enhanced cooperation of the States whose currency is the euro as established under the provisions of Article 236.*** ***Once the participation of a State with a derogation is confirmed by the Commission, that State shall be considered to be a State whose currency is the euro within the meaning and for the purposes of Articles 201, 203, 236, 237, 238 and 239 and of Protocol No 12.***
Articles 140–144	Articles 242–246 (ex-Articles 140–144 TFEU) .....

PART V
THE POLICIES OF THE UNION

CHAPTER ONE

The first chapter in the part of the Fundamental Law which establishes the general policies of the Union contains provisions of horizontal application.

Here it is proposed to strengthen the imperative of employment policy (Article 249) and to combat climate change (Article 251).

	GENERAL PROVISIONS
Articles 7–8 TFEU	Articles 247–248 (ex-Articles 7–8 TFEU) .....
Article 9 In defining and implementing its policies and activities, the Union shall ***take into account*** requirements linked to the promotion of a high level of employment, the guarantee of adequate social protection, the fight against social exclusion, and a high level of education, training and protection of human health.	Article 249 (ex-Article 9 TFEU) In defining and implementing its policies and activities, the Union shall ***integrate*** requirements linked to the promotion of a high level of employment, the guarantee of adequate social protection, the fight against social exclusion, and a high level of education, training and protection of human health.
Article 10	Article 250 (ex-Article 10 TFEU) .....
Article 11 Environmental protection requirements must be integrated into the definition and implementation of the Union's policies and activities, in particular with a view to promoting sustainable development.	Article 251 (ex-Article 11 TFEU) Environmental protection requirements must be integrated into the definition and implementation of the Union's policies and activities, in particular with a view to promoting sustainable development ***and to combatting climate change.***
Articles 12–17	Articles 252–257 (ex-Articles 12–17 TFEU) .....

NON-DISCRIMINATION AND CITIZENSHIP OF THE UNION

CHAPTER TWO

This chapter deals with the civic rights which are enjoyed by citizens of the European Union.

In important adjustments, it is here proposed to change the special laws of the Council into normal laws, adopted by co-decision between Council and Parliament – for example, in Article 259 for anti-discrimination policies, in Article 261 for freedom of movement, in Article 262 for the right to vote and stand in municipal and European Parliamentary elections, and in Article 263 for consular protection.

We adopt a more permissive approach to the addition of new rights, and provide that the EU institutions can be addressed in any European language (and not just in the EU's 23 'official' languages).

In order to redress an injustice whereby many Europeans living abroad are deprived of the right to vote either for their original national parliament or for the national parliament of the state in which they reside, we propose to extend, under certain residency conditions, the right of EU citizens living in states other than their own to vote for their relevant State parliament (Articles 260(2)(d) and 262(3)).

NON-DISCRIMINATION AND CITIZENSHIP OF THE UNION	CITIZENSHIP OF THE UNION
Article 18	Article 258 (ex-Article 18 TFEU) .....
Article 19	Article 259 (ex-Article 19 TFEU)
1. Without prejudice to the other provisions of the Treaties and within the limits of the powers conferred by them upon the Union, the Council, ***acting unanimously*** in accordance with a special legislative procedure ***and after obtaining the consent of the European Parliament***, may take appropriate action to combat discrimination based on sex, racial or ethnic origin, religion or belief, disability, age or sexual orientation.	Without prejudice to the other provisions of the Fundamental Law and within the limits of the powers conferred by them upon the Union, ***the European Parliament and*** the Council, acting in accordance with ***the*** special legislative procedure, may take appropriate action to combat discrimination based on sex, racial or ethnic origin, religion or belief, disability, age or sexual orientation.
2. By way of derogation from paragraph 1, the European Parliament and the Council, acting in accordance with the ordinary legislative procedure, may adopt ***the basic principles of Union*** incentive measures, ***excluding any harmonisation of the laws and regulations of the Member States***, to support action taken by the Member States in order to contribute to the achievement of the objectives referred to in paragraph 1.	2. By way of derogation from paragraph 1, the European Parliament and the Council, acting in accordance with the ordinary legislative procedure, may adopt incentive measures to support action taken by the States ***which contributes*** to the achievement of the objectives referred to in paragraph 1.
Article 20	Article 260 (ex-Article 20 TFEU)
1. Citizenship of the Union is hereby established. Every person holding the nationality of a Member State shall be a citizen of the Union. Citizenship of the Union shall be additional to and not replace national citizenship.	1. Citizenship of the Union is hereby established. Every person holding the nationality of a State shall be a citizen of the Union. Citizenship of the Union shall be additional to and not replace national citizenship.
2. Citizens of the Union shall enjoy ***the rights and be subject to the duties provided for in the Treaties. They shall have, inter alia:***	2. Citizens of the Union ***shall enjoy these specific rights:***
(a) the right to move and reside freely within the territory of the Member States;	(a) the right to move and reside freely within the territory of the States;

(b) the right to vote and to stand as candidates in elections to the European Parliament and in municipal elections in their Member State of residence, under the same conditions as nationals of that State; (c) the right to enjoy, in the territory of a third country in which the Member State of which they are nationals is not represented, the protection of the diplomatic and consular authorities of any Member State on the same conditions as the nationals of that State; (d) the right to petition the European Parliament, to apply to the European Ombudsman, and to address the institutions and advisory bodies of the Union in any ***of the Treaty languages*** and to obtain a reply in the same language. These rights shall be exercised in accordance with the conditions and limits defined by the Treaties and by the measures adopted thereunder.	(b) the right to vote and to stand as candidates in municipal elections in their State of residence, under the same conditions as nationals of that State; (c) the right to vote and to stand as candidates in elections to the European Parliament ***in any State***, under the same conditions as nationals of that State; ***(d) the right to vote in parliamentary elections in their State of residence, under the same conditions as nationals of that State;*** (e) the right to enjoy, in the territory of a third country in which the State of which they are nationals is not represented, the protection of the diplomatic and consular authorities of any State on the same conditions as the nationals of that State; (f) the right to petition the European Parliament, to apply to the European Ombudsman, and to address the institutions and advisory bodies of the Union ***in any European language*** and to obtain a reply in the same language. These rights shall be exercised in accordance with the conditions and limits defined by the Fundamental Law and by the measures adopted thereunder.
Article 21	Article 261 (ex-Article 21 TFEU)
1. Every citizen of the Union shall have the right to move and reside freely within the territory of the Member States, subject to the limitations and conditions laid down in the Treaties and by the measures adopted to give them effect. 2. If action by the Union should prove necessary to attain this objective and the Treaties have not provided the necessary powers, the European Parliament and the Council, acting in accordance with the ordinary legislative procedure, may adopt provisions with a view to facilitating the exercise of the rights referred to in paragraph 1.	1. Every citizen of the Union shall have the right to move and reside freely within the territory of the States, subject to the limitations and conditions laid down in the Fundamental Law and by the measures adopted to give them effect. 2. If action by the Union should prove necessary to attain this objective and the Fundamental Law have not provided the necessary powers, the European Parliament and the Council, acting in accordance with the ordinary legislative procedure, may adopt provisions with a view to facilitating the exercise of the rights referred to in paragraph 1.

3. For the same purposes as those referred to in paragraph 1 and if the Treaties have not provided the necessary powers, the Council, acting in accordance with ***a*** special legislative procedure, may adopt measures concerning social security or social protection. ***The Council shall act unanimously after consulting the European Parliament.***	3. For the same purposes as those referred to in paragraph 1 and if the Fundamental Law has not provided the necessary powers, ***the European Parliament and*** the Council, acting in accordance with ***the*** special legislative procedure, may adopt measures concerning social security or social protection.
Article 22	Article 262 (ex-Article 22 TFEU)
1. Every citizen of the Union residing in a Member State of which he is not a national shall have the right to vote and to stand as a candidate at municipal elections in the Member State in which he resides, under the same conditions as nationals of that State. This right shall be exercised subject to detailed arrangements adopted by the Council, ***acting unanimously*** in accordance with a special legislative procedure ***and after consulting the European Parliament; these arrangements may provide for derogations where warranted by problems specific to a Member State.***	1. Every citizen of the Union residing in a State of which he is not a national shall have the right to vote and to stand as a candidate at municipal elections in the State in which he resides, under the same conditions as nationals of that State. This right shall be exercised subject to detailed arrangements adopted by the ***European Parliament and the Council***, acting in accordance with the special legislative procedure.
2. Without prejudice to Article 223(1) and to the provisions adopted for its implementation, every citizen of the Union residing in a Member State of which he is not a national shall have the right to vote and to stand as a candidate in elections to the European Parliament in the Member State in which he resides, under the same conditions as nationals of that State. This right shall be exercised subject to detailed arrangements adopted by the Council, ***acting unanimously*** in accordance with ***a*** special legislative procedure ***and after consulting the European Parliament; these arrangements may provide for derogations where warranted by problems specific to a Member State.***	2. Without prejudice to Article 23(1) and to the provisions adopted for its implementation, every citizen of the Union residing in a State of which he is not a national shall have the right to vote and to stand as a candidate in elections to the European Parliament in the State in which he resides, under the same conditions as nationals of that State. This right shall be exercised subject to detailed arrangements adopted by the ***European Parliament and*** the Council, acting in accordance with ***the*** special legislative procedure.

	3. Every citizen of the Union shall have the right to vote in elections to the State parliament of the State either of which he or she is a national or in which he or she resides. This right shall be exercised subject to detailed arrangements adopted by the European Parliament and the Council, acting in accordance with the special legislative procedure. These arrangements may provide for derogations where warranted by problems specific to a State.
Article 23	Article 263 (ex-Article 23 TFEU)
Every citizen of the Union shall, in the territory of a third country in which the Member State of which he is a national is not represented, be entitled to protection by the diplomatic or consular authorities of any Member State, on the same conditions as the nationals of that State. Member States shall adopt the necessary provisions and start the international negotiations required to secure this protection. The Council, acting in accordance with ***a*** special legislative procedure ***and after consulting the European Parliament, may*** adopt directives establishing the coordination and cooperation measures necessary to facilitate such protection.	Every citizen of the Union shall, in the territory of a third country in which the State of which he or she is a national is not represented, be entitled to protection by the diplomatic or consular authorities of any State, on the same conditions as the nationals of that State. States shall adopt the necessary provisions and start the international negotiations required to secure this protection. ***The European Parliament and*** the Council, acting in accordance with ***the ordinary*** legislative procedure, ***shall*** adopt directives establishing the coordination and cooperation measures necessary to facilitate such protection.
Article 24	Article 264 (ex-Article 24 TFEU) .....

Article 25	Article 265 (ex-Article 25 TFEU)
The Commission shall report to the European Parliament, to the Council and to the Economic and Social Committee every three years on the application of the provisions of this Part. This report shall take account of the development of the Union.	The Commission shall report to the European Parliament and to the Council every three years on the application of the provisions of this Part. This report shall take account of the development of the Union.
On this basis, and without prejudice to the other provisions of the Treaties, the Council, acting ***unanimously*** in accordance with ***a*** special legislative procedure ***and after obtaining the consent of the European Parliament***, may adopt provisions to strengthen or to add to the rights listed in Article 20(2). ***These provisions shall enter into force after their approval by the Member States in accordance with their respective constitutional requirements.***	On this basis, and without prejudice to the other provisions of the Fundamental Law, ***the European Parliament and*** the Council, acting in accordance with ***the*** special legislative procedure, may adopt provisions to strengthen or to add to the rights listed in Article 260(2).

THE INTERNAL MARKET

CHAPTER THREE

These articles establish the main principles of the internal market. As executive duties now falling on the Council are transferred to the Commission, we give both chambers of the legislature an equal, if limited, right to revoke the Commission's decisions before their entry into force. Examples of this new system, which is comparable in some respects to the operation of delegated acts, are found in Articles 266(3), 272 and 300.

In the light of ECJ jurisprudence, we propose to add a new clause (Article 267) which clarifies and affirms the right of the social partners to engage in collective labour agreements.

Faithful to the principle of equality between the two chambers of the legislature, we give the Parliament, under the special legislative procedure, the right of co-decision on measures which constitute a step backwards in the matter of liberalisation of capital with third countries (Article 298).

THE INTERNAL MARKET	THE INTERNAL MARKET
Article 26	Article 266 (ex-Article 26 TFEU)
1. The Union shall adopt measures with the aim of establishing or ensuring the functioning of the internal market, ***in accordance with the relevant provisions of the Treaties.***	1. The Union shall adopt measures with the aim of establishing or ensuring the functioning of the internal market.
2. The internal market shall comprise an area without internal frontiers in which the free movement of goods, persons, services and capital is ***ensured in accordance with the provisions of the Treaties.***	2. The internal market shall comprise an area without internal frontiers in which the free movement of goods, persons, services and capital is ***assured.***

3. The ***Council, on a proposal from the*** Commission, shall determine the guidelines and conditions necessary to ensure balanced progress in all the sectors concerned.	3. The ***Commission*** shall determine the guidelines and conditions necessary to ensure balanced progress in all the sectors concerned. ***The decisions of the Commission shall enter into force after a period of four weeks if no objection has been expressed either by the European Parliament, acting pursuant to Article 12(8), or by the Council, acting pursuant to Article 14(5).***
	Article 267 ***The free movement of goods, persons, services and capital may not impair the exercise of social rights and principles as provided for in Union and State law. These include the right to negotiate and enforce collective agreements and to take collective action, and the autonomy of the social partners to exercise these rights.***
Article 27	Article 268 (ex-Article 27 TFEU) .....
FREE MOVEMENT OF GOODS	FREE MOVEMENT OF GOODS
Articles 28–30	Articles 269–271 (ex-Articles 28–30 TFEU) .....
Article 31 Common Customs Tariff duties shall be fixed by ***the Council on a proposal from*** the Commission.	Article 272 (ex-Article 31 TFEU) Common Customs Tariff duties shall be fixed by the ***Commission. The decisions of the Commission shall enter into force after a period of four weeks if no objection has been expressed either by the European Parliament, acting pursuant to Article 12(8), or by the Council, acting pursuant to Article 14(5).***
Articles 32–37	Articles 273–278 (ex-Articles 32–37 TFEU) .....
FREE MOVEMENT OF PERSONS, SERVICES AND CAPITAL	FREE MOVEMENT OF PERSONS, SERVICES AND CAPITAL
Articles 45–63	Articles 279–297 (ex-Articles 45–63 TFEU) .....

Article 64	Article 298 (ex-Article 64 TFEU)
1. The provisions of Article 63 shall be without prejudice to the application to third countries of any restrictions which exist on 31 December 1993 under national or Union law adopted in respect of the movement of capital to or from third countries involving direct investment – including in real estate – establishment, the provision of financial services or the admission of securities to capital markets. In respect of restrictions existing under national law in Bulgaria, Estonia and Hungary, the relevant date shall be 31 December 1999.	1. The provisions of Article 297 shall be without prejudice to the application to third countries of any restrictions which exist on 31 December 1993 under national or Union law adopted in respect of the movement of capital to or from third countries involving direct investment – including in real estate – establishment, the provision of financial services or the admission of securities to capital markets. In respect of restrictions existing under national law in Bulgaria, Estonia and Hungary, the relevant date shall be 31 December 1999.
2. Whilst endeavouring to achieve the objective of free movement of capital between Member States and third countries to the greatest extent possible and without prejudice to the other Chapters of the Treaties, the European Parliament and the Council, acting in accordance with the ordinary legislative procedure, shall adopt the measures on the movement of capital to or from third countries involving direct investment – including investment in real estate – establishment, the provision of financial services or the admission of securities to capital markets.	2. Whilst endeavouring to achieve the objective of free movement of capital between States and third countries to the greatest extent possible and without prejudice to the other Chapters of the Fundamental Law, the European Parliament and the Council, acting in accordance with the ordinary legislative procedure, shall adopt the measures on the movement of capital to or from third countries involving direct investment – including investment in real estate – establishment, the provision of financial services or the admission of securities to capital markets.
3. Notwithstanding paragraph 2, ***only*** the Council, acting in accordance with ***a*** special legislative procedure, may ***unanimously, and after consulting the European Parliament,*** adopt measures which constitute a step backwards in Union law as regards the liberalisation of the movement of capital to or from third countries.	3. Notwithstanding paragraph 2, ***where measures are adopted*** which constitute a step backwards in Union law as regards the liberalisation of the movement of capital to or from third countries, ***the European Parliament and the Council shall act according to the special legislative procedure.***
Article 65	Article 299 (ex-Article 65 TFEU) .....

Article 66	Article 300 (ex-Article 66 TFEU)
Where, in exceptional circumstances, movements of capital to or from third countries cause, or threaten to cause, serious difficulties for the operation of economic and monetary union, ***the Council, on a proposal from*** the Commission and after consulting the European Central Bank, may take safeguard measures with regard to third countries for a period not exceeding six months if such measures are strictly necessary.	Where, in exceptional circumstances, movements of capital to or from third countries cause, or threaten to cause, serious difficulties for the operation of economic and monetary union, the ***Commission***, after consulting the European Central Bank, may take safeguard measures with regard to third countries for a period not exceeding six months if such measures are strictly necessary. ***The decisions of the Commission may be revoked either by the European Parliament, acting pursuant to Article 12(8), or by the Council, acting pursuant to Article 14(5).***

COMPETITION, TAXATION AND APPROXIMATION OF LAWS

CHAPTER FOUR

Throughout this chapter, which features important building blocks of the single market, we normalise the legislative procedure (co-decision). We transfer residual executive powers of the Council to the Commission, subject to the power of revocation by the legislature (Article 312). Special laws of the Council are abolished in the cases of Articles 303, 307, 309, 313 and 317.

Nevertheless, in Article 303 provision is made for a new EU competition authority to be established at arm's length from the Commission to operate the Union's competition policy. This change reflects the more political role of the Commission, and the necessity, in these circumstances, for the Commission to drop its quasi-judicial functions with respect to market supervision.

In Article 313, legislation on both direct and indirect taxation is made subject to the ordinary legislative procedure. Besides making a major contribution to simplification (including the repeal of ex-Article 115 TFEU), the Union acquires a greater ability to use tax as an instrument to bolster the internal market.

Article 314 on the approximation of laws, has been and will continue to be the key article in the construction of the integrated single market. We eliminate the prohibition (ex-paragraph 2) on legislation relating to the fiscal aspects of the free movement of labour. This will increase the capacity of the EU to act to facilitate the mobility of labour by introducing minimum terms and conditions for the treatment of taxation, mortgages, pensions and welfare benefits.

COMMON RULES ON COMPETITION, TAXATION AND APPROXIMATION OF LAWS	COMPETITION, TAXATION AND APPROXIMATION OF LAWS
Articles 101–102	Articles 301–302 (ex-Articles 101–102 TFEU) .....
Article 103	Article 303 (ex-Article 103 TFEU)
1. The appropriate regulations or directives to give effect to the principles set out in Articles 101 and 102 shall be laid down by the ***Council, on a proposal from the Commission and after consulting the European Parliament.***	1. ***The European Parliament and the Council, acting in accordance with the ordinary legislative procedure, shall by way of*** regulations or directives give effect to the principles set out in Articles 301 and 302.
	2. ***A European competition authority shall be established with the powers necessary to implement the competition law of the Union. The competition authority shall report annually to the Commission, the European Parliament and the Council.*** ***Any natural or legal person may appeal against decisions of the European competition authority to the Court of Justice in accordance with Article 58 where the decision directly concerns them.***
2. The regulations or directives referred to in paragraph 1 shall be designed in particular:	3. The regulations or directives referred to in paragraph 1 shall be designed in particular:
(a) to ensure compliance with the prohibitions laid down in Article 101(1) and in Article 102 by making provision for fines and periodic penalty payments;	(a) to ensure compliance with the prohibitions laid down in Article 301(1) and in Article 302 by making provision for fines and periodic penalty payments;
(b) to lay down detailed rules for the application of Article 101(3), taking into account the need to ensure effective supervision on the one hand, and to simplify administration to the greatest possible extent on the other;	(b) to lay down detailed rules for the application of Article 301(3), taking into account the need to ensure effective supervision on the one hand, and to simplify administration to the greatest possible extent on the other;
(c) to define, if need be, in the various branches of the economy, the scope of the provisions of Articles 101 and 102;	(c) to define, if need be, in the various branches of the economy, the scope of the provisions of Articles 301 and 302;

(d) to define the respective functions of the Commission and of the Court of Justice of the European Union in applying the provisions laid down in this paragraph; (e) to determine the relationship between national laws and the provisions contained in this Section or adopted pursuant to this Article.	(d) to define the respective functions of the Commission, ***the competition authority*** and of the Court of Justice of the European Union in applying the provisions laid down in this paragraph; (e) to determine the relationship between State laws and the provisions contained in this Section or adopted pursuant to this Article.
Article 104	Article 304 (ex-Article 104 TFEU) .....
Article 105 1. Without prejudice to Article 104, the Commission shall ensure the application of the principles laid down in Articles 101 and 102. On application by a Member State or on its own initiative, and in cooperation with the competent authorities in the Member States, which shall give it their assistance, the Commission shall investigate cases of suspected infringement of these principles. If it finds that there has been an infringement, it shall propose appropriate measures to bring it to an end. 2. If the infringement is not brought to an end, the Commission shall record such infringement of the principles in a reasoned decision. The Commission may publish its decision and authorise Member States to take the measures, the conditions and details of which it shall determine, needed to remedy the situation. 3. The Commission may adopt regulations relating to the categories of agreement in respect of which the Council has adopted a regulation or a directive pursuant to Article 103(2)(b).	Article 305 (ex-Article 105 TFEU) 1. Without prejudice to Article 304, the Commission ***and the European competition authority*** shall ensure the application of the principles laid down in Articles 301 and 302. On application by a State or on its own initiative, and in cooperation with the competent authorities in the States, which shall give it their assistance, the ***European competition authority*** shall investigate cases of suspected infringement of these principles. If it finds that there has been an infringement, it shall propose appropriate measures to bring it to an end. 2. If the infringement is not brought to an end, the ***European competition authority*** shall record such infringement of the principles in a reasoned decision. The ***European competition authority*** may publish its decision and authorise States to take the measures, the conditions and details of which it shall determine, needed to remedy the situation. 3. The Commission may adopt regulations relating to the categories of agreement in respect of which the ***European Parliament and the*** Council have adopted a regulation or a directive pursuant to Article 303(2)(b).
Article 106	Article 306 (ex-Article 106 TFEU) .....

Article 107	Article 307 (ex-Article 107 TFEU)
1. Save as otherwise provided in the Treaties, any aid granted by a Member State or through State resources in any form whatsoever which distorts or threatens to distort competition by favouring certain undertakings or the production of certain goods shall, in so far as it affects trade between Member States, be incompatible with the internal market.	1. Save as otherwise provided in the Fundamental Law, any aid granted by a State or through State resources in any form whatsoever which distorts or threatens to distort competition by favouring certain undertakings or the production of certain goods shall, in so far as it affects trade between States, be incompatible with the internal market.
2. The following shall be compatible with the internal market:	2. The following shall be compatible with the internal market:
(a) aid having a social character, granted to individual consumers, provided that such aid is granted without discrimination related to the origin of the products concerned;	(a) aid having a social character, granted to individual consumers, provided that such aid is granted without discrimination related to the origin of the products concerned;
(b) aid to make good the damage caused by natural disasters or exceptional occurrences;	(b) aid to make good the damage caused by natural disasters or exceptional occurrences;
(c) aid granted to the economy of certain areas of the Federal Republic of Germany affected by the division of Germany, in so far as such aid is required in order to compensate for the economic disadvantages caused by that division. Five years after the entry into force of the Treaty of Lisbon, the Council, acting on a proposal from the Commission, may adopt a decision repealing this point.	
3. The following may be considered to be compatible with the internal market:	3. The following may be considered to be compatible with the internal market:
(a) aid to promote the economic development of areas where the standard of living is abnormally low or where there is serious underemployment, and of the regions referred to in Article 349, in view of their structural, economic and social situation;	(a) aid to promote the economic development of areas where the standard of living is abnormally low or where there is serious underemployment, and of the regions referred to in Article 128, in view of their structural, economic and social situation;
(b) aid to promote the execution of an important project of common European interest or to remedy a serious disturbance in the economy of a Member State;	(b) aid to promote the execution of an important project of common European interest or to remedy a serious disturbance in the economy of a State;

(c) aid to facilitate the development of certain economic activities or of certain economic areas, where such aid does not adversely affect trading conditions to an extent contrary to the common interest; (d) aid to promote culture and heritage conservation where such aid does not affect trading conditions and competition in the Union to an extent that is contrary to the common interest; (e) such other categories of aid as may be specified by ***decision of the Council on a proposal from*** the Commission.	(c) aid to facilitate the development of certain economic activities or of certain economic areas, where such aid does not adversely affect trading conditions to an extent contrary to the common interest; (d) aid to promote culture and heritage conservation where such aid does not affect trading conditions and competition in the Union to an extent that is contrary to the common interest; (e) such other categories of aid as may be specified by ***the European Parliament and the Council, acting by way of a regulation, in accordance with the ordinary legislative procedure.***
Article 108	Article 308 (ex-Article 108 TFEU) .....
Article 109 The Council, ***on a proposal from the Commission and after consulting the European Parliament***, may make any appropriate regulations for the application of Articles 107 and 108 and may in particular determine the conditions in which Article 108(3) shall apply and the categories of aid exempted from this procedure.	Article 309 (ex-Article 109 TFEU) The ***European Parliament and the Council, in accordance with the ordinary legislative procedure***, may make any appropriate regulations for the application of Articles 307 and 308 and may in particular determine the conditions in which Article 308(3) shall apply and the categories of aid exempted from this procedure.
Articles 110–111	Articles 310–311 (ex-Articles 110–111 TFEU) .....
Article 112 In the case of charges other than turnover taxes, excise duties and other forms of indirect taxation, remissions and repayments in respect of exports to other Member States may not be granted and countervailing charges in respect of imports from Member States may not be imposed unless the measures contemplated have been previously approved for a limited period by ***the Council on a proposal from*** the Commission.	Article 312 (ex-Article 112 TFEU) In the case of charges other than turnover taxes, excise duties and other forms of indirect taxation, remissions and repayments in respect of exports to other States may not be granted and countervailing charges in respect of imports from States may not be imposed unless the measures contemplated have been previously approved for a limited period by the ***Commission.***

	The decision of the Commission may be revoked either by the European Parliament, acting pursuant to Article 12(8), or by the Council, acting pursuant to Article 14(5).
Article 113	Article 313 (ex-Article 113 TFEU)
The Council ***shall, acting unanimously*** in accordance with ***a special*** legislative procedure ***and after consulting the European Parliament and the Economic and Social Committee***, adopt provisions for the harmonisation of legislation concerning turnover taxes, excise duties and other forms of indirect taxation to the extent that such harmonisation is necessary to ensure the establishment and the functioning of the internal market and to avoid distortion of competition.	***The European Parliament and Council shall, acting in accordance with the ordinary legislative procedure***, adopt provisions for the harmonisation of legislation concerning ***direct taxation and*** turnover taxes, excise duties and other forms of indirect taxation to the extent that such harmonisation is necessary to ensure the establishment and the functioning of the internal market and to avoid distortion of competition.
Article 114	Article 314 (ex-Article 114 TFEU)
1. Save where otherwise provided in the Treaties, the following provisions shall apply for the achievement of the objectives set out in Article 26. The European Parliament and the Council shall, acting in accordance with the ordinary legislative procedure ***and after consulting the Economic and Social Committee***, adopt the measures for the approximation of the provisions laid down by law, regulation or administrative action in Member States which have as their object the establishment and functioning of the internal market. ***2. Paragraph 1 shall not apply to fiscal provisions, to those relating to the free movement of persons nor to those relating to the rights and interests of employed persons.***	1. Save where otherwise provided in the Fundamental Law, the following provisions shall apply for the achievement of the objectives set out in Article 266. The European Parliament and the Council shall, acting in accordance with the ordinary legislative procedure, adopt the measures for the approximation of the provisions laid down by law, regulation or administrative action in States which have as their object the establishment and functioning of the internal market.

3. The Commission, in its proposals envisaged in paragraph 1 concerning health, safety, environmental protection and consumer protection, will take as a base a high level of protection, taking account in particular of any new development based on scientific facts. Within their respective powers, the European Parliament and the Council will also seek to achieve this objective.

4. If, after the adoption of a harmonisation measure by the European Parliament and the Council, by the Council or by the Commission, a Member State deems it necessary to maintain national provisions on grounds of major needs referred to in Article 36, or relating to the protection of the environment or the working environment, it shall notify the Commission of these provisions as well as the grounds for maintaining them.

5. Moreover, without prejudice to paragraph 4, if, after the adoption of a harmonisation measure by the European Parliament and the Council, by the Council or by the Commission, a Member State deems it necessary to introduce national provisions based on new scientific evidence relating to the protection of the environment or the working environment on grounds of a problem specific to that Member State arising after the adoption of the harmonisation measure, it shall notify the Commission of the envisaged provisions as well as the grounds for introducing them.

6. The Commission shall, within six months of the notifications as referred to in paragraphs 4 and 5, approve or reject the national provisions involved after having verified whether or not they are a means of arbitrary discrimination or a disguised restriction on trade between Member States and whether or not they shall constitute an obstacle to the functioning of the internal market.

2. The Commission, in its proposals envisaged in paragraph 1 concerning health, safety, environmental protection and consumer protection, will take as a base a high level of protection, taking account in particular of any new development based on scientific facts. Within their respective powers, the European Parliament and the Council will also seek to achieve this objective.

3. If, after the adoption of a harmonisation measure by the European Parliament and the Council or by the Commission, a State deems it necessary to maintain national provisions on grounds of major needs referred to in Article 277, or relating to the protection of the environment or the working environment, it shall notify the Commission of these provisions as well as the grounds for maintaining them.

4. Moreover, without prejudice to paragraph 3, if, after the adoption of a harmonisation measure by the European Parliament and the Council or by the Commission, a State deems it necessary to introduce national provisions based on new scientific evidence relating to the protection of the environment or the working environment on grounds of a problem specific to that State arising after the adoption of the harmonisation measure, it shall notify the Commission of the envisaged provisions as well as the grounds for introducing them.

5. The Commission shall, within six months of the notifications as referred to in paragraphs 3 and 4, approve or reject the national provisions involved after having verified whether or not they are a means of arbitrary discrimination or a disguised restriction on trade between States and whether or not they shall constitute an obstacle to the functioning of the internal market.

In the absence of a decision by the Commission within this period the national provisions referred to in paragraphs 4 and 5 shall be deemed to have been approved. When justified by the complexity of the matter and in the absence of danger for human health, the Commission may notify the Member State concerned that the period referred to in this paragraph may be extended for a further period of up to six months. 7. When, pursuant to paragraph 6, a Member State is authorised to maintain or introduce national provisions derogating from a harmonisation measure, the Commission shall immediately examine whether to propose an adaptation to that measure. 8. When a Member State raises a specific problem on public health in a field which has been the subject of prior harmonisation measures, it shall bring it to the attention of the Commission which shall immediately examine whether to propose appropriate measures to the Council. 9. By way of derogation from the procedure laid down in Articles 258 and 259, the Commission and any Member State may bring the matter directly before the Court of Justice of the European Union if it considers that another Member State is making improper use of the powers provided for in this Article. 10. The harmonisation measures referred to above shall, in appropriate cases, include a safeguard clause authorising the Member States to take, for one or more of the non-economic reasons referred to in Article 36, provisional measures subject to a Union control procedure.	In the absence of a decision by the Commission within this period the national provisions referred to in paragraphs 3 and 4 shall be deemed to have been approved. When justified by the complexity of the matter and in the absence of danger for human health, the Commission may notify the State concerned that the period referred to in this paragraph may be extended for a further period of up to six months. 6. When, pursuant to paragraph 5, a State is authorised to maintain or introduce national provisions derogating from a harmonisation measure, the Commission shall immediately examine whether to propose an adaptation to that measure. 7. When a State raises a specific problem on public health in a field which has been the subject of prior harmonisation measures, it shall bring it to the attention of the Commission which shall immediately examine whether to propose appropriate measures to the ***European Parliament and*** Council. 8. By way of derogation from the procedure laid down in Articles 54 and 55, the Commission and any State may bring the matter directly before the Court of Justice of the European Union if it considers that another State is making improper use of the powers provided for in this Article. 9. The harmonisation measures referred to above shall, in appropriate cases, include a safeguard clause authorising the States to take, for one or more of the non-economic reasons referred to in Article 277, provisional measures subject to a Union control procedure.
Article 115	[delete]

Articles 116–117	Articles 315–316 (ex-Articles 116–117 TFEU) .....
Article 118	Article 317 (ex-Article 118 TFEU)
In the context of the establishment and functioning of the internal market, the European Parliament and the Council, acting in accordance with the ordinary legislative procedure, shall establish measures for the creation of European intellectual property rights to provide uniform protection of intellectual property rights throughout the Union and for the setting up of centralised Union-wide authorisation, coordination and supervision arrangements. The Council, acting in accordance with ***a*** special legislative procedure, shall by means of regulations establish language arrangements for the European intellectual property rights. The Council shall act unanimously after consulting the European Parliament.	In the context of the establishment and functioning of the internal market, the European Parliament and the Council, acting in accordance with the ordinary legislative procedure, shall establish measures for the creation of European intellectual property rights to provide uniform protection of intellectual property rights throughout the Union and for the setting up of centralised Union-wide authorisation, coordination and supervision arrangements. ***The European Parliament and*** the Council, acting in accordance with ***the*** special legislative procedure, shall by means of regulations establish language arrangements for the European intellectual property rights.

EMPLOYMENT

CHAPTER FIVE

The revised Article 318 upgrades employment to be regarded as a common policy of the Union with the clear objective of 'achieving a high level of employment'. The change allows for the deletion of ex-Article 147 TFEU.

In an important change to the decision-making procedures, the powers of the Commission to drive the policy are enhanced (Article 320). The annual employment guidelines will become a legislative act. The Commission will make a proposal for recommendations to the Council. Parliament may amend the Commission's proposal unless its amendments are rejected by a double majority of Commission and Council. This procedure is based on that used for the macro-economic guidelines (Article 220), which remain a non-binding recommendation (pursuant to Article 81). In the case of the employment guidelines, however, the EU has no possibility to impose sanctions where its recommendations are ignored. Nevertheless, the possibility of more intensive EU action is foreseen in certain critical circumstances.

This is particularly so with respect of the euro states. In Article 321 we lift the prohibition against the harmonisation of national laws at least for the eurozone.

EMPLOYMENT	EMPLOYMENT
Article 145	Article 318 (ex-Articles 145 & 147 TFEU)
Member States and the Union shall, ***in accordance with this Title, work towards developing a coordinated strategy for employment and particularly for promoting*** a skilled, trained and adaptable workforce and labour markets responsive to economic change ***with a view to achieving the objectives defined in Article 3 of the Treaty on European Union.***	***The Union shall establish a common policy aimed at achieving a high level of employment, particularly through the development of*** a skilled, trained and adaptable workforce and labour markets responsive to economic change. The objective of a high level of employment shall be taken into consideration in the formulation and implementation of Union policies and activities.
Article 146	Article 319 (ex-Article 146 TFEU) .....
Article 147	[delete]
Article 148	Article 320 (ex-Article 148 TFEU)
	1. ***States shall regard their employment policies as a matter of common concern, and shall coordinate them within the context of a European semester.***
1. The European Council shall each year consider the employment situation in the Union and adopt conclusions thereon, on the basis of a joint annual report by the Council and the Commission.	2. The European Council shall each year consider the employment situation in the Union and adopt conclusions thereon, on the basis of a joint annual report by the Council and the Commission.
2. On the basis of the conclusions of the European Council, the Council, on a proposal from the Commission ***and after consulting the European Parliament, the Economic and Social Committee, the Committee of the Regions and the Employment Committee referred to in Article 150***, shall each year ***draw up*** guidelines which the Member States shall take into account in their employment policies. These guidelines shall be consistent with the broad guidelines ***adopted pursuant to Article 121(2).***	Having considered the conclusions of the European Council, ***the European Parliament and*** the Council, on a proposal of the Commission ***and in accordance with the ordinary legislative procedure***, shall each year ***adopt*** guidelines which the States shall take into account in their employment policies. These employment guidelines shall be consistent with the broad ***macro-economic*** policy guidelines adopted pursuant to Article 220(2).

3. Each Member State shall provide the Council and the Commission with an annual report on the principal measures taken to implement its employment policy in the light of the guidelines for employment as referred to in paragraph 2.	3. Each State shall provide the Council and the Commission with an annual report on the principal measures taken to implement its employment policy in the light of the guidelines for employment as referred to in paragraph 2.
4. The ***Council***, on the basis of the reports referred to in paragraph 3 and having received the views of the Employment Committee, shall each year carry out an examination of the implementation of the employment policies of the Member States in the light of the guidelines for employment. The Council, on a ***recommendation from*** the Commission, may, if it considers it appropriate in the light of that examination, make recommendations to Member States.	4. The ***Commission***, on the basis of the reports referred to in paragraph 3 and having received the views of the Employment Committee, shall each year carry out an examination of the implementation of the employment policies of the States in the light of the guidelines for employment. The Council, on a ***proposal of*** the Commission, may, if it considers it appropriate in the light of that examination, make recommendations to States. ***The recommendations shall be made public.*** ***In the case that a State fails to follow the recommendations, the Council may decide, on a proposal of the Commission, to take more intensive action.***
	5. At any stage of the procedure, the European Parliament may request the right to be heard and may propose amendments to the Commission's proposal for recommendations. The Council may reject those amendments if the Commission delivers a negative opinion. Otherwise the Commission's proposal shall be deemed to have been adopted by the Council in its amended version. ***The Council shall act without the participation in the vote of the State concerned. A qualified majority shall be defined in accordance with Article 109.***
5. On the basis of the results of that examination, the Council and the Commission shall make a joint annual report to the European Council on the employment situation in the Union and on the implementation of the guidelines for employment.	6. On the basis of the results of the examination ***referred to in paragraph 4***, the Council and the Commission shall make the joint annual report to the European Council on the employment situation in the Union and on the implementation of the guidelines for employment.

Article 149	Article 321 (ex-Article 149 TFEU)
The European Parliament and the Council, acting in accordance with the ordinary legislative procedure ***and after consulting the Economic and Social Committee and the Committee of the Regions***, may adopt incentive measures designed to encourage cooperation between Member States and to support their action in the field of employment through initiatives aimed at developing exchanges of information and best practices, providing comparative analysis and advice as well as promoting innovative approaches and evaluating experiences, in particular by recourse to pilot projects.	The European Parliament and the Council, acting in accordance with the ordinary legislative procedure, may adopt incentive measures designed to encourage cooperation between States and to support their action in the field of employment through initiatives aimed at developing exchanges of information and best practices, providing comparative analysis and advice as well as promoting innovative approaches and evaluating experiences, in particular by recourse to pilot projects.
Those measures shall not include harmonisation of the laws and regulations of the Member States.	***For States whose currency is the euro***, those measures ***may*** include harmonisation of the laws and regulations of ***those*** States.
Article 150	Article 322 (ex-Article 150 TFEU) .....

EUROPEAN SOCIETY

CHAPTER SIX

In this chapter we group the policies which impact upon the quality of European life. In all areas, the Fundamental Law adopts a more confident tone than that of the Lisbon Treaty, and drops certain constraints on the scope of these societal policies which limit their effectiveness at the European level.

In the key Article 325, we cross, as it were, the *passerelle* (ex-Article 153(2) TFEU) and introduce either the special or ordinary legislative procedure in areas which are to date covered by special laws of the Council. We drop the complete exclusion of the harmonisation of national laws, leaving it up to the EU legislature to act should it choose to do so. We drop the prohibition against EU legislation on pay in order to widen the scope of EU competence in the social policy field (Article 325(5)).

The provisions on education, vocational training, youth and sport, on culture and on public health are streamlined and made subject to the normal co-decision procedures. We propose to sharpen the focus of these policies. The provision on consumer protection needs no amendment.

SOCIAL POLICY	SOCIAL POLICY
Articles 151–152	Articles 323–324 (ex-Articles 151–152 TFEU) .....
Article 153	Article 325 (ex-Article 153 TFEU)
1. With a view to achieving the objectives of Article 151, ***the Union shall support and complement the activities of the Member States*** in the following fields:	1. With a view to achieving the objectives of Article 324, ***the social policy of the Union shall comprise action*** in the following fields:
(a) improvement in particular of the working environment to protect workers' health and safety;	(a) improvement in particular of the working environment to protect workers' health and safety;
(b) working conditions;	(b) working conditions;

(c) social security and social protection of workers;

(d) protection of workers where their employment contract is terminated;

(e) the information and consultation of workers;

(f) representation and collective defence of the interests of workers and employers, including co-determination, subject to paragraph 5;

(g) conditions of employment for third-country nationals legally residing in Union territory;

(h) the integration of persons excluded from the labour market, ***without prejudice to Article 166;***

(i) equality between men and women with regard to labour market opportunities and treatment at work;

(j) the combating of social exclusion;

(k) the modernisation of social protection systems without prejudice to point (c).

2. To this end, the European Parliament and the Council:

(a) may adopt measures designed to encourage cooperation between Member States through initiatives aimed at improving knowledge, developing exchanges of information and best practices, promoting innovative approaches and evaluating experiences, ***excluding any harmonisation of the laws and regulations of the Member States***;

(c) social security and social protection of workers;

(d) protection of workers where their employment contract is terminated;

(e) the information and consultation of workers;

(f) representation and collective defence of the interests of workers and employers, including co-determination, subject to paragraph 5;

(g) conditions of employment for third-country nationals legally residing in Union territory;

(h) the integration of persons excluded from the labour market;

(i) equality between men and women with regard to labour market opportunities and treatment at work;

(j) the combating of social exclusion;

(k) the modernisation of social protection systems.

2. To this end, the European Parliament and the Council:

(a) may adopt measures designed to encourage cooperation between States through initiatives aimed at improving knowledge, developing exchanges of information and best practices, promoting innovative approaches and evaluating experiences;

(b) may adopt, ***in the fields referred to in paragraph 1(a) to (i)***, by means of directives, minimum requirements ***for gradual implementation***, having regard to the conditions and technical rules obtaining in each of the Member States. Such directives shall avoid imposing administrative, financial and legal constraints in a way which would hold back the creation and development of small and medium-sized undertakings.

The European Parliament and the Council shall act in accordance with the ordinary legislative procedure ***after consulting the Economic and Social Committee and the Committee of the Regions.***

In the fields referred to in paragraph 1(c), (d), (f) and (g), the ***Council*** shall act ***unanimously***, in accordance with a special legislative procedure, ***after consulting the European Parliament and the said Committees.***

The Council, acting unanimously on a proposal from the Commission, after consulting the European Parliament, may decide to render the ordinary legislative procedure applicable to paragraph 1(d), (f) and (g).

3. A Member State may entrust management and labour, at their joint request, with the implementation of directives adopted pursuant to paragraph 2, or, where appropriate, with the implementation of a ***Council*** decision adopted in accordance with Article 155.

In this case, it shall ensure that, no later than the date on which a directive or a decision must be transposed or implemented, management and labour have introduced the necessary measures by agreement, the Member State concerned being required to take any necessary measure enabling it at any time to be in a position to guarantee the results imposed by that directive or that decision.

(b) may adopt, by means of directives, ***measures comprising*** minimum requirements, having regard to the conditions and technical rules obtaining in each of the States. Such directives shall avoid imposing administrative, financial and legal constraints in a way which would hold back the creation and development of small and medium-sized undertakings.

The European Parliament and the Council shall act in accordance with the ordinary legislative procedure.

In the fields referred to in paragraph 1(c), (d), (f) and (g), ***they*** shall act in accordance with ***the*** special legislative procedure.

3. A State may entrust management and labour, at their joint request, with the implementation of directives adopted pursuant to paragraph 2, or, where appropriate, with the implementation of a decision adopted in accordance with Article 327.

In this case, it shall ensure that, no later than the date on which a directive or a decision must be transposed or implemented, management and labour have introduced the necessary measures by agreement, the State concerned being required to take any necessary measure enabling it at any time to be in a position to guarantee the results imposed by that directive or that decision.

4. The provisions adopted pursuant to this Article: – shall not affect the right of Member States to define the fundamental principles of their social security systems and must not significantly affect the financial equilibrium thereof, – shall not prevent any Member State from maintaining or introducing more stringent protective measures compatible with the Treaties. 5. The provisions of this Article shall not apply to ***pay***, the right of association, the right to strike or the right to impose lock-outs.	4. The provisions adopted pursuant to this Article: – shall not affect the right of States to define the fundamental principles of their social security systems and must not significantly affect the financial equilibrium thereof, – shall not prevent any State from maintaining or introducing more stringent protective measures compatible with the Fundamental Law. 5. The provisions of this Article shall not apply to the right of association, the right to strike or the right to impose lock-outs.
Article 154	Article 326 (ex-Article 154) .....
Article 155 1. Should management and labour so desire, the dialogue between them at Union level may lead to contractual relations, including agreements. 2. Agreements concluded at Union level shall be implemented either in accordance with the procedures and practices specific to management and labour and the Member States or, in matters covered by Article 153, at the joint request of the signatory parties, ***by a Council decision on a proposal from the Commission. The European Parliament shall be informed.*** The Council shall act unanimously where the agreement in question contains one or more provisions relating to one of the areas for which unanimity is required pursuant to Article 153(2).	Article 327 (ex-Article 155 TFEU) 1. Should management and labour so desire, the dialogue between them at Union level may lead to contractual relations, including agreements. 2. Agreements concluded at Union level shall be implemented either in accordance with the procedures and practices specific to management and labour and the States or, in matters covered by Article 326, at the joint request of the signatory parties, ***by the European Parliament and the Council, acting in accordance with the ordinary legislative procedure.*** ***The European Parliament and*** the Council shall act ***in accordance with the special legislative procedure*** where the agreement in question contains one or more provisions relating to ***Article 325(1)(c), (d), (f) and (g).***
Articles 156–159	Articles 328–331 (ex-Articles 156–159) .....

Articles 160–161	[delete]
THE EUROPEAN SOCIAL FUND	THE EUROPEAN SOCIAL FUND
Articles 162–164	Articles 332–334 (ex-Articles 162–164 TFEU) .....
EDUCATION, VOCATIONAL TRAINING, YOUTH AND SPORT	EDUCATION, VOCATIONAL TRAINING, YOUTH AND SPORT
Article 165	Article 335 (ex-Article 165 TFEU)
1. The Union shall contribute to the development of quality education ***by encouraging cooperation between Member States and, if necessary, by supporting and supplementing their action, while fully respecting the responsibility of the Member States for the content of teaching and the organisation of education systems and their cultural and linguistic diversity.*** The Union shall contribute to the promotion of European ***sporting issues***, while taking account of the specific nature of sport, its structures based on voluntary activity and its social and educational function.	1. The Union shall contribute to the development of quality education ***and life-long learning.*** The Union shall contribute to the promotion of European ***sport***, while taking account of ***its*** specific nature, its structures based on voluntary activity and its social and educational function.
2. Union action shall be aimed at:	2. Union action shall be aimed at:
– developing the European dimension in education, particularly through the teaching and dissemination of the languages ***of the Member States***,	– developing the European dimension in education, particularly through the teaching and dissemination of ***European*** languages,
– encouraging mobility of students and teachers, by encouraging inter alia, the academic recognition of diplomas and periods of study,	– encouraging mobility of students and teachers, by encouraging inter alia, the academic recognition of diplomas and periods of study,
– promoting cooperation between educational establishments,	– promoting cooperation between educational establishments,
– developing exchanges of information and experience on issues common to the education systems of the Member States,	– developing exchanges of information and experience on issues common to the education systems of the States,

– encouraging the development of youth exchanges and of exchanges of socio-educational instructors, and encouraging the participation of young people in democratic life in Europe,	– encouraging the development of youth exchanges and of exchanges of socio-educational instructors, and encouraging the participation of young people in democratic life in Europe,
– encouraging the development of distance education,	– encouraging the development of distance education,
– developing the European dimension in sport, by promoting fairness and openness ***in sporting competitions and cooperation between bodies responsible for sports, and by protecting the physical and moral integrity of sportsmen and sportswomen, especially the youngest sportsmen and sportswomen.***	– developing the European dimension ***and identity*** in sport, by promoting fairness and openness.
3. The Union and the Member States shall foster cooperation with third countries and the competent international organisations in the field of education and sport, in particular the Council of Europe.	3. The Union and the States shall foster cooperation with third countries and the competent international organisations in the field of education and sport, in particular the Council of Europe.
4. ***In order to contribute to the achievement of*** the objectives referred to in this Article: – ***the European Parliament and the Council, acting in accordance with the ordinary legislative procedure, after consulting the Economic and Social Committee and the Committee of the Regions, shall adopt incentive measures, excluding any harmonisation of the laws and regulations of the Member States,*** – ***the Council, on a proposal from the Commission, shall adopt recommendations.***	4. The European Parliament and the Council, acting in accordance with the ordinary legislative procedure, ***shall adopt measures to achieve the objectives referred to in this Article.***
Article 166	Article 336 (ex-Article 166 TFEU)
1. The Union shall implement a vocational training policy ***which shall support and supplement the action of the Member States, while fully respecting the responsibility of the Member States for the content and organisation of vocational training.***	1. The Union shall implement ***a vocational training policy.***

2. Union action shall aim to:	2. Union action shall aim to:
– facilitate adaptation to industrial changes, in particular through vocational training and retraining,	– facilitate adaptation to industrial changes, in particular through vocational training and retraining,
– improve initial and continuing vocational training in order to facilitate vocational integration and reintegration into the labour market,	– improve initial and continuing vocational training in order to facilitate vocational integration and reintegration into the labour market,
– facilitate access to vocational training and encourage mobility of instructors and trainees and particularly young people,	– facilitate access to vocational training and encourage mobility of instructors and trainees and particularly young people,
– stimulate cooperation on training between educational or training establishments and firms,	– stimulate cooperation on training between educational or training establishments and firms,
– develop exchanges of information and experience on issues common to the training systems of the Member States.	– develop exchanges of information and experience on issues common to the training systems of the States.
3. The Union and the Member States shall foster cooperation with third countries and the competent international organisations in the sphere of vocational training.	3. The Union and the States shall foster cooperation with third countries and the competent international organisations in the sphere of vocational training.
4. The European Parliament and the Council, acting in accordance with the ordinary legislative procedure ***and after consulting the Economic and Social Committee and the Committee of the Regions***, shall adopt measures to ***contribute to the achievement of*** the objectives referred to in this Article, ***excluding any harmonisation of the laws and regulations of the Member States, and the Council, on a proposal from the Commission, shall adopt recommendations.***	4. The European Parliament and the Council, acting in accordance with the ordinary legislative procedure, shall adopt measures to ***achieve the objectives referred to in this Article.***
CULTURE	CULTURE
Article 167	Article 337 (ex-Article 167 TFEU)
1. The Union shall contribute to the flowering of ***the cultures of the Member States***, while respecting ***their*** national and regional diversity ***and at the same time bringing the common cultural heritage to the fore.***	1. The Union shall contribute to the flowering of ***European culture***, while respecting its national and regional diversity.

2. Action by the Union shall be aimed at encouraging cooperation between Member States ***and, if necessary, supporting and supplementing their action*** in the following areas:

– improvement of the knowledge and dissemination of the culture and history of the European peoples,

– conservation and safeguarding of cultural heritage of European significance,

– non-commercial cultural exchanges,

– artistic and literary creation, ***including in the audiovisual sector.***

3. The Union and the Member States shall foster cooperation with third countries and the competent international organisations in the sphere of culture, in particular the Council of Europe.

4. The Union shall take cultural aspects into account in its action under other provisions of the Treaties, in particular in order to respect and to promote the diversity of its cultures.

5. In order to contribute to the achievement of the objectives referred to in this Article:

– the European Parliament and the Council acting in accordance with the ordinary legislative procedure ***and after consulting the Committee of the Regions***, shall adopt incentive measures, ***excluding any harmonisation of the laws and regulations of the Member States,***

– ***the Council, on a proposal from the Commission, shall adopt recommendations.***

2. Action by the Union shall be aimed at encouraging cooperation between States in the following areas:

– improvement of the knowledge and dissemination of the culture and history of the European peoples,

– conservation and safeguarding of cultural heritage of European significance,

– non-commercial cultural exchanges,

– artistic and literary creation.

3. The Union and the States shall foster cooperation with third countries and the competent international organisations in the sphere of culture, in particular the Council of Europe.

4. The Union shall take cultural aspects into account in its action under other provisions of the Fundamental Law, in particular in order to respect and to promote the diversity of its cultures.

5. In order to contribute to the achievement of the objectives referred to in this Article, the European Parliament and the Council, acting in accordance with the ordinary legislative procedure, shall adopt incentive measures.

Other measures shall be adopted in accordance with the special legislative procedure.

PUBLIC HEALTH	PUBLIC HEALTH
Article 168	Article 338 (ex-Article 168 TFEU)
1. A high level of human health protection shall be ensured in the definition and implementation of all Union policies and activities.	1. A high level of human health protection shall be ensured in the definition and implementation of all Union policies and activities.
Union action, which shall complement national policies, shall be directed towards improving public health, preventing physical and mental illness and diseases, and obviating sources of danger to physical and mental health. Such action shall cover the fight against the major health scourges, by promoting research into their causes, their transmission and their prevention, as well as health information and education, and monitoring, early warning of and combating serious cross-border threats to health.	Union action, which shall complement State policies, shall be directed towards improving public health, preventing physical and mental illness and diseases, and obviating sources of danger to physical and mental health. Such action shall cover the fight against the major health scourges, by promoting research into their causes, their transmission and their prevention, as well as health information and education, and monitoring, early warning of and combating serious cross-border threats to health.
The Union shall ***complement the Member States'*** action in reducing drugs-related health damage, including information and prevention.	The Union shall ***take*** action in reducing drugs-related health damage, including information and prevention.
2. The Union shall encourage ***cooperation between the Member States in the areas referred to in this Article and, if necessary,*** lend support ***to their action. It shall in particular encourage cooperation between the Member States to improve*** the complementarity of their health services in cross-border areas.	2. The Union shall encourage ***and lend support to the States in improving*** the complementarity of their health services in cross-border areas.
Member States shall, in liaison with the Commission, coordinate among themselves their policies and programmes in the areas referred to in paragraph 1. The Commission may, ***in close contact with the Member States,*** take any useful initiative to promote ***such*** coordination, in particular initiatives aiming at the establishment of guidelines and indicators, the organisation of exchange of best practice, and the preparation of the necessary elements for periodic monitoring and evaluation. The European Parliament shall be kept fully informed.	***The Commission may take any useful initiatives to promote the coordination of State policies and programmes in the field of public health,*** in particular initiatives aiming at the establishment of guidelines and indicators, the organisation of exchange of best practice, and the preparation of the necessary elements for periodic monitoring and evaluation. The European Parliament shall be kept fully informed.

3. The Union and the Member States shall foster cooperation with third countries and the competent international organisations in the sphere of public health.

4. ***By way of derogation from Article 2(5) and Article 6(a) and in accordance with Article 4(2)(k)*** the European Parliament and the Council, acting in accordance with the ordinary legislative procedure ***and after consulting the Economic and Social Committee and the Committee of the Regions***, shall contribute to the achievement of the objectives referred to in this Article ***through adopting in order to meet common safety concerns***:

(a) measures setting high standards of quality and safety of organs and substances of human origin, blood and blood derivatives; these measures shall not prevent any Member State from maintaining or introducing more stringent protective measures;

(b) measures in the veterinary and phytosanitary fields which have as their direct objective the protection of public health;

(c) measures setting high standards of quality and safety for medicinal products and devices for medical use.

3. The Union and the States shall foster cooperation with third countries and the competent international organisations in the sphere of public health.

4. The European Parliament and the Council, acting in accordance with the ordinary legislative procedure, shall contribute to the achievement of the objectives referred to in this Article ***by adopting measures in the following areas***:

(a) measures setting high standards of quality and safety of organs and substances of human origin, blood and blood derivatives; these measures shall not prevent any State from maintaining or introducing more stringent protective measures;

(b) measures in the veterinary and phytosanitary fields which have as their direct objective the protection of public health;

(c) measures setting high standards of quality and safety for medicinal products and devices for medical use;

(d) incentive measures designed to protect and improve human health and in particular to combat the major cross-border health scourges, measures concerning monitoring, early warning of and combating serious cross-border threats to health, and measures which have as their direct objective the protection of public health regarding tobacco and the abuse of alcohol.

5. ***The European Parliament and the Council, acting in accordance with the ordinary legislative procedure and after consulting the Economic and Social Committee and the Committee of the Regions, may also adopt*** incentive measures designed to protect and improve human health and in particular to combat the major cross-border health scourges, measures concerning monitoring, early warning of and combating serious cross-border threats to health, and measures which have as their direct objective the protection of public health regarding tobacco and the abuse of alcohol, ***excluding any harmonisation of the laws and regulations of the Member States.***	
6. ***The Council, on a proposal from the Commission, may also adopt recommendations for the purposes set out in this Article.***	
7. Union action shall respect the responsibilities of the Member States for the definition of their health policy and for the organisation and delivery of health services and medical care. The responsibilities of the Member States shall include the management of health services and medical care and the allocation of the resources assigned to them. The measures referred to in paragraph 4(a) shall not affect national provisions on the donation or medical use of organs and blood.	5. Union action shall respect the responsibilities of the States for the definition of their health policy and for the organisation and delivery of health services and medical care. The responsibilities of the States shall include the management of health services and medical care and the allocation of the resources assigned to them. The measures referred to in paragraph 4(a) shall not affect national provisions on the donation or medical use of organs and blood.
CONSUMER PROTECTION	CONSUMER PROTECTION
Article 169	Article 339 (ex-Article 169 TFEU)
1. In order to promote the interests of consumers and to ensure a high level of consumer protection, the Union shall contribute to protecting the health, safety and economic interests of consumers, as well as to promoting their right to information, education and to organise themselves in order to safeguard their interests.	1. In order to promote the interests of consumers and to ensure a high level of consumer protection, the Union shall contribute to protecting the health, safety and economic interests of consumers, as well as to promoting their right to information, education and to organise themselves in order to safeguard their interests.

2. The Union shall contribute to the attainment of the objectives referred to in paragraph 1 through:	2. The Union shall contribute to the attainment of the objectives referred to in paragraph 1 through:
(a) measures adopted pursuant to Article 114 in the context of the completion of the internal market;	(a) measures adopted pursuant to Article 314 in the context of the completion of the internal market;
(b) measures which support, supplement and monitor the policy pursued by the Member States.	(b) measures which support, supplement and monitor the policy pursued by the States.
3. The European Parliament and the Council, acting in accordance with the ordinary legislative procedure ***and after consulting the Economic and Social Committee***, shall adopt the measures referred to in paragraph 2(b).	3. The European Parliament and the Council, acting in accordance with the ordinary legislative procedure, shall adopt the measures referred to in paragraph 2(b).
4. Measures adopted pursuant to paragraph 3 shall not prevent any Member State from maintaining or introducing more stringent protective measures. Such measures must be compatible with the Treaties. The Commission shall be notified of them.	4. Measures adopted pursuant to paragraph 3 shall not prevent any State from maintaining or introducing more stringent protective measures. Such measures must be compatible with the Fundamental Law. The Commission shall be notified of them.

AGRICULTURE AND FISHERIES

CHAPTER SEVEN

The main innovation in this chapter is to separate fisheries from agriculture, giving the common fisheries policy its distinct set of objectives (Article 342). This change signals the enhanced political importance of the fisheries sector, and will assist in the modernisation of the EU's common fisheries policy.

The objectives of the CAP are modernised, which should ease the process of reform.

Consistent with the logic of the Fundamental Law, the authority to fix farm prices and fish quotas is transferred from the Council, on a proposal of the Commission, to the Commission itself (Article 346(3)).

AGRICULTURE AND FISHERIES	AGRICULTURE AND FISHERIES
Article 38	Article 340 (ex-Article 38 TFEU)
1. The Union shall define and implement a common agriculture and fisheries policy.	1. The Union shall define and implement a common agriculture and fisheries policy.
The internal market shall extend to agriculture, fisheries and trade in agricultural products. 'Agricultural products' means the products of the soil, of stock farming and of fisheries and products of first-stage processing directly related to these products. ***References to the common agricultural policy or to agriculture, and the use of the term 'agricultural', shall be understood as also referring to fisheries, having regard to the specific characteristics of this sector.***	The internal market shall extend to agriculture, fisheries and trade in agricultural products. 'Agricultural products' means the products of the soil, of stock farming and products of first-stage processing directly related to these products. ***'Fishery products' means aquatic organisms resulting from any fishing activity or products derived thereof.***
2. Save as otherwise provided in Articles 39 to 44, the rules laid down for the establishment and functioning of the internal market shall apply to agricultural products.	2. Save as otherwise provided in Articles 341 to 347, the rules laid down for the establishment and functioning of the internal market shall apply to agricultural ***and fishery*** products.

3. The products subject to the provisions of Articles 39 to 44 are listed in Annex I.	3. The products subject to the provisions of Articles 341 to 347 are listed in Annex I.
4. The operation and development of the internal market for agricultural products must be accompanied by the establishment of a common agricultural policy.	4. The operation and development of the internal market for agricultural ***and fishery*** products must be accompanied by the establishment of a common agricultural policy ***and a common fisheries policy.***
Article 39	Article 341 (ex-Article 39 TFEU)
1. The objectives of the common agricultural policy shall be:	1. The objectives of the common agricultural policy shall be:
(a) to increase agricultural productivity by promoting technical progress and by ensuring the rational development of agricultural production and the optimum utilisation of the factors of production, in particular labour;	(a) to increase agricultural productivity by promoting technical progress and by ensuring the rational development of agricultural production and the optimum utilisation of the factors of production, in particular labour;
(b) thus to ensure a fair standard of living for the agricultural community, ***in particular by increasing the individual earnings of persons engaged in agriculture***;	(b) thus to ensure a fair standard of living for the agricultural community;
(c) to stabilise markets;	(c) to stabilise markets;
(d) to assure the availability of supplies;	(d) to assure the ***security of food supplies***;
(e) to ensure ***that supplies reach consumers at reasonable prices.***	(e) to ensure ***food safety and animal welfare.***
2. In working out the common agricultural policy and the special methods for its application, account shall be taken of: (a) the particular nature of agricultural activity, which results from the social structure of agriculture and from structural and natural disparities between the various agricultural regions; ***(b) the need to effect the appropriate adjustments by degrees;*** ***(c) the fact that in the Member States agriculture constitutes a sector closely linked with the economy as a whole.***	2. In working out the common agricultural policy and the special methods for its application, account shall be taken of the particular nature of agricultural activity, which results from the social structure of agriculture and from structural and natural disparities between the various agricultural regions.

	Article 342 ***1. The objectives of the common fisheries policy shall be:*** ***(a) to sustain fish stocks and conserve marine biological resources;*** ***(b) to manage fisheries by contributing to long-term social, economic and environmental sustainability;*** ***(c) to ensure a fair standard of living for the fisheries sector;*** ***(d) to stabilise markets;*** ***(e) to assure the security of fish supplies;*** ***(f) to ensure food safety and the welfare of fish.*** ***2. In working out the common fisheries policy and the special methods for its application, account shall be taken of the particular nature of fishing activity, which results from the social structure of the fisheries sector and from structural and natural disparities between the various maritime regions.***
Article 40 1. In order to attain the objectives set out in Article 39, a common organisation of agricultural markets shall be established. This organisation shall take one of the following forms, depending on the product concerned: (a) common rules on competition; (b) compulsory coordination of the various national market organisations; (c) a European market organisation.	Article 343 (ex-Article 40 TFEU) 1. In order to attain the objectives set out in Article 341, a common organisation of agricultural markets shall be established. This organisation shall take one of the following forms, depending on the product concerned: (a) common rules on competition; (b) compulsory coordination of the various national market organisations; (c) a European market organisation. ***In order to attain the objectives set out in Article 342, a common organisation of the markets in fishery and aquaculture products shall be established.***

2. The common organisation established in accordance with paragraph 1 may include all measures required to attain the objectives set out in Article 39, in particular regulation of prices, aids for the production and marketing of the various products, storage and carryover arrangements and common machinery for stabilising imports or exports.	2. The common ***organisations*** established in accordance with paragraph 1 may include all measures required to attain the objectives set out in Articles 341 ***and 342***, in particular regulation of prices, aids for the production and marketing of the various products, ***marketing standards, consumer information***, storage and carryover arrangements and common machinery for stabilising imports or exports.
The common organisation shall be limited to pursuit of the objectives set out in Article 39 and shall exclude any discrimination between producers or consumers within the Union.	The common organisations shall be limited to pursuit of the objectives set out in Articles 341 ***and 342*** and shall exclude any discrimination between producers or consumers within the Union.
Any common price policy shall be based on common criteria and uniform methods of calculation.	Any common price policy shall be based on common criteria and uniform methods of calculation.
3. In order to enable the common organisation referred to in paragraph 1 to attain its objectives, one or more agricultural guidance and guarantee funds may be set up.	3. In order to enable the common ***organisations*** referred to in paragraph 1 to attain ***their*** objectives, one or more agricultural guidance and guarantee funds ***and a fisheries and maritime fund*** may be set up.
Article 41	Article 344 (ex-Article 41 TFEU)
To enable the objectives set out in Article 39 to be attained, provision may be made within the framework of the common agricultural policy for measures such as:	To enable the objectives set out in Articles 341 ***and 342*** to be attained, provision may be made within the framework of the common agricultural ***and fisheries policies*** for measures such as:
(a) an effective coordination of efforts in the spheres of vocational training, of research and of the dissemination of agricultural knowledge; this may include joint financing of projects or institutions;	(a) an effective coordination of efforts in the spheres of vocational training, of ***scientific*** research and of the dissemination of knowledge; this may include joint financing of projects or institutions ***as well as data sharing***;
(b) joint measures to promote consumption of certain products.	(b) joint measures to promote consumption of certain products.

Article 42	Article 345 (ex-Article 42 TFEU)
The provisions of the Chapter relating to rules on competition shall apply to production of and trade in agricultural products only to the extent determined by the European Parliament and the Council within the framework of Article 43(2) and in accordance with the procedure laid down therein, account being taken of the objectives set out in Article 39.	The provisions of the Chapter relating to rules on competition shall apply to production of and trade in agricultural ***and fishery*** products only to the extent determined by the European Parliament and the Council within the framework of Article 346(2) and in accordance with the procedure laid down therein, account being taken of the objectives set out in Articles 341 ***and 342.***
The Council, on a proposal from the Commission, may authorise the granting of aid:	The ***Commission*** may authorise the granting of aid:
(a) for the protection of enterprises handicapped by structural or natural conditions; (b) within the framework of economic development programmes.	(a) for the protection of enterprises handicapped by structural or natural conditions; (b) within the framework of economic development programmes.
Article 43	Article 346 (ex-Article 43 TFEU)
1. The Commission shall submit proposals for working out and implementing the common agricultural policy, including the replacement of the national organisations by one of the forms of common organisation provided for in Article 40(1), ***and for implementing the measures specified in this Title.***	1. The Commission shall submit proposals for implementing the common agricultural ***and fisheries policies***, including the replacement of the national organisations by one of the forms of common organisation provided for in Article 343(1).
These proposals shall take account of the interdependence of the agricultural matters ***mentioned in this Title.***	These proposals shall take account of the interdependence of agricultural ***and fisheries*** matters.
2. The European Parliament and the Council, acting in accordance with the ordinary legislative procedure and after consulting the Economic and Social Committee, shall establish the common organisation of agricultural markets provided for in Article 40(1) and the other provisions necessary for the pursuit of the objectives of the common agricultural policy and the common fisheries policy.	2. The European Parliament and the Council, acting in accordance with the ordinary legislative procedure, shall establish the common ***organisations*** of agricultural ***and fishery*** markets provided for in Article 343(1) and the other provisions necessary for the pursuit of the objectives of the common agricultural policy and the common fisheries policy.

3. The ***Council, on a proposal from the*** Commission, shall adopt measures on fixing prices, levies, aid and quantitative limitations and on the fixing and allocation of fishing opportunities.	3. The ***Commission*** shall adopt measures on fixing prices, levies, aid and quantitative limitations and on the fixing and allocation of fishing opportunities.
4. In accordance with paragraph 2, the national market organisations may be replaced by the common organisation provided for in Article 40(1) if:	4. In accordance with paragraph 2, the national market organisations may be replaced by the common ***organisations*** provided for in Article 343(1) if:
(a) the common organisation offers Member States which are opposed to this measure and which have an organisation of their own for the production in question equivalent safeguards for the employment and standard of living of the producers concerned, account being taken of the adjustments that will be possible and the specialisation that will be needed with the passage of time;	(a) the common organisation offers States which are opposed to this measure and which have an organisation of their own for the production in question equivalent safeguards for the employment and standard of living of the producers concerned, account being taken of the adjustments that will be possible and the specialisation that will be needed with the passage of time;
(b) such an organisation ensures conditions for trade within the Union similar to those existing in a national market.	(b) such an organisation ensures conditions for trade within the Union similar to those existing in a national market.
5. If a common organisation for certain raw materials is established before a common organisation exists for the corresponding processed products, such raw materials as are used for processed products intended for export to third countries may be imported from outside the Union.	5. If a common organisation for certain raw materials is established before a common organisation exists for the corresponding processed products, such raw materials as are used for processed products intended for export to third countries may be imported from outside the Union.
Article 44	Article 347 (ex-Article 44 TFEU) .....

TRANSPORT

CHAPTER EIGHT

The chapter on transport dates from the Treaty of Rome, at a time when Europe's borders were almost closed, and is anomalous. We propose that transport is treated like any other service industry under normal internal market rules.

To the goals of the common transport policy we add a provision to allow the EU to take charge of modernising cross-border transport systems according to high standards of technology and ecology (Article 348(1)(d)). We insert in the same operational article the two still relevant substantive clauses from ex-Article 95(2) and ex-Article 97(3) TFEU.

Article 90	[delete]
Article 91	Article 348 (ex-Article 91 TFEU)
1. ***For the purpose of implementing Article 90, and*** taking into account the distinctive features of transport, the European Parliament and the Council shall, acting in accordance with the ordinary legislative procedure and after consulting the Economic and Social Committee and the Committee of the Regions, lay down: (a) common rules applicable to international transport to or from the territory of a Member State or passing across the territory of one or more Member States; (b) the conditions under which non-resident carriers may operate transport services within a Member State; (c) measures to improve transport safety; (d) any other appropriate provisions.	1. Taking into account the distinctive features of transport, the European Parliament and the Council shall, acting in accordance with the ordinary legislative procedure, lay down: (a) common rules applicable to international transport to or from the territory of a State or passing across the territory of one or more States; (b) the conditions under which non-resident carriers may operate transport services within a State; (c) measures to improve transport safety; ***(d) measures to modernise intra-state transport across the Union according to the highest standards of ecology and technology;*** (e) any other appropriate provisions.

2. When the measures referred to in paragraph 1 are adopted, account shall be taken of cases where their application might seriously affect the standard of living and level of employment in certain regions, and the operation of transport facilities.	*2. In the case of transport within the Union, discrimination which takes the form of carriers charging different rates and imposing different conditions for the carriage of the same goods over the same transport links on grounds of the country of origin or of destination of the goods in question shall be prohibited.* *3. Charges or dues in respect of the crossing of frontiers which are charged by a carrier in addition to the transport rates shall not exceed a reasonable level after taking the costs actually incurred thereby into account.*
Article 92	[delete]
Article 93	Article 349 (ex-Article 93 TFEU) .....
Articles 94–95	[delete]
Article 96	Article 350 (ex-Article 96 TFEU) .....
Articles 97–100	[delete]

TRANS-EUROPEAN NETWORKS

CHAPTER NINE

Similarly to the previous chapter on transport, we upgrade the role of the Commission and widen the scope of the ordinary legislative procedure with respect to the building of trans-European networks. We insert a mention of project bonds, particularly apt for cross-border investment.

Article 170	Article 351 (ex-Article 170 TFEU) .....
Article 171	Article 352 (ex-Article 171 TFEU)
1. In order to achieve the objectives referred to in Article 170, the Union:	1. In order to achieve the objectives referred to in Article 351, the Union:
– shall establish a series of guidelines covering the objectives, priorities and broad lines of measures envisaged in the sphere of trans-European networks; these guidelines shall identify projects of common interest,	– shall establish a series of guidelines covering the objectives, priorities and broad lines of measures envisaged in the sphere of trans-European networks; these guidelines shall identify projects of common interest,
– shall implement any measures that may prove necessary to ensure the interoperability of the networks, in particular in the field of technical standardisation,	– shall implement any measures that may prove necessary to ensure the interoperability of the networks, in particular in the field of technical standardisation,
– may support projects of common interest ***supported by Member States***, which are identified in the framework of the guidelines referred to in the first indent, particularly through feasibility studies, loan guarantees or interest-rate subsidies; the Union may also contribute, through the Cohesion Fund set up pursuant to Article 177, to the financing of specific projects in Member States in the area of transport infrastructure.	– may support projects of common interest which are identified in the framework of the guidelines referred to in the first indent, particularly through feasibility studies, loan guarantees, interest-rate subsidies ***or project bonds***; the Union may also contribute, through the Cohesion Fund set up pursuant to Article 358, to the financing of specific projects in States in the area of transport infrastructure.

The Union's activities shall take into account the potential economic viability of the projects.	The Union's activities shall take into account the potential economic viability of the projects.
2. ***Member States shall, in liaison with the Commission, coordinate among themselves*** the policies pursued at national level which may have a significant impact on the achievement of the objectives referred to in Article 170. The Commission may, in close cooperation with the Member State, take any useful initiative to promote such coordination.	2. ***The Commission shall coordinate*** the policies pursued at State level which may have a significant impact on the achievement of the objectives referred to in Article 351. The Commission may, in close cooperation with the State, take any useful initiative to promote such coordination.
3. The Union may decide to cooperate with third countries to promote projects of mutual interest and to ensure the interoperability of networks.	3. The Union may decide to cooperate with third countries to promote projects of mutual interest and to ensure the interoperability of networks.
Article 172	Article 353 (ex-Article 172 TFEU)
The guidelines and other measures referred to in Article 171(1) shall be adopted by the European Parliament and the Council, acting in accordance with the ordinary legislative procedure ***and after consulting the Economic and Social Committee and the Committee of the Regions.***	The guidelines and other measures referred to in Article 352 shall be adopted by the European Parliament and the Council, acting in accordance with the ordinary legislative procedure.
Guidelines and projects of common interest which relate to the territory of a Member State shall require the approval of the Member State concerned.	Guidelines and projects of common interest which relate to the territory of a Member State shall require the approval of the Member State concerned.

INDUSTRY

CHAPTER TEN

In the logic of the Fundamental Law, we streamline the Union's industrial policy by strengthening the powers of the Commission to drive matters, as well as by removing the prohibition on the harmonisation of national laws (Article 354(3)).

A new sub-clause refers to the new technologies.

One may note in the context of general industrial policy the abolition of a specific article of the Treaty of Lisbon on tourism on the grounds of its superfluity (ex-Article 195 TFEU).

Article 173	Article 354 (ex-Article 173 TFEU)
1. The Union ***and the Member States shall ensure that the conditions necessary for the competitiveness of the Union's industry exist.***	1. The Union ***shall contribute to the development of Europe's industry.***
For that purpose, in accordance with a system of open and competitive markets, ***their*** action shall be aimed at:	For that purpose, in accordance with a system of open and competitive markets, its action shall be aimed at:
– speeding up the adjustment of industry to structural changes,	– speeding up the adjustment of industry to structural changes,
– encouraging an environment favourable to initiative and to the development of undertakings throughout the Union, particularly small and medium-sized undertakings,	– encouraging an environment favourable to initiative and to the development of undertakings throughout the Union, particularly small and medium-sized undertakings,
– encouraging an environment favourable to cooperation between undertakings,	– encouraging an environment favourable to cooperation between undertakings,
– fostering better exploitation of the industrial potential of policies of innovation, research and technological development.	– fostering better exploitation of the industrial potential of policies of innovation, research and technological development,
	– developing a strategy to help new technologies deliver sustainable economic growth.

2. ***The Member States shall consult each other in liaison with the Commission and, where necessary, shall coordinate their action.*** The Commission may take any useful initiative to promote such coordination, in particular initiatives aiming at the establishment of guidelines and indicators, the organisation of exchange of best practice, and the preparation of the necessary elements for periodic monitoring and evaluation. The European Parliament shall be kept fully informed.	2. The Commission may take any useful initiative to promote ***the*** coordination ***of the industrial policies of the States***, in particular initiatives aiming at the establishment of guidelines and indicators, the organisation of exchange of best practice, and the preparation of the necessary elements for periodic monitoring and evaluation. The European Parliament ***and the Council*** shall be kept fully informed.
3. The Union shall contribute to the achievement of the objectives set out in paragraph 1 through the policies and activities it pursues under other provisions of the Treaties. The European Parliament and the Council, acting in accordance with the ordinary legislative procedure ***and after consulting the Economic and Social Committee, may decide on specific measures in support of action taken in the Member States to achieve the objectives set out in paragraph 1, excluding any harmonisation of the laws and regulations of the Member States.***	3. The Union shall contribute to the achievement of the objectives set out in paragraph 1 through the policies and activities it pursues under other provisions of the Fundamental Law. ***The European Parliament and the Council, acting in accordance with the ordinary legislative procedure, shall adopt measures to achieve the objectives referred to in this Article.***
This Title shall not provide a basis for the introduction by the Union of any measure which could lead to a distortion of competition or contains tax provisions or provisions relating to the rights and interests of employed persons.	This Article shall not provide a basis for the introduction by the Union of any measure which could lead to a distortion of competition or contains tax provisions or provisions relating to the rights and interests of employed persons.

ECONOMIC, SOCIAL AND TERRITORIAL COHESION

CHAPTER ELEVEN

In this chapter the legislative procedure is normalised and the focus sharpened.

Article 174	Article 355 (ex-Article 174 TFEU)
In order to promote its overall harmonious development, the Union shall develop and pursue its actions leading to the strengthening of its economic, social and territorial cohesion.	In order to promote its overall harmonious development, the Union shall develop and pursue its actions leading to the strengthening of its economic, social and territorial cohesion.
In particular, the Union shall aim at reducing disparities between the levels of development of the various regions and the backwardness of the least favoured regions.	In particular, the Union shall aim at reducing disparities between the levels of development of the various regions and the backwardness of the least favoured regions.
Among the regions concerned, particular attention shall be paid to rural areas, areas affected by industrial transition, and regions which suffer from severe and permanent natural or demographic handicaps such as the northernmost regions with very low population density and island, cross-border and mountain regions.	Among the regions concerned, particular attention shall be paid to rural areas, areas affected by industrial transition, and regions which suffer from severe and permanent natural or demographic handicaps such as the northernmost regions with very low population density and island, cross-border and mountain regions.

Article 175	Article 356 (ex-Article 175 TFEU)
Member States shall conduct their economic policies ***and shall coordinate them*** in such a way as, ***in addition***, to attain the objectives set out in Article 174. ***The formulation and implementation of the Union's policies and actions and the implementation of the internal market shall take into account the objectives set out in Article 174 and shall contribute to their achievement.*** The Union shall also support the achievement of these objectives by the action it takes through the Structural Funds (European Agricultural Guidance and Guarantee Fund, Guidance Section; European Social Fund; European Regional Development Fund), the European Investment Bank and the other existing Financial Instruments.	***The Union*** shall conduct ***its*** economic policies ***and implement the internal market*** in such a way as to attain the objectives set out in Article 355. The Union shall also support the achievement of these objectives by the action it takes through the Structural Funds (European Agricultural Guidance and Guarantee Fund, Guidance Section; European Social Fund; European Regional Development Fund), the European Investment Bank and the other existing Financial Instruments.
The Commission shall submit a report to the European Parliament, the Council, the Economic and Social Committee and the Committee of the Regions every three years on the progress made towards achieving economic, social and territorial cohesion and on the manner in which the various means provided for in this Article have contributed to it. This report shall, if necessary, be accompanied by appropriate proposals.	The Commission shall submit a report to the European Parliament, the Council every three years on the progress made towards achieving economic, social and territorial cohesion and on the manner in which the various means provided for in this Article have contributed to it. This report shall, if necessary, be accompanied by appropriate proposals.
If specific actions prove necessary outside the Funds and without prejudice to the measures decided upon within the framework of the other Union policies, such actions may be adopted by the ***Council*** acting in accordance with the ordinary legislative procedure ***and after consulting the Economic and Social Committee and the Committee of the Regions.***	If specific actions prove necessary outside the Funds and without prejudice to the measures decided upon within the framework of the other Union policies, such actions may be adopted ***by the European Parliament and*** the Council acting in accordance with the ordinary legislative procedure.
Articles 176–178	Articles 357–359 (ex-Articles 176–178 TFEU) .....

RESEARCH AND TECHNOLOGICAL DEVELOPMENT AND SPACE

CHAPTER TWELVE

Consistent with the changes made to the competences of the EU with respect to R&D (Article 19), the special law of the Council used by the Lisbon Treaty for the establishment of the multi-annual EU research programmes is replaced by the ordinary legislative procedure.

Articles 179–181	Articles 360–362 (ex-Articles 179–181 TFEU) .....
Article 182	Article 363 (ex-Article 182 TFEU)
1. A multiannual framework programme, setting out all the activities of the Union, shall be adopted by the European Parliament and the Council, acting in accordance with the ordinary legislative procedure after consulting the Economic and Social Committee.	1. A multiannual framework programme, setting out all the activities of the Union, shall be adopted by the European Parliament and the Council, acting in accordance with the ordinary legislative procedure.
The framework programme shall:	The framework programme shall:
– establish the scientific and technological objectives to be achieved by the activities provided for in Article 180 and fix the relevant priorities,	– establish the scientific and technological objectives to be achieved by the activities provided for in Article 361 and fix the relevant priorities,
– indicate the broad lines of such activities,	– indicate the broad lines of such activities,
– fix the maximum overall amount and the detailed rules for Union financial participation in the framework programme and the respective shares in each of the activities provided for.	– fix the maximum overall amount and the detailed rules for Union financial participation in the framework programme and the respective shares in each of the activities provided for.
2. The framework programme shall be adapted or supplemented as the situation changes.	2. The framework programme shall be adapted or supplemented as the situation changes.

3. The framework programme shall be implemented through specific programmes developed within each activity. Each specific programme shall define the detailed rules for implementing it, fix its duration and provide for the means deemed necessary. The sum of the amounts deemed necessary, fixed in the specific programmes, may not exceed the overall maximum amount fixed for the framework programme and each activity. ***4. The Council, acting in accordance with a special legislative procedure and after consulting the European Parliament and the Economic and Social Committee, shall adopt the specific programmes.*** ***5. As a complement to the activities planned in the multiannual framework programme, the European Parliament and the Council, acting in accordance with the ordinary legislative procedure and after consulting the Economic and Social Committee, shall establish the measures necessary for the implementation of the European research area.***	3. The framework programme shall be implemented through specific programmes developed within each activity. Each specific programme shall define the detailed rules for implementing it, fix its duration and provide for the means deemed necessary. The sum of the amounts deemed necessary, fixed in the specific programmes, may not exceed the overall maximum amount fixed for the framework programme and each activity.
Articles 183–187	Articles 364–368 (ex-Articles 183–187 TFEU) .....
Article 188 ***The Council, on a proposal from the Commission and after consulting the European Parliament and the Economic and Social Committee, shall adopt the provisions referred to in Article 187.*** The European Parliament and the Council, acting in accordance with the ordinary legislative procedure ***and after consulting the Economic and Social Committee***, shall adopt the provisions referred to in Articles 183, 184 and 185. Adoption of the supplementary programmes shall require the agreement of the Member States concerned.	Article 369 (ex-Article 188 TFEU) The European Parliament and the Council, acting in accordance with the ordinary legislative procedure, shall adopt the provisions referred to in Articles 364, 365 and 366. Adoption of the supplementary programmes shall require the agreement of the States concerned.

Article 189	Article 370 (ex-Article 189 TFEU)
1. To promote scientific and technical progress, industrial competitiveness and the implementation of its policies, the Union shall draw up a European space policy. To this end, it may promote joint initiatives, support research and technological development and coordinate the efforts needed for the exploration and exploitation of space.	1. To promote scientific and technical progress, industrial competitiveness and the implementation of its policies, the Union shall draw up a European space policy. To this end, it may promote joint initiatives, support research and technological development and coordinate the efforts needed for the exploration and exploitation of space.
2. To contribute to attaining the objectives referred to in paragraph 1, the European Parliament and the Council, acting in accordance with the ordinary legislative procedure, shall establish the necessary measures, which may take the form of a European space programme, excluding any harmonisation of the laws and regulations of the Member States.	2. To contribute to attaining the objectives referred to in paragraph 1, the European Parliament and the Council, acting in accordance with the ordinary legislative procedure, shall establish the necessary measures, which may take the form of a European space programme.
3. The Union shall establish any appropriate relations with the European Space Agency.	3. The Union shall establish any appropriate relations with the European Space Agency.
4. This Article shall be without prejudice to the other provisions of this Title.	
Article 190	Article 371 (ex-Article 190 TFEU) .....

ENVIRONMENT

CHAPTER THIRTEEN

Combating climate change is added to the objectives of EU environment policy, and its decision-making procedures normalised. In Article 373, the special legislative procedure is proposed to replace the special law of the Council for the particularly sensitive areas of the policy which tread on national planning law. Consequent on the changes made in Article 313, the special character of fiscal law is dropped.

The financing of EU environment policy becomes an integral part of the EU budget (deletion of ex-Article 192(4) TFEU).

Article 191	Article 372 (ex-Article 191 TFEU)
1. Union policy on the environment shall contribute to pursuit of the following objectives:	1. Union policy on the environment shall contribute to pursuit of the following objectives:
	– ***combating climate change,***
– preserving, protecting and improving the quality of the environment,	– preserving, protecting and improving the quality of the environment,
– protecting human health,	– protecting human health,
– prudent and rational utilisation of natural resources,	– prudent and rational utilisation of natural resources,
– promoting measures at international level to deal with regional or worldwide environmental problems, and in particular combating climate change.	– promoting measures at international level to deal with regional or worldwide environmental problems, and in particular combating climate change.

2. Union policy on the environment shall aim at a high level of protection taking into account the diversity of situations in the various regions of the Union. It shall be based on the precautionary principle and on the principles that preventive action should be taken, that environmental damage should as a priority be rectified at source and that the polluter should pay.	2. Union policy on the environment shall aim at a high level of protection taking into account the diversity of situations in the various regions of the Union. It shall be based on the precautionary principle and on the principles that preventive action should be taken, that environmental damage should as a priority be rectified at source and that the polluter should pay.
In this context, harmonisation measures answering environmental protection requirements shall include, where appropriate, a safeguard clause allowing Member States to take provisional measures, for non-economic environmental reasons, subject to a procedure of inspection by the Union.	In this context, harmonisation measures answering environmental protection requirements shall include, where appropriate, a safeguard clause allowing States to take provisional measures, for non-economic environmental reasons, subject to a procedure of inspection by the Union.
3. In preparing its policy on the environment, the Union shall take account of:	3. In preparing its policy on the environment, the Union shall take account of:
– available scientific and technical data,	– available scientific and technical data,
– environmental conditions in the various regions of the Union,	– environmental conditions in the various regions of the Union,
– the potential benefits and costs of action or lack of action,	– the potential benefits and costs of action or lack of action,
– the economic and social development of the Union as a whole and the balanced development of its regions.	– the economic and social development of the Union as a whole and the balanced development of its regions.
4. Within their respective spheres of competence, the Union and the Member States shall cooperate with third countries and with the competent international organisations. The arrangements for Union cooperation may be the subject of agreements between the Union and the third parties concerned.	4. Within their respective spheres of competence, the Union and the States shall cooperate with third countries and with the competent international organisations. The arrangements for Union ***policy*** may be the subject of agreements between the Union and the third parties concerned.
The previous subparagraph shall be without prejudice to Member States' competence to negotiate in international bodies and to conclude international agreements.	

Article 192	Article 373 (ex-Article 192 TFEU)
1. The European Parliament and the Council, acting in accordance with the ordinary legislative procedure ***and after consulting the Economic and Social Committee and the Committee of the Regions***, shall decide what action is to be taken by the Union in order to achieve the objectives referred to in Article 191.	1. The European Parliament and the Council, acting in accordance with the ordinary legislative procedure, shall decide what action is to be taken by the Union in order to achieve the objectives referred to in Article 372.
2. ***By way of derogation from the decision-making procedure provided for in paragraph 1 and without prejudice to Article 114,*** the Council acting ***unanimously*** in accordance with ***a*** special legislative procedure ***and after consulting the European Parliament, the Economic and Social Committee and the Committee of the Regions***, shall adopt:	2. Without prejudice to Article 313, ***the European Parliament and*** the Council, acting in accordance with ***the*** special legislative procedure, shall adopt:
(a) ***provisions primarily of a fiscal nature;***	
(b) measures affecting:	(a) measures affecting:
– town and country planning,	– town and country planning,
– quantitative management of water resources or affecting, directly or indirectly, the availability of those resources,	– quantitative management of water resources or affecting, directly or indirectly, the availability of those resources,
– land use, with the exception of waste management;	– land use, with the exception of waste management;
(c) measures significantly affecting a Member State's choice between different energy sources and the general structure of its energy supply.	(b) measures significantly affecting a State's choice between different energy sources and the general structure of its energy supply.
The Council, acting unanimously on a proposal from the Commission and after consulting the European Parliament, the Economic and Social Committee and the Committee of the Regions, may make the ordinary legislative procedure applicable to the matters referred to in the first subparagraph.	

3. General action programmes setting out priority objectives to be attained shall be adopted by the European Parliament and the Council, acting in accordance with the ordinary legislative procedure ***and after consulting the Economic and Social Committee and the Committee of the Regions.***	3. General action programmes setting out priority objectives to be attained and the measures necessary for their implementation shall be adopted by the European Parliament and the Council, acting in accordance with the ordinary legislative procedure.
The measures necessary for the implementation of these programmes shall be adopted under the terms of paragraph 1 or 2, as the case may be.	
4. Without prejudice to certain measures adopted by the Union, the Member States shall finance and implement the environment policy.	
5. Without prejudice to the principle that the polluter should pay, if a measure based on the provisions of paragraph 1 involves costs deemed disproportionate for the public authorities of a Member State, such measure shall lay down appropriate provisions in the form of:	4. Without prejudice to the principle that the polluter should pay, if a measure based on the provisions of paragraph 1 involves costs deemed disproportionate for the public authorities of a Member State, such measure shall lay down appropriate provisions in the form of:
– temporary derogations, and/or	– temporary derogations, and/or
– financial support from the Cohesion Fund set up pursuant to Article 177.	– financial support from the Cohesion Fund set up pursuant to Article 358.
Article 193	Article 374 (ex-Article 193 TFEU) .....

ENERGY

CHAPTER FOURTEEN

Consistent with the changes proposed to environment policy, the energy chapter is revised to drop the absolute prohibition that EU policy must not affect a State's right to determine its own choice of energy supply (Article 375(2)). The special legislative procedure replaces the special law of the Council in these cases.

Article 376 encapsulates the vestigial and important powers of the Union conferred under the Euratom Treaty in the matter of nuclear safety – which, under Article 19, becomes an exclusive competence of the Union.

This chapter as amended is a significant extension of the Union's competence in energy supply policy and is commensurate with its existing powers on the demand side. The focus shifts from protecting individual and largely uncoordinated state interests to having dutiful care towards the environmental and energy interests of the Union as a whole. Without such a change the idea of a 'European energy community' will remain a chimera.

Article 194	Article 375 (ex-Article 194 TFEU)
1. In the context of the establishment and functioning of the internal market and with regard for the need to preserve and improve the environment, Union policy on energy shall aim, in a spirit of solidarity between Member States, to:	1. In the context of the establishment and functioning of the internal market and with regard for the need to preserve and improve the environment, ***the common energy policy of the Union*** shall aim, in a spirit of solidarity between States, to:
(a) ensure the functioning of the energy market;	(a) ensure the functioning of the energy market;
(b) ensure security of energy supply in the Union;	(b) ensure security of energy supply in the Union;
(c) promote energy efficiency and energy saving and the development of new and renewable forms of energy; and	(c) promote energy efficiency and energy saving and the development of new and renewable forms of energy; and
(d) promote the interconnection of energy networks.	(d) promote the interconnection of energy networks.

2. Without prejudice to the application of other provisions of the Treaties, the European Parliament and the Council, acting in accordance with the ordinary legislative procedure, shall establish the measures necessary to achieve the objectives in paragraph 1. ***Such measures shall be adopted after consultation of the Economic and Social Committee and the Committee of the Regions.***	2. Without prejudice to the application of other provisions of the Fundamental Law, the European Parliament and the Council, acting in accordance with the ordinary legislative procedure, shall establish the measures necessary to achieve the objectives in paragraph 1.
Such measures ***shall*** not affect a Member State's ***right to determine*** the conditions for exploiting its energy resources, its choice between different energy sources and the general structure of its energy supply, ***without prejudice*** to Article 192(2)(c).	***Where such measures may*** affect a State's ***determination of*** the conditions for exploiting its energy resources, its choice between different energy sources and the general structure of its energy supply, ***the European Parliament and the Council shall act in accordance with the special legislative procedure, pursuant*** to Article 373(2)(b).
3. By way of derogation from paragraph 2, the Council, acting in accordance with ***a*** special legislative procedure, shall ***unanimously and after consulting the European Parliament***, establish the measures referred to therein when they are primarily of a fiscal nature.	
	Article 376 *1. The Union shall establish a common policy in the field of atomic energy aimed at achieving the following objectives:* *(a) promote research and ensure the dissemination of technical information,* *(b) establish uniform safety standards for the nuclear industry,* *(c) ensure that nuclear materials are not diverted to purposes other than those for which they are intended,* *(d) exercise the right of ownership conferred upon it with respect to special fissile materials,* *(e) establish with other countries and international organisations such relations as will maintain progress in the peaceful uses of nuclear energy.*

	2. States shall consult the Commission ex ante on plans to develop nuclear installations. Each State shall provide the Commission with data relating to any plan for the disposal of radioactive waste in whatever form as will make it possible to determine whether the implementation of such plans is liable to result in the radioactive contamination of the water, soil or airspace. The Commission may carry out inspections within the States. *3. The Commission shall make proposals to the States with regard to the level of radioactivity. In cases of urgency, the Commission shall issue a decision requiring the State concerned to take, within a period laid down by the Commission, all necessary measures to prevent infringement of the health and safety regulations as determined by Union law.* *4. An agency shall be established to monitor the respect for safety and security standards relating to nuclear installations.* *5. The European Parliament and the Council, acting in accordance with the ordinary legislative procedure, shall lay down regulations and directives necessary to achieve these objectives.*
TOURISM	
Article 195	[delete]

PART VI

FREEDOM, SECURITY AND JUSTICE WITHIN THE UNION

CHAPTER ONE

Major changes are made to the treaty in respect of the Union as an area of freedom, security and justice.

In general, we strengthen the role of the Commission and follow the logic of the rest of the Fundamental Law, which is to make the two chambers of the legislature co-equal and to normalise qualified majority voting in the Council plus co-decision with the Parliament (the ordinary legislative procedure). Where the Commission takes over executive powers from the Council, the legislature is given the power of revocation (Article 383). It is proposed to abolish the right of a quarter of the states to make legislative initiatives in the area of freedom, security and justice (ex-Article 76 TFEU).

Greater emphasis is placed on the principle of mutual recognition (Article 378).

In cases of emergency inflow of refugees, we empower the Commission to adopt provisional measures (Article 385). As far as the integration of immigrant populations is concerned, and action against crime, we drop the prohibition on the harmonisation of national law (Articles 386(4) and 391, respectively).

Sensitive issues, such as in the field of family law, will be enacted by the special legislative procedure, but the veto given by the Lisbon Treaty to any one national parliament is eliminated (Article 388(3)). Likewise, in matters of criminal justice and police, the 'emergency brake' given to any one state is dropped – as is the 'automatic throttle' towards enhanced cooperation (Articles 389(3), 390(3), 393(1) and 394(3)).

We take the step, only prefigured in the Lisbon Treaty, of proposing that Eurojust takes on the form of an EU public prosecutor, with wider powers, by eliminating the special law of the Council and the veto power of the European Council (Article 393) (1) and (4).

AREA OF FREEDOM, SECURITY AND JUSTICE	AREA OF FREEDOM, SECURITY AND JUSTICE
Article 67	Article 377 (ex-Article 67 TFEU)
1. The Union shall constitute an area of freedom, security and justice with respect for fundamental rights and the different legal systems and traditions of the Member States.	1. The Union shall constitute an area of freedom, security and justice with respect for fundamental rights and the different legal systems and traditions of the States.
2. It shall ensure the absence of internal border controls for persons and shall frame a common policy on asylum, immigration and external border control, based on solidarity between Member States, which is fair towards third-country nationals. For the purpose of this Title, stateless persons shall be treated as third-country nationals.	2. It shall ensure the absence of internal border controls for persons and shall frame a common policy on asylum, immigration and external border control, based on solidarity between States ***and citizens***, which is fair towards third-country nationals. For the purpose of this Chapter, stateless persons shall be treated as third-country nationals.
3. The Union shall endeavour to ensure a high level of security through measures to prevent and combat crime, racism and xenophobia, and through measures for coordination and cooperation between police and judicial authorities and other competent authorities, as well as through the mutual recognition of judgments in criminal matters and, if necessary, through the approximation of criminal laws.	3. The Union shall endeavour to ensure a high level of security through measures to prevent and combat crime, racism and xenophobia, and through measures for coordination and cooperation between police and judicial authorities and other competent authorities, as well as through the mutual recognition of judgments in criminal matters and, if necessary, through the approximation of criminal laws.
4. The Union shall facilitate access to justice, in particular through the principle of mutual recognition of judicial and extrajudicial decisions in civil matters.	4. The Union shall facilitate access to justice, in particular through the principle of mutual recognition of judicial and extrajudicial decisions in civil matters.
Articles 68–69	[delete]

Article 70	Article 378 (ex-Article 70 TFEU)
Without prejudice to Articles 258, 259 and 260, the Council may, ***on a proposal from the Commission***, adopt measures laying down the arrangements whereby Member States, in collaboration with the Commission, ***conduct objective and impartial evaluation of the implementation of the Union policies referred to in this Title by Member States' authorities, in particular in order to*** facilitate full application of the principle of mutual recognition. ***The European Parliament and national Parliaments shall be informed of the content and results of the evaluation.***	Without prejudice to Articles 54, 55 and 56, ***the European Parliament and*** the Council, ***acting in accordance with the ordinary legislative procedure,*** may adopt measures laying down the arrangements whereby States, in collaboration with the Commission, facilitate full application of the principle of mutual recognition.
Articles 71–72	Articles 379–380 (ex-Articles 71–72 TFEU) .....
Article 73	Article 381 (ex-Article 73 TFEU)
It shall be open to Member States to organise between themselves and under their responsibility such forms of cooperation and coordination as they deem appropriate between the competent departments of their administrations responsible for safeguarding national security.	It shall be open to States, ***after consulting the Commission***, to organise between themselves and under their responsibility such forms of cooperation and coordination as they deem appropriate between the competent departments of their administrations responsible for safeguarding national security. ***The European Parliament and the parliaments of the States shall be kept informed.***
Article 74	Article 382 (ex-Article 74 TFEU)
The Council shall adopt measures to ensure administrative cooperation between the relevant departments of the Member States in the ***areas covered by this Title***, as well as between those departments and the Commission. ***It shall act on a Commission proposal, subject to Article 76, and after consulting the European Parliament.***	***The European Parliament and the Council, in accordance with the ordinary legislative procedure, shall adopt measures*** to ensure administrative cooperation between the relevant departments of the States in the ***area of freedom, security and justice***, as well as between those departments and the Commission.

Article 75	Article 383 (ex-Article 75 TFEU)
Where necessary to achieve the objectives set out in Article 67, as regards preventing and combating terrorism and related activities, the European Parliament and the Council, acting by means of regulations in accordance with the ordinary legislative procedure, shall define a framework for administrative measures with regard to capital movements and payments, such as the freezing of funds, financial assets or economic gains belonging to, or owned or held by, natural or legal persons, groups or non-State entities.	Where necessary to achieve the objectives set out in Article 377, as regards preventing and combating terrorism and related activities, the European Parliament and the Council, acting by means of regulations in accordance with the ordinary legislative procedure, shall define a framework for administrative measures with regard to capital movements and payments, such as the freezing of funds, financial assets or economic gains belonging to, or owned or held by, natural or legal persons, groups or non-State entities.
The ***Council, on a proposal from the*** Commission, shall adopt measures to implement the framework referred to in the first paragraph.	The ***Commission*** shall adopt measures to implement the framework referred to in the first paragraph. ***The decisions of the Commission shall enter into force after a period of two weeks if no objection has been expressed either by the European Parliament, acting pursuant to Article 12(8), or by the Council, acting pursuant to Article 14(5).***
The acts referred to in this Article shall include necessary provisions on legal safeguards.	The acts referred to in this Article shall include necessary provisions on legal safeguards.
Article 76	 [delete]

POLICIES ON BORDER CHECKS, ASYLUM AND IMMIGRATION	BORDERS CONTROLS
Article 77	Article 384 (ex-Article 77 TFEU)
1. The Union shall ***develop*** a policy with a view to:	1. The Union shall ***establish*** a policy with a view to:
(a) ensuring the absence of any controls on persons, whatever their nationality, when crossing internal borders;	(a) ensuring the absence of any controls on persons, whatever their nationality, when crossing internal borders;
(b) carrying out checks on persons and efficient monitoring of the crossing of external borders;	(b) carrying out checks on persons and efficient monitoring of the crossing of external borders;
(c) the gradual introduction of an integrated management system for external borders.	(c) the gradual introduction of an integrated management system for external borders.
2. For the purposes of paragraph 1, the European Parliament and the Council, acting in accordance with the ordinary legislative procedure, shall adopt measures concerning:	2. The European Parliament and the Council, acting in accordance with the ordinary legislative procedure, shall adopt measures concerning:
(a) the common policy on visas and other short-stay residence permits;	(a) the common policy on visas and other short-stay residence permits;
(b) the checks to which persons crossing external borders are subject;	(b) the checks to which persons crossing external borders are subject;
(c) the conditions under which nationals of third countries shall have the freedom to travel within the Union for a short period;	(c) the conditions under which nationals of third countries shall have the freedom to travel within the Union for a short period;
(d) any measure necessary for the gradual establishment of an integrated management system for external borders;	(d) any measure necessary for the gradual establishment of an integrated management system for external borders;
(e) the absence of any controls on persons, whatever their nationality, when crossing internal borders.	(e) the issuance of passports, identity cards, residence permits or any other such document;
	(f) the absence of any controls on persons, whatever their nationality, when crossing internal borders.

3. If action by the Union should prove necessary to facilitate the exercise of the right referred to in Article 20(2)(a), and if the Treaties have not provided the necessary powers, the ***Council***, acting in accordance with ***a*** special legislative procedure, may adopt provisions concerning passports, identity cards, residence permits or any other such document. ***The Council shall act unanimously after consulting the European Parliament.***	3. If action by the Union should prove necessary to facilitate the exercise of the right referred to in Article 260(2)(a), and if the Fundamental Law has not provided the necessary powers, ***the European Parliament and*** the Council, acting in accordance with ***the*** special legislative procedure, may adopt provisions concerning passports, identity cards, residence permits or any other such document.
4. This Article shall not affect the competence of the Member States concerning the geographical demarcation of their borders, in accordance with international law.	4. This Article shall not affect the competence of the States concerning the geographical demarcation of their borders, in accordance with international law.
	ASYLUM
Article 78	Article 385 (ex-Article 78 TFEU)
1. The Union shall ***develop*** a common policy on asylum, subsidiary protection and temporary protection with a view to offering appropriate status to any third-country national requiring international protection and ensuring compliance with the principle of non-refoulement. This policy must be in accordance with the Geneva Convention of 28 July 1951 and the Protocol of 31 January 1967 relating to the status of refugees, and other relevant treaties.	1. The Union shall ***establish*** a common policy on asylum, subsidiary protection and temporary protection with a view to offering appropriate status to any third-country national requiring international protection and ensuring compliance with the principle of non-refoulement. This policy must be in accordance with the Geneva Convention of 28 July 1951 and the Protocol of 31 January 1967 relating to the status of refugees, and other relevant treaties.
2. For the purposes of paragraph 1, the European Parliament and the Council, acting in accordance with the ordinary legislative procedure, shall adopt measures for a common European asylum system comprising:	2. For the purposes of paragraph 1, the European Parliament and the Council, acting in accordance with the ordinary legislative procedure, shall adopt measures for a common European asylum system comprising:
(a) a uniform status of asylum for nationals of third countries, valid throughout the Union;	(a) a uniform status of asylum for nationals of third countries, valid throughout the Union;
(b) a uniform status of subsidiary protection for nationals of third countries who, without obtaining European asylum, are in need of international protection;	(b) a uniform status of subsidiary protection for nationals of third countries who, without obtaining European asylum, are in need of international protection;

(c) a common system of temporary protection for displaced persons in the event of a massive inflow;	(c) a common system of temporary protection for displaced persons in the event of a massive inflow;
(d) common procedures for the granting and withdrawing of uniform asylum or subsidiary protection status;	(d) common procedures for the granting and withdrawing of uniform asylum or subsidiary protection status;
(e) criteria and mechanisms for determining which Member State is responsible for considering an application for asylum or subsidiary protection;	(e) criteria and mechanisms for determining which State is responsible for considering an application for asylum or subsidiary protection;
(f) standards concerning the conditions for the reception of applicants for asylum or subsidiary protection;	(f) standards concerning the conditions for the reception of applicants for asylum or subsidiary protection;
(g) partnership and cooperation with third countries for the purpose of managing inflows of people applying for asylum or subsidiary or temporary protection.	(g) partnership and cooperation with third countries for the purpose of managing inflows of people applying for asylum or subsidiary or temporary protection.
3. In the event of one or more Member States being confronted by an emergency situation characterised by a sudden inflow of nationals of third countries, the ***Council, on a proposal from the*** Commission, may adopt provisional measures for the benefit of the Member State(s) concerned. It shall act after consulting the European Parliament.	3. In the event of one or more States being confronted by an emergency situation characterised by a sudden inflow of nationals of third countries, the ***Commission*** may adopt provisional measures for the benefit of the State(s) concerned. It shall act after consulting the European Parliament ***and the Council.***
	IMMIGRATION
Article 79	Article 386 (ex-Article 79 TFEU)
1. The Union shall ***develop*** a common immigration policy aimed at ensuring, at all stages, the efficient management of migration flows, fair treatment of third-country nationals residing legally in Member States, and the prevention of, and enhanced measures to combat, illegal immigration and trafficking in human beings.	1. The Union shall ***establish*** a common immigration policy aimed at ensuring, at all stages, the efficient management of migration flows, fair treatment of third-country nationals residing legally in States, and the prevention of, and enhanced measures to combat, illegal immigration and trafficking in human beings.

2. For the purposes of paragraph 1, the European Parliament and the Council, acting in accordance with the ordinary legislative procedure, shall adopt measures in the following areas:	2. For the purposes of paragraph 1, the European Parliament and the Council, acting in accordance with the ordinary legislative procedure, shall adopt measures in the following areas:
(a) the conditions of entry and residence, and standards on the issue by Member States of long-term visas and residence permits, including those for the purpose of family reunification;	(a) the conditions of entry and residence, and standards on the issue by States of long-term visas and residence permits, including those for the purpose of family reunification;
(b) the definition of the rights of third-country nationals residing legally in a Member State, including the conditions governing freedom of movement and of residence in other Member States;	(b) the definition of the rights of third-country nationals residing legally in a State, including the conditions governing freedom of movement and of residence in other States;
(c) illegal immigration and unauthorised residence, including removal and repatriation of persons residing without authorisation;	(c) illegal immigration and unauthorised residence, including removal and repatriation of persons residing without authorisation;
(d) combatting trafficking in persons, in particular women and children.	(d) combatting trafficking in persons, in particular women and children.
3. The Union may conclude agreements with third countries for the readmission to their countries of origin or provenance of third-country nationals who do not or who no longer fulfil the conditions for entry, presence or residence in the territory of one of the Member States.	3. The Union may conclude agreements with third countries for the readmission to their countries of origin or provenance of third-country nationals who do not or who no longer fulfil the conditions for entry, presence or residence in the territory of one of the States.
4. The European Parliament and the Council, acting in accordance with the ordinary legislative procedure, may establish measures to provide incentives and support for the action of Member States with a view to promoting the integration of third-country nationals residing legally in their territories, ***excluding any harmonisation of the laws and regulations of the Member States.***	4. The European Parliament and the Council, acting in accordance with the ordinary legislative procedure, may establish measures to provide incentives and support for the action of States with a view to promoting the integration of third-country nationals residing legally in their territories.
5. This Article shall not affect the right of Member States to determine volumes of admission of third-country nationals coming from third countries to their territory in order to seek work, whether employed or self-employed.	

Article 80	Article 387 (ex-Article 80 TFEU) .....
JUDICIAL COOPERATION IN CIVIL MATTERS	JUDICIAL COOPERATION IN CIVIL MATTERS
Article 81	Article 388 (ex-Article 81 TFEU)
1. The Union shall ***develop*** judicial cooperation in civil matters having cross-border implications, based on the principle of mutual recognition of judgments and of decisions in extrajudicial cases. Such cooperation may include the adoption of measures for the approximation of the laws and regulations of the Member States.	1. The Union shall ***establish*** judicial cooperation in civil matters having cross-border implications, based on the principle of mutual recognition of judgments and of decisions in extrajudicial cases. Such cooperation may include the adoption of measures for the approximation of the laws and regulations of the States.
2. For the purposes of paragraph 1, the European Parliament and the Council, acting in accordance with the ordinary legislative procedure, shall adopt measures, particularly when necessary for the proper functioning of the internal market, aimed at ensuring:	2. For the purposes of paragraph 1, the European Parliament and the Council, acting in accordance with the ordinary legislative procedure, shall adopt measures, particularly when necessary for the proper functioning of the internal market, aimed at ensuring:
(a) the mutual recognition and enforcement between Member States of judgments and of decisions in extrajudicial cases;	(a) the mutual recognition and enforcement between States of judgments and of decisions in extrajudicial cases;
(b) the cross-border service of judicial and extrajudicial documents;	(b) the cross-border service of judicial and extrajudicial documents;
(c) the compatibility of the rules applicable in the Member States concerning conflict of laws and of jurisdiction;	(c) the compatibility of the rules applicable in the States concerning conflict of laws and of jurisdiction;
(d) cooperation in the taking of evidence;	(d) cooperation in the taking of evidence;
(e) effective access to justice;	(e) effective access to justice;
(f) the elimination of obstacles to the proper functioning of civil proceedings, if necessary by promoting the compatibility of the rules on civil procedure applicable in the Member States;	(f) the elimination of obstacles to the proper functioning of civil proceedings, if necessary by promoting the compatibility of the rules on civil procedure applicable in the States;
(g) the development of alternative methods of dispute settlement;	(g) the development of alternative methods of dispute settlement;

(h) support for the training of the judiciary and judicial staff.	(h) support for the training of the judiciary and judicial staff.
3. Notwithstanding paragraph 2, measures concerning family law with cross-border implications shall be established by the Council, acting in accordance with a special legislative procedure. ***The Council shall act unanimously after consulting the European Parliament.***	3. Notwithstanding paragraph 2, measures concerning family law with cross-border implications shall be established by ***the European Parliament*** and the Council ***in accordance with the special legislative procedure.***
The Council, on a proposal from the Commission, may adopt a decision determining those aspects of family law with cross-border implications which may be the subject of acts adopted by the ordinary legislative procedure. The Council shall act unanimously after consulting the European Parliament.	
The proposal referred to in the second subparagraph shall be notified to the national Parliaments. If a national Parliament makes known its opposition within six months of the date of such notification, the decision shall not be adopted. In the absence of opposition, the Council may adopt the decision.	
JUDICIAL COOPERATION IN CRIMINAL MATTERS	JUDICIAL COOPERATION IN CRIMINAL MATTERS
Article 82	Article 389 (ex-Article 82 TFEU)
1. Judicial cooperation in criminal matters in the Union shall be based on the principle of mutual recognition of judgments and judicial decisions and shall include the approximation of the laws and regulations of the Member States in the areas referred to in paragraph 2 and in Article 83.	1. Judicial cooperation in criminal matters in the Union shall be based on the principle of mutual recognition of judgments and judicial decisions and shall include the approximation of the laws and regulations of the States in the areas referred to in paragraph 2 and in Article 390.
The European Parliament and the Council, acting in accordance with the ordinary legislative procedure, shall adopt measures to:	The European Parliament and the Council, acting in accordance with the ordinary legislative procedure, shall adopt measures to:
(a) lay down rules and procedures for ensuring recognition throughout the Union of all forms of judgments and judicial decisions;	(a) lay down rules and procedures for ensuring recognition throughout the Union of all forms of judgments and judicial decisions;

(b) prevent and settle conflicts of jurisdiction between Member States;

(c) support the training of the judiciary and judicial staff;

(d) facilitate cooperation between judicial or equivalent authorities of the Member States in relation to proceedings in criminal matters and the enforcement of decisions.

2. To the extent necessary to facilitate mutual recognition of judgments and judicial decisions and police and judicial cooperation in criminal matters having a cross-border dimension, the European Parliament and the Council may, by means of directives adopted in accordance with the ordinary legislative procedure, establish minimum rules. Such rules shall take into account the differences between the legal traditions and systems of the Member States.

They shall concern:

(a) mutual admissibility of evidence between Member States;

(b) the rights of individuals in criminal procedure;

(c) the rights of victims of crime;

(d) any other specific aspects of criminal procedure which the Council has identified in advance by a decision; for the adoption of such a decision, the Council shall act unanimously after obtaining the consent of the European Parliament.

Adoption of the minimum rules referred to in this paragraph shall not prevent Member States from maintaining or introducing a higher level of protection for individuals.

(b) prevent and settle conflicts of jurisdiction between States;

(c) support the training of the judiciary and judicial staff;

(d) facilitate cooperation between judicial or equivalent authorities of the States in relation to proceedings in criminal matters and the enforcement of decisions.

2. To the extent necessary to facilitate mutual recognition of judgments and judicial decisions and police and judicial cooperation in criminal matters having a cross-border dimension, the European Parliament and the Council may, by means of directives adopted in accordance with the ordinary legislative procedure, establish minimum rules. Such rules shall take into account the differences between the legal traditions and systems of the States.

They shall concern ***inter alia***:

(a) mutual admissibility of evidence between States;

(b) the rights of individuals in criminal procedure;

(c) the rights of victims of crime.

Adoption of the minimum rules referred to in this paragraph shall not prevent States from maintaining or introducing a higher level of protection for individuals.

3. Where a member of the Council considers that a draft directive as referred to in paragraph 2 would affect fundamental aspects of its criminal justice system, ***it may request that the draft directive be referred to the European Council. In that case, the ordinary legislative procedure shall be suspended. After discussion, and in case of a consensus, the European Council shall, within four months of this suspension, refer the draft back to the Council, which shall terminate the suspension of the ordinary legislative procedure.***

Within the same timeframe, in case of disagreement, and if at least nine Member States wish to establish enhanced cooperation on the basis of the draft directive concerned, they shall notify the European Parliament, the Council and the Commission accordingly. In such a case, the authorisation to proceed with enhanced cooperation referred to in Article 20(2) of the Treaty on European Union and Article 329(1) of this Treaty shall be deemed to be granted and the provisions on enhanced cooperation shall apply.

3. Where a member of the Council considers that a draft directive as referred to in paragraph 2 would affect fundamental aspects of its criminal justice system, ***the law shall be adopted in accordance with the special legislative procedure.***

Article 83

1. The European Parliament and the Council may, by means of directives adopted in accordance with the ordinary legislative procedure, establish minimum rules concerning the definition of criminal offences and sanctions in the areas of particularly serious crime with a cross-border dimension resulting from the nature or impact of such offences or from a special need to combat them on a common basis.

These areas of crime are the following: terrorism, trafficking in human beings and sexual exploitation of women and children, illicit drug trafficking, illicit arms trafficking, money laundering, corruption, counterfeiting of means of payment, computer crime and organised crime.

Article 390
(ex-Article 83 TFEU)

1. The European Parliament and the Council may, by means of directives adopted in accordance with the ordinary legislative procedure, establish minimum rules concerning the definition of criminal offences and sanctions in the areas of particularly serious crime with a cross-border dimension resulting from the nature or impact of such offences or from a special need to combat them on a common basis.

These areas of crime are the following: terrorism, trafficking in human beings and sexual exploitation of women and children, illicit drug trafficking, illicit arms trafficking, money laundering, corruption, counterfeiting of means of payment, computer crime and organised crime.

On the basis of developments in crime, the Council ***may*** adopt a decision identifying other areas of crime that meet the criteria specified in this paragraph. ***It shall act unanimously after obtaining the consent of the European Parliament.***	On the basis of developments in crime, the ***Commission may propose to the European Parliament and*** the Council a decision identifying other areas of crime that meet the criteria specified in this paragraph. ***The Council shall act by a majority of three quarters of the States. The Parliament shall act by a majority of its component Members.***
2. If the approximation of criminal laws and regulations of the Member States proves essential to ensure the effective implementation of a Union policy in an area which has been subject to harmonisation measures, directives may establish minimum rules with regard to the definition of criminal offences and sanctions in the area concerned. ***Such directives shall be adopted by the same ordinary or special legislative procedure as was followed for the adoption of the harmonisation measures in question, without prejudice to Article 76.***	2. If the approximation of criminal laws and regulations of the States proves essential to ensure the effective implementation of a Union policy in an area which has been subject to harmonisation measures, directives may establish minimum rules with regard to the definition of criminal offences and sanctions in the area concerned.
3. Where a member of the Council considers that a draft directive as referred to in paragraph 1 or 2 would affect fundamental aspects of its criminal justice system, ***it may request that the draft directive be referred to the European Council. In that case, the ordinary legislative procedure shall be suspended. After discussion, and in case of a consensus, the European Council shall, within four months of this suspension, refer the draft back to the Council, which shall terminate the suspension of the ordinary legislative procedure.*** ***Within the same timeframe, in case of disagreement, and if at least nine Member States wish to establish enhanced cooperation on the basis of the draft directive concerned, they shall notify the European Parliament, the Council and the Commission accordingly. In such a case, the authorisation to proceed with enhanced cooperation referred to in Article 20(2) of the Treaty on European Union and Article 329(1) of this Treaty shall be deemed to be granted and the provisions on enhanced cooperation shall apply.***	3. Where a member of the Council considers that a draft directive as referred to in paragraph 1 or 2 would affect fundamental aspects of its criminal justice system, ***the law shall be adopted in accordance with the special legislative procedure.***

Article 84	Article 391 (ex-Article 84 TFEU)
The European Parliament and the Council, acting in accordance with the ordinary legislative procedure, may establish measures to promote and support the action of Member States in the field of crime prevention, ***excluding any harmonisation of the laws and regulations of the Member States.***	The European Parliament and the Council, acting in accordance with the ordinary legislative procedure, may establish measures to promote and support the action of the States in the field of crime prevention.
Article 85	Article 392 (ex-Article 85 TFEU) .....
Article 86	Article 393 (ex-Article 86 TFEU)
1. In order to combat crimes affecting the financial interests of the Union, the Council, by means of regulations adopted in accordance with a special legislative procedure, may establish a European Public Prosecutor's Office from Eurojust. ***The Council shall act unanimously after obtaining the consent of the European Parliament.*** ***In the absence of unanimity in the Council, a group of at least nine Member States may request that the draft regulation be referred to the European Council. In that case, the procedure in the Council shall be suspended. After discussion, and in case of a consensus, the European Council shall, within four months of this suspension, refer the draft back to the Council for adoption.*** ***Within the same timeframe, in case of disagreement, and if at least nine Member States wish to establish enhanced cooperation on the basis of the draft regulation concerned, they shall notify the European Parliament, the Council and the Commission accordingly. In such a case, the authorisation to proceed with enhanced cooperation referred to in Article 20(2) of the Treaty on European Union and Article 329(1) of this Treaty shall be deemed to be granted and the provisions on enhanced cooperation shall apply.***	1. In order to combat crimes affecting the financial interests of the Union, ***the European Parliament and*** the Council, by means of regulations adopted in accordance with ***the*** special legislative procedure, may establish a European Public Prosecutor's Office from Eurojust.

2. The European Public Prosecutor's Office shall be responsible for investigating, prosecuting and bringing to judgment, where appropriate in liaison with Europol, the perpetrators of, and accomplices in, offences against the Union's financial interests, as determined by the regulation provided for in paragraph 1. It shall exercise the functions of prosecutor in the competent courts of the Member States in relation to such offences.

3. The regulations referred to in paragraph 1 shall determine the general rules applicable to the European Public Prosecutor's Office, the conditions governing the performance of its functions, the rules of procedure applicable to its activities, as well as those governing the admissibility of evidence, and the rules applicable to the judicial review of procedural measures taken by it in the performance of its functions.

4. The ***European Council*** may, at the same time or subsequently, adopt a decision amending paragraph 1 in order to extend the powers of the European Public Prosecutor's Office to include serious crime having a cross-border dimension and amending accordingly paragraph 2 as regards the perpetrators of, and accomplices in, serious crimes affecting more than one Member State. ***The European Council shall act unanimously after obtaining the consent of the European Parliament and after consulting the Commission.***

2. The European Public Prosecutor's Office shall be responsible for investigating, prosecuting and bringing to judgment, where appropriate in liaison with Europol, the perpetrators of, and accomplices in, offences against the Union's financial interests, as determined by the regulation provided for in paragraph 1. It shall exercise the functions of prosecutor in the competent courts of the States in relation to such offences.

3. The regulations referred to in paragraph 1 shall determine the general rules applicable to the European Public Prosecutor's Office, the conditions governing the performance of its functions, the rules of procedure applicable to its activities, as well as those governing the admissibility of evidence, and the rules applicable to the judicial review of procedural measures taken by it in the performance of its functions.

4. ***The European Parliament and the Council, in accordance with the special legislative procedure***, may, at the same time or subsequently, adopt a decision amending paragraph 1 in order to extend the powers of the European Public Prosecutor's Office to include serious crime having a cross-border dimension and amending accordingly paragraph 2 as regards the perpetrators of, and accomplices in, serious crimes affecting more than one State.

POLICE COOPERATION	POLICE COOPERATION
Article 87	Article 394 (ex-Article 87 TFEU)
1. The Union shall establish police cooperation involving all the Member States' competent authorities, including police, customs and other specialised law enforcement services in relation to the prevention, detection and investigation of criminal offences.	1. The Union shall establish police cooperation involving all the States' competent authorities, including police, customs and other specialised law enforcement services in relation to the prevention, detection and investigation of criminal offences.
2. For the purposes of paragraph 1, the European Parliament and the Council, acting in accordance with the ordinary legislative procedure, may establish measures concerning:	2. For the purposes of paragraph 1, the European Parliament and the Council, acting in accordance with the ordinary legislative procedure, may establish measures concerning:
(a) the collection, storage, processing, analysis and exchange of relevant information;	(a) the collection, storage, processing, analysis and exchange of relevant information;
(b) support for the training of staff, and cooperation on the exchange of staff, on equipment and on research into crime-detection;	(b) support for the training of staff, and cooperation on the exchange of staff, on equipment and on research into crime-detection;
(c) common investigative techniques in relation to the detection of serious forms of organised crime.	(c) common investigative techniques in relation to the detection of serious forms of organised crime.
3. The Council, acting in accordance with a special legislative procedure, may establish measures concerning operational cooperation between the authorities referred to in this Article. ***The Council shall act unanimously after consulting the European Parliament.***	3. ***The European Parliament and*** the Council, ***by means of regulations adopted in accordance with the special legislative procedure***, may establish measures concerning operational cooperation between the authorities referred to in this Article.
In case of the absence of unanimity in the Council, a group of at least nine Member States may request that the draft measures be referred to the European Council. In that case, the procedure in the Council shall be suspended. After discussion, and in case of a consensus, the European Council shall, within four months of this suspension, refer the draft back to the Council for adoption.	

Within the same timeframe, in case of disagreement, and if at least nine Member States wish to establish enhanced cooperation on the basis of the draft measures concerned, they shall notify the European Parliament, the Council and the Commission accordingly. In such a case, the authorisation to proceed with enhanced cooperation referred to in Article 20(2) of the Treaty on European Union and Article 329(1) of this Treaty shall be deemed to be granted and the provisions on enhanced cooperation shall apply.	
The specific procedure provided for in the second and third subparagraphs shall not apply to acts which constitute a development of the Schengen acquis.	
Article 88	Article 395 (ex-Article 88 TFEU)
1. Europol's mission shall be to support and strengthen action by the Member States' police authorities and other law enforcement services and their mutual cooperation in preventing and combating serious crime affecting two or more Member States, terrorism and forms of crime which affect a common interest covered by a Union policy.	1. Europol's mission shall be to support and strengthen action by the States' police authorities and other law enforcement services and their mutual cooperation in preventing and combating serious crime affecting two or more States, terrorism and forms of crime which affect a common interest covered by a Union policy.
2. The European Parliament and the Council, by means of regulations adopted in accordance with the ordinary legislative procedure, shall determine Europol's structure, operation, field of action and tasks. These tasks may include:	2. The European Parliament and the Council, by means of regulations adopted in accordance with the ordinary legislative procedure, shall determine Europol's structure, operation, field of action and tasks. These tasks may include:
(a) the collection, storage, processing, analysis and exchange of information, in particular that forwarded by the authorities of the Member States or third countries or bodies;	(a) the collection, storage, processing, analysis and exchange of information, in particular that forwarded by the authorities of the States or third countries or bodies;
(b) the coordination, organisation and implementation of investigative and operational action carried out jointly with the Member States' competent authorities or in the context of joint investigative teams, where appropriate in liaison with Eurojust.	(b) the coordination, organisation and implementation of investigative and operational action carried out jointly with the States' competent authorities or in the context of joint investigative teams, where appropriate in liaison with Eurojust.

These regulations shall also lay down the procedures for scrutiny of Europol's activities by the European Parliament, together with national Parliaments. 3. Any operational action by Europol must be carried out in liaison and in agreement with the authorities of the Member State or States whose territory is concerned. The application of coercive measures shall be the exclusive responsibility of the competent national authorities.	These regulations shall also lay down the procedures for scrutiny of Europol's activities by the European Parliament, together with national Parliaments. 3. Any operational action by Europol must be carried out in liaison and in agreement with the authorities of the State or States whose territory is concerned. The application of coercive measures shall be the exclusive responsibility of the competent national authorities.
Article 89	Article 396 (ex-Article 89 TFEU)
The Council, acting in accordance with ***a*** special legislative procedure, shall lay down the conditions and limitations under which the competent authorities of the Member States referred to in Articles 82 and 87 may operate in the territory of another Member State in liaison and in agreement with the authorities of that State. ***The Council shall act unanimously after consulting the European Parliament.***	***The European Parliament and Council, acting in accordance with the special legislative procedure***, shall lay down the conditions and limitations under which the competent authorities of the States referred to in Articles 389 and 394 may operate in the territory of another State in liaison and in agreement with the authorities of that State.

CIVIL PROTECTION

CHAPTER TWO

We lift the prohibition on the harmonisation of national legislation.

CIVIL PROTECTION	CIVIL PROTECTION
Article 196	Article 397 (ex-Article 196 TFEU)
1. The Union shall encourage cooperation between Member States in order to improve the effectiveness of systems for preventing and protecting against natural or man-made disasters.	1. The Union shall encourage cooperation between States in order to improve the effectiveness of systems for preventing and protecting against natural or man-made disasters.
Union action shall aim to:	Union action shall aim to:
(a) support and complement Member States' action at national, regional and local level in risk prevention, in preparing their civil-protection personnel and in responding to natural or man-made disasters within the Union;	(a) support and complement States' action at national, regional and local level in risk prevention, in preparing their civil-protection personnel and in responding to natural or man-made disasters within the Union;
(b) promote swift, effective operational cooperation within the Union between national civil protection services;	(b) promote swift, effective operational cooperation within the Union between national civil protection services;
(c) promote consistency in international civil-protection work.	(c) promote consistency in international civil-protection work.
2. The European Parliament and the Council, acting in accordance with the ordinary legislative procedure shall establish the measures necessary to help achieve the objectives ***referred to in paragraph 1, excluding any harmonisation of the laws and regulations of the Member States.***	2. The European Parliament and the Council, acting in accordance with the ordinary legislative procedure shall establish the measures necessary to help achieve the objectives ***of this Article.***

ADMINISTRATIVE COOPERATION

CHAPTER THREE

It is proposed to strengthen the imperative towards closer cooperation between national administrations in their implementation of EU law, and to drop the prohibition on the harmonisation of national legislation.

ADMINISTRATIVE COOPERATION	ADMINISTRATIVE COOPERATION
Article 197	Article 398 (ex-Article 197 TFEU)
1. Effective implementation of Union law by the Member States, which is essential for the proper functioning of the Union, shall be regarded as a matter of common interest.	1. Effective implementation of Union law by the States, which is essential for the proper functioning of the Union, shall be regarded as a matter of common ***concern***.
2. The Union may support the efforts of Member States to improve their administrative capacity to implement Union law. Such action may include facilitating the exchange of information and of civil servants as well as supporting training schemes. ***No Member State shall be obliged to avail itself of such support***. The European Parliament and the Council, acting by means of regulations in accordance with the ordinary legislative procedure, shall establish the necessary measures to this end, ***excluding any harmonisation of the laws and regulations of the Member States***.	2. The Union ***shall*** support the efforts of States to improve their administrative capacity to implement Union law. Such action may include facilitating the exchange of information and of civil servants as well as supporting training schemes. The European Parliament and the Council, acting by means of regulations in accordance with the ordinary legislative procedure, shall establish the necessary measures to this end.
3. This Article shall be without prejudice to the obligations of the Member States to implement Union law or to the prerogatives and duties of the Commission. It shall also be without prejudice to other provisions of the Treaties providing for administrative cooperation among the Member States and between them and the Union.	3. This Article shall be without prejudice to the obligations of the States to implement Union law or to the prerogatives and duties of the Commission. It shall also be without prejudice to other provisions of the Fundamental Law providing for administrative cooperation among the States and between them and the Union.

PART VII

ASSOCIATION OF THE OVERSEAS TERRITORIES

This chapter concerns the overseas dominions of Denmark (including Greenland), France, the Netherlands and the UK.

For the development of the EU's relations with these territories, we propose the special legislative procedure.

Articles 198–202	Articles 399–403 (ex-Articles 198–202 TFEU) .....
Article 203	Article 404 (ex-Article 203 TFEU)
The Council, ***acting unanimously on a proposal from the Commission***, shall, on the basis of the experience acquired under the association of the countries and territories with the Union and of the principles set out in the Treaties, lay down provisions as regards the detailed rules and the procedure for the association of the countries and territories with the Union. ***Where the provisions in question are adopted by the Council in accordance with a special legislative procedure, it shall act unanimously on a proposal from the Commission and after consulting the European Parliament.***	***The European Parliament and*** the Council, acting ***in accordance with the special legislative procedure***, shall, on the basis of the experience acquired under the association of the countries and territories with the Union and of the principles set out in the Fundamental Law, lay down provisions as regards the detailed rules and the procedure for the association of the countries and territories with the Union.
Article 204	Article 405 (ex-Article 204 TFEU) .....

PART VIII

THE EXTERNAL ACTION OF THE UNION

CHAPTER ONE

The general description of the objectives of the Union's external action adds to paragraph 1 of Article 406 the provision on neighbourhood policy found in ex-Article 8 TEU.

The Fundamental Law adjusts the role of the European Council to focus the heads of government on setting the strategic orientation of the Union in international affairs, leaving to the Commission and Council the job of taking operational decisions. We also seek to strengthen the collegial ties of the Foreign Minister to the Commission, and to enhance the role of the Commission to initiate and coordinate policy.

GENERAL PROVISIONS ON THE UNION'S EXTERNAL ACTION AND SPECIFIC PROVISIONS ON THE COMMON FOREIGN AND SECURITY POLICY	GENERAL PROVISIONS
Article 21	Article 406 (ex-Articles 8 & 21 TEU)
1. The Union's action on the international scene shall be guided by the principles which have inspired its own creation, development and enlargement, and which it seeks to advance in the wider world: democracy, the rule of law, the universality and indivisibility of human rights and fundamental freedoms, respect for human dignity, the principles of equality and solidarity, and respect for the principles of the United Nations Charter and international law.	1. The Union's action on the international scene shall be guided by the principles which have inspired its own creation, development and enlargement, and which it seeks to advance in the wider world: democracy, the rule of law, the universality and indivisibility of human rights and fundamental freedoms, respect for human dignity, the principles of equality and solidarity, and respect for the principles of the United Nations Charter and international law.

The Union shall seek to develop relations and build partnerships with third countries, and international, regional or global organisations which share the principles referred to in the first subparagraph. It shall promote multilateral solutions to common problems, in particular in the framework of the United Nations.	The Union shall seek to develop relations and build partnerships with third countries, and international, regional or global organisations which share the principles referred to in the first subparagraph. It shall promote multilateral solutions to common problems, in particular in the framework of the United Nations.
	The Union shall seek to develop a special relationship with neighbouring countries, aiming to establish an area of prosperity and good neighbourliness, founded on the values of the Union and characterised by close and peaceful relations based on cooperation.
2. The Union shall define and pursue common policies and actions, and shall work for a high degree of cooperation in all fields of international relations, in order to:	2. The Union shall define and pursue common policies and actions, and shall work for a high degree of cooperation in all fields of international relations, in order to:
(a) safeguard its values, fundamental interests, security, independence and integrity;	(a) safeguard its values, fundamental interests, security, independence and integrity;
(b) consolidate and support democracy, the rule of law, human rights and the principles of international law;	(b) consolidate and support democracy, the rule of law, human rights and the principles of international law;
(c) preserve peace, prevent conflicts and strengthen international security, in accordance with the purposes and principles of the United Nations Charter, with the principles of the Helsinki Final Act and with the aims of the Charter of Paris, including those relating to external borders;	(c) preserve peace, prevent conflicts and strengthen international security, in accordance with the purposes and principles of the United Nations Charter, with the principles of the Helsinki Final Act and with the aims of the Charter of Paris, including those relating to external borders;
(d) foster the sustainable economic, social and environmental development of developing countries, with the primary aim of eradicating poverty;	(d) foster the sustainable economic, social and environmental development of developing countries, with the primary aim of eradicating poverty;
(e) encourage the integration of all countries into the world economy, including through the progressive abolition of restrictions on international trade;	(e) encourage the integration of all countries into the world economy, including through the progressive abolition of restrictions on international trade;

(f) help develop international measures to preserve and improve the quality of the environment and the sustainable management of global natural resources, in order to ensure sustainable development;	(f) help develop international measures to preserve and improve the quality of the environment and the sustainable management of global natural resources, in order to ensure sustainable development;
(g) assist populations, countries and regions confronting natural or man-made disasters; and	(g) assist populations, countries and regions confronting natural or man-made disasters; and
(h) promote an international system based on stronger multilateral cooperation and good global governance.	(h) promote an international system based on stronger multilateral cooperation and good global governance.
3. ***The Union shall respect the principles and pursue the objectives set out in paragraphs 1 and 2 in the development and implementation of the different areas of the Union's external action covered by this Title and by Part Five of the Treaty on the Functioning of the European Union, and of the external aspects of its other policies.*** The Union shall ensure consistency between the different areas of its external action and between these and its other policies. ***The Council and the Commission, assisted by the High Representative of the Union for Foreign Affairs and Security Policy, shall ensure that consistency and shall cooperate to that effect.***	3. The Union shall ensure consistency between the different areas of its external action and between these and its other policies.
Article 22	Article 407 (ex-Article 22 TEU)
1. On the basis of the principles and objectives set out in Article 21, the European Council shall identify the strategic interests and objectives of the Union. Decisions of the European Council on the strategic interests and objectives of the Union shall relate to the common foreign and security policy and to other areas of the external action of the Union. Such decisions may concern the relations of the Union with a specific country or region or may be thematic in approach. ***They shall define their duration, and the means to be made available by the Union and the Member States.***	On the basis of the principles and objectives set out in Article 406, ***and on the basis of proposals made by the Commission***, the European Council shall identify the strategic interests and objectives of the Union. ***The identification by*** the European Council ***of*** the strategic interests and objectives of the Union shall relate to the common foreign and security policy and to other areas of the external action of the Union. Such ***orientations*** may concern the relations of the Union with a specific country or region or may be thematic in approach.

The European Council shall act unanimously on a recommendation from the Council, adopted by the latter under the arrangements laid down for each area. Decisions of the European Council shall be implemented in accordance with the procedures provided for in the Treaties. ***2. The High Representative of the Union for Foreign Affairs and Security Policy, for the area of common foreign and security policy, and the Commission, for other areas of external action, may submit joint proposals to the Council.***	
Article 23	[delete]

COMMON FOREIGN AND SECURITY POLICY

CHAPTER TWO

Article 408 elides the treatment of CFSP more closely to that of other Union policies, for example, and importantly, by lifting the restriction on the authority of the European Court of Justice in this area. It also takes a more positive stance on the goal of a common defence policy.

To rectify one of the obvious weaknesses of Lisbon, we give to the Foreign Minister two political deputies (Article 411).

The convoluted decision-making procedure of the Lisbon treaty is greatly simplified in Article 412. Consistent with our approach throughout the Fundamental Law, it is foreseen that the Council will normally act by qualified majority vote. This does not preclude the fact that the foreign ministers in Council will have a consensual approach to decisions in foreign policy, but it does lighten the shadow of a unilateral national veto. Recourse to the European Council is to be a last resort in cases of serious disagreement. Parliament is given the right of consent to decisions of the Council in the field of CFSP, subject to the observance of strict time-limits.

In Article 414 we strengthen the role of the Foreign Minister in speaking for the Union in international fora, not least at the UN.

The role of the European Parliament is further enhanced, in that it will now be informed and consulted over the conduct of operations in addition to the 'main aspects and basic choices' (Article 415). Parliament also has a strengthened role on the budgetary aspects of CFSP (Article 417).

Article 24	Article 408 (ex-Article 24 TEU)
1. The Union's competence in matters of common foreign and security policy shall cover all areas of foreign policy and all questions relating to the Union's security, including the progressive framing of a common defence policy ***that might lead*** to a common defence.	1. The Union's competence in matters of common foreign and security policy shall cover all areas of foreign policy and all questions relating to the Union's security, including the progressive framing of a common defence policy ***leading*** to a common defence.
The common foreign and security policy is subject to specific rules and procedures. It shall be defined and implemented by the European Council and the Council acting unanimously, except where the Treaties provide otherwise. The adoption of legislative acts shall be excluded. The common foreign and security policy shall be put into effect by the High Representative of the Union for Foreign Affairs and Security Policy and by Member States, in accordance with the Treaties. The specific role of the European Parliament and of the Commission in this area is defined by the Treaties. The Court of Justice of the European Union shall not have jurisdiction with respect to these provisions, with the exception of its jurisdiction to monitor compliance with Article 40 of this Treaty and to review the legality of certain decisions as provided for by the second paragraph of Article 275 of the Treaty on the Functioning of the European Union.	
2. Within the framework of the principles and objectives of its external action, the Union shall conduct, define and implement a common foreign and security policy, based on the development of mutual political solidarity among Member States, the identification of questions of general interest and the achievement of an ever-increasing degree of convergence of Member States' actions.	2. Within the framework of the principles and objectives of its external action, the Union shall conduct, define and implement a common foreign and security policy, based on the development of mutual political solidarity among the States, the identification of questions of general interest and the achievement of an ever-increasing degree of convergence.
3. The Member States shall support the Union's external and security policy actively and unreservedly in a spirit of loyalty and mutual solidarity and shall comply with the Union's action in this area.	3. The States shall support the Union's external and security policy actively and unreservedly in a spirit of loyalty and mutual solidarity and shall comply with the Union's action in this area.

The Member States shall work together to enhance and develop their mutual political solidarity. They shall refrain from any action which is contrary to the interests of the Union or likely to impair its effectiveness as a cohesive force in international relations. The Council and the High Representative shall ensure compliance with these principles.	The States shall work together to enhance and develop their mutual political solidarity. They shall refrain from any action which is contrary to the interests of the Union or likely to impair its effectiveness as a cohesive force in international relations. The Council and the Foreign Minister shall ensure compliance with these principles.
Article 25 The Union shall conduct the common foreign and security policy by: (a) defining the general guidelines; (b) adopting decisions defining: (i) actions to be undertaken by the Union; (ii) positions to be taken by the Union; (iii) ***arrangements for the implementation of the decisions referred to in points (i) and (ii);*** and by (c) strengthening systematic cooperation between Member States in the conduct of policy.	Article 409 (ex-Article 25 TEU) The Union shall conduct the common foreign and security policy by defining general guidelines, adopting decisions defining actions and positions, and by strengthening systematic cooperation between the States in the conduct of policy. ***Where the international situation requires operational action by the Union, the Council shall adopt the necessary decisions on the basis of proposals made by the Commission.*** ***Where a State has to take urgent action in cases of imperative need, it shall inform the Commission immediately.***
Article 26 1. ***The European Council shall identify the Union's strategic interests, determine the objectives of and define general guidelines for the common foreign and security policy, including for matters with defence implications. It shall adopt the necessary decisions.***	Article 410 (ex-Article 26 TEU)

If international developments so require, the President of the European Council shall convene an extraordinary meeting of the European Council in order to define the strategic lines of the Union's policy in the face of such developments.	
2. The Council shall frame the common foreign and security policy and take the decisions necessary for defining and implementing it on the basis of the general guidelines and strategic lines defined by the European Council.	1. ***On the basis of proposals of the Commission, and in accordance with the general guidelines and strategic lines defined by the European Council***, the Council shall frame the common foreign and security policy.
The Council and the High Representative of the Union for Foreign Affairs and Security Policy shall ensure the unity, consistency and effectiveness of action by the Union.	The Council and the Foreign Minister shall ensure the unity, consistency and effectiveness of action by the Union.
3. The common foreign and security policy shall be put into effect by the High Representative and by the Member States, using national and Union resources.	2. The common foreign and security policy shall be put into effect by the Foreign Minister and by the States, using ***State*** and Union resources.
Article 27	Article 411 (ex-Article 27 TEU)
1. The High Representative of the Union for Foreign Affairs and Security Policy, who shall chair the Foreign Affairs Council, shall contribute through his proposals to the development of the common foreign and security policy and shall ensure implementation of the decisions adopted by ***the European Council and*** the Council.	1. The Foreign Minister, who shall chair the Foreign Affairs Council, shall contribute through his or her proposals to the development of the common foreign and security policy and shall ***coordinate the activities of the States within the Council***. The Foreign Minister shall ensure implementation of the decisions adopted by the Council.
2. The High Representative shall represent the Union for matters relating to the common foreign and security policy. He shall conduct political dialogue with third parties on the Union's behalf and shall express the Union's position in international organisations and at international conferences.	2. The Foreign Minister shall represent the Union for matters relating to the common foreign and security policy. He or she shall conduct political dialogue with third parties on the Union's behalf and shall express the Union's position in international organisations and at international conferences.

3. In fulfilling his mandate, the High Representative shall be assisted by a European External Action Service. This service shall work in cooperation with the diplomatic services of the Member States ***and shall comprise officials from relevant departments of the General Secretariat of the Council and of the Commission as well as staff seconded from national diplomatic services of the Member States. The organisation and functioning of the European External Action Service shall be established by a decision of the Council. The Council shall act on a proposal from the High Representative after consulting the European Parliament and after obtaining the consent of the Commission.***	3. In fulfilling his or her mandate, the Foreign Minister shall be assisted by the Foreign Service. This service shall work in cooperation with the diplomatic services of the States. 4. ***The Foreign Minister shall have political deputies. One deputy minister shall chair the Political and Security Committee responsible for the political control and strategic direction of crisis management operations. The deputy ministers may represent the Foreign Minister at the European Parliament and Council.*** ***The deputy foreign ministers will be nominated by the President of the Commission after having consulted the Council. They will take up their appointment having been subject to a hearing and a vote of approval by the responsible committee of the European Parliament.***
Articles 28–30	[delete]
Article 31	Article 412 (ex-Article 31 TEU)
1. Decisions ***under this Chapter*** shall be taken by ***the European Council and*** the Council ***acting unanimously***, except where ***this Chapter*** provides otherwise. ***The adoption of legislative acts shall be excluded.***	1. Decisions ***in common foreign and security policy*** shall be taken by the Council, ***on proposals by the Commission, with the consent of the European Parliament***, except where ***the Fundamental Law*** provides otherwise. ***The Council shall act in accordance with the voting procedure laid down in Article 14(5).***
When abstaining in a vote, any member of the Council may qualify its abstention by making a formal declaration under the present subparagraph. In that case, it shall not be obliged to apply the decision, but shall accept that the decision commits the Union. In a spirit of mutual solidarity, the Member State concerned shall refrain from any action likely to conflict with or impede Union action based on that decision and the other Member States shall respect its position. ***If the members of the Council qualifying their abstention in this way represent at least one third of the Member States comprising at least one third of the population of the Union, the decision shall not be adopted.***	When abstaining in a vote, any member of the Council may qualify its abstention by making a formal declaration under the present subparagraph. In that case, it shall not be obliged to apply the decision, but shall accept that the decision commits the Union. In a spirit of mutual solidarity, the State concerned shall refrain from any action likely to conflict with or impede Union action based on that decision and the other states shall respect its position.

2. *By derogation from the provisions of paragraph 1, the Council shall act by qualified majority:*

– *when adopting a decision defining a Union action or position on the basis of a decision of the European Council relating to the Union's strategic interests and objectives, as referred to in Article 22(1),*

– *when adopting a decision defining a Union action or position, on a proposal which the High Representative of the Union for Foreign Affairs and Security Policy has presented following a specific request from the European Council, made on its own initiative or that of the High Representative,*

– *when adopting any decision implementing a decision defining a Union action or position,*

– *when appointing a special representative in accordance with Article 33.*

If a member of the Council declares that, for vital and stated reasons of national policy, it intends to oppose the adoption of a decision to be taken by qualified majority, a vote shall not be taken. The High Representative will, in close consultation with the Member State involved, search for a solution acceptable to it. If he does not succeed, the Council may, acting by a qualified majority, request that the matter be referred to the European Council for a decision by unanimity.

3. *The European Council may unanimously adopt a decision stipulating that the Council shall act by a qualified majority in cases other than those referred to in paragraph 2.*

4. *Paragraphs 2 and 3 shall not apply to decisions having military or defence implications.*

5. *For procedural questions, the Council shall act by a majority of its members.*

2. If a member of the Council declares that, for vital and stated reasons of national policy, it intends to oppose the adoption of a decision to be taken by qualified majority, a vote shall not be taken. The Foreign Minister will, in close consultation with the State involved, search for a solution acceptable to it. If the Foreign Minister does not succeed, the Council may, acting by a qualified majority, request that the matter be referred to the European Council for a decision by unanimity.

3. ***The European Parliament shall act in accordance with the voting procedure laid down in Article 12(7). The Parliament shall deliver its decision within a time-limit which will be set depending on the urgency of the matter and will be specified in the draft decision of the Council. In the absence of a decision by Parliament within that time-limit, the Council may adopt the decision.***

Article 32	Article 413 (ex-Article 32 TEU)
Member States shall consult one another within the European Council and the Council on any matter of foreign and security policy of general interest in order to determine a common approach. Before undertaking any action on the international scene or entering into any commitment which could affect the Union's interests, each Member State shall consult the ***others within the European Council or the Council.*** Member States shall ensure, through the convergence of their actions, that the Union is able to assert its interests and values on the international scene. Member States shall show mutual solidarity. ***When the European Council or the Council has defined a common approach of the Union within the meaning of the first paragraph, the High Representative of the Union for Foreign Affairs and Security Policy and the Ministers for Foreign Affairs of the Member States shall coordinate their activities within the Council.*** The diplomatic missions of the Member States and the Union delegations in third countries and at international organisations shall cooperate and shall contribute to formulating and implementing the common approach.	The States shall consult one another within the European Council and the Council on any matter of foreign and security policy of general interest in order to determine a common approach. Before undertaking any action on the international scene or entering into any commitment which could affect the Union's interests, each State shall consult ***the Commission.*** States shall ensure, through the convergence of their actions, that the Union is able to assert its interests and values on the international scene. States shall show mutual solidarity. The diplomatic missions of the States and the Union delegations in third countries and at international organisations shall cooperate and shall contribute to formulating and implementing the common approach.
Article 33	[delete]
Article 34	Article 414 (ex-Article 34 TEU)
1. Member States shall coordinate their action in international organisations and at international conferences. They shall uphold the Union's positions in such forums. The High Representative of the Union for Foreign Affairs and Security Policy shall organise this coordination.	1. ***The Foreign Minister*** shall coordinate the action of the Union in international organisations and at international conferences, and shall uphold the Union's positions in such forums.

In international organisations and at international conferences where not all the Member States participate, those which do take part shall uphold the Union's positions.	In international organisations and at international conferences where not all the States participate, those which do take part shall uphold the Union's positions.
2. In accordance with Article 24(3), Member States represented in international organisations or international conferences where not all the Member States participate shall keep the other Member States and the High Representative informed of any matter of common interest.	2. In accordance with Article 408(3), States represented in international organisations or international conferences where not all the States participate shall keep the other States and the Foreign Minister informed of any matter of common interest.
Member States which are also members of the United Nations Security Council will concert and keep the other Member States and the High Representative fully informed. Member States which are members of the Security Council will, in the execution of their functions, defend the positions and the interests of the Union, without prejudice to their responsibilities under the provisions of the United Nations Charter.	States which are also members of the United Nations Security Council will concert and keep the other States and the Foreign Minister fully informed. States which are members of the Security Council will, in the execution of their functions, defend the positions and the interests of the Union, without prejudice to their responsibilities under the provisions of the United Nations Charter.
When the Union has defined a position on a subject which is on the United Nations Security Council agenda, ***those Member States which sit on the Security Council shall request that the High Representative be invited to*** present the Union's position.	When the Union has defined a position on a subject which is on the United Nations Security Council agenda, ***the Foreign Minister shall*** present the Union's position.
Article 35	[delete]
Article 36	Article 415 (ex-Article 36 TEU)
The High Representative of the Union for Foreign Affairs and Security Policy shall regularly consult the European Parliament on the main aspects and the basic choices of the common foreign and security policy and the common security and defence policy ***and inform it of how those policies evolve***. He shall ensure that the views of the European Parliament are duly taken into ***consideration***. Special representatives may be involved in briefing the European Parliament.	The Foreign Minister shall regularly ***inform and*** consult the European Parliament on the main aspects, basic choices ***and operational decisions of the common foreign, security and defence policies***. The Foreign Minister shall ensure that the views of the European Parliament are duly taken into ***account***. ***The deputy ministers*** and special representatives may also be involved in briefing the European Parliament.

The European Parliament may address questions or make recommendations to the Council or the High Representative. Twice a year it shall hold a debate on progress in implementing the common foreign and security policy, including the common security and defence policy.	The European Parliament may address questions or make recommendations to ***the Commission*** or the Council. Twice a year it shall hold a debate on progress in implementing the common foreign, ***security and defence policies of the Union***.
Article 37	Article 416 (ex-Article 37 TEU)
The Union may conclude agreements with one or more States or international organisations in areas covered by this Chapter.	The Union may conclude agreements with one or more States or international organisations in ***the field of common foreign, security and defence policies***.
Articles 38–40	[delete]
Article 41	Article 417 (ex-Article 41 TEU)
1. Administrative expenditure to which the implementation of this Chapter gives rise for the institutions shall be charged to the Union budget.	1. Administrative expenditure to which the implementation of this Chapter gives rise for the institutions shall be charged to the Union budget.
2. Operating expenditure to which the implementation of this Chapter gives rise shall also be charged to the Union budget, except for such expenditure arising from operations having military or defence implications ***and*** cases where the Council acting unanimously decides ***otherwise***.	2. Operating expenditure to which the implementation of this Chapter gives rise shall also be charged to the Union budget, except for such expenditure arising from operations having military or defence implications ***in*** cases where the Council, acting unanimously ***on a proposal of the Commission***, so decides.
In cases where expenditure is not charged to the Union budget, it shall be charged to the Member States in accordance with the gross national product scale, unless the Council acting unanimously decides otherwise. As for expenditure arising from operations having military or defence implications, Member States whose representatives in the Council have made a formal declaration under Article 31(1), second subparagraph, shall not be obliged to contribute to the financing thereof.	In cases where ***military or defence related*** expenditure is not charged to the Union budget, it shall be charged to the States in accordance with the gross national product scale. States whose representatives in the Council have made a formal declaration under Article 412(1) shall not be obliged to contribute to the financing thereof.

3. The Council shall adopt a decision establishing the specific procedures for guaranteeing rapid access to appropriations in the Union budget for urgent financing of initiatives in the framework of the common foreign and security ***policy, and in particular for preparatory activities for the tasks referred to in Article 42(1) and Article 43. It shall act after consulting the European Parliament.***

Preparatory activities for the tasks referred to in Article 42(1) and Article 43 which are not charged to the Union budget shall be financed by a start-up fund made up of Member States' contributions.

The Council shall adopt by a qualified majority, on a proposal from the High Representative of the Union for Foreign Affairs and Security Policy, decisions establishing:

(a) the procedures for setting up and financing the start-up fund, in particular the amounts allocated to the fund;

(b) the procedures for administering the start-up fund;

(c) the financial control procedures.

When the task planned in accordance with Article 42(1) and Article 43 cannot be charged to the Union budget, the Council shall authorise the High Representative to use the fund. The High Representative shall report to the Council on the implementation of this remit.

3. ***The European Parliament and the Council, acting in accordance with the ordinary legislative procedure, shall enact a law laying down*** the specific procedures for guaranteeing rapid access to appropriations in the Union budget for urgent financing of initiatives in the framework of the ***common foreign, security and defence policies.***

The regulation shall establish mechanisms for the coordination of the financial contributions of the States and for the financial accountability of the scheme to the European Parliament and State Parliaments and to the Court of Auditors.

COMMON SECURITY AND DEFENCE POLICY

CHAPTER THREE

In the adjustments to this chapter, we encourage the evolution of the Union towards adopting a common defence policy.

The position of the Commission, including the Foreign Minister, is rationalised in order that it can contribute more to the development of CSDP.

The battlegroups gain a legal base (Article 418) and the role of the European Defence Agency is strengthened through the involvement of the European Parliament (Article 421). Parliament also gains consultative powers in the establishment of a permanent military core group of the Union (Article 422).

Article 42	Article 418 (ex-Article 42 TEU)
1. The common security and defence policy shall ***be an integral part of the common foreign and security policy. It shall*** provide the Union with an operational capacity drawing on civilian and military assets. The Union may use them on missions outside the Union for peace-keeping, conflict prevention and strengthening international security in accordance with the principles of the United Nations Charter. The performance of these tasks shall be undertaken using capabilities provided by the Member States.	1. The common security and defence policy shall provide the Union with an operational capacity drawing on civilian and military assets. The Union may use them on missions outside the Union for peace-keeping, conflict prevention and strengthening international security in accordance with the principles of the United Nations Charter. The performance of these tasks shall be undertaken using capabilities provided by the States.

2. The common security and defence policy shall ***include*** the progressive framing of a common Union defence ***policy. This will lead to a common defence, when the European Council, acting unanimously, so decides. It shall in that case recommend to the Member States the adoption of such a decision in accordance with their respective constitutional requirements.***

The policy of the Union ***in accordance with this Section shall not prejudice the specific character of the security and defence policy of certain Member States and*** shall respect the obligations of certain Member States, which see their common defence realised in the North Atlantic Treaty Organisation (NATO), under the North Atlantic Treaty and be compatible with the common security and defence policy established within that framework.

3. Member States shall make civilian and military capabilities available to the Union for the implementation of the common security and defence policy, ***to contribute to the objectives defined by the Council.*** Those Member States which together establish multinational forces may also make them available to the common security and defence policy.

Member States shall undertake progressively to improve their military capabilities. The Agency in the field of defence capabilities development, research, acquisition and armaments (hereinafter referred to as 'the European Defence Agency') shall identify operational requirements, shall promote measures to satisfy those requirements, shall contribute to identifying and, where appropriate, implementing any measure needed to strengthen the industrial and technological base of the defence sector, shall participate in defining a European capabilities and armaments policy, and shall assist the Council in evaluating the improvement of military capabilities.

2. The common security and defence policy shall ***involve*** the progressive framing of a common Union defence. It shall not prejudice the specific character of the security and defence policy of certain States.

The ***defence*** policy of the Union shall respect the obligations of ***those*** States which see their common defence realised in the North Atlantic Treaty Organisation (NATO), under the North Atlantic Treaty and be compatible with the common security and defence policy established within that framework. Union defence policy shall be consistent with commitments to NATO, which, for those States which are members of it, remains the foundation of their collective defence and the forum for its implementation.

3. States shall make civilian and military capabilities available to the Union for the implementation of the common security and defence policy.

Those States which together establish multinational forces may also make them available to the common security and defence policy.

A European battlegroup may be formed by three or more States as laid down in Protocol No 8 on permanent structured cooperation.

States shall undertake progressively to improve their military capabilities. The Agency in the field of defence capabilities development, research, acquisition and armaments (hereinafter 'the European Defence Agency') shall identify operational requirements, shall promote measures to satisfy those requirements, shall contribute to identifying and, where appropriate, implementing any measure needed to strengthen the industrial and technological base of the defence sector, shall participate in defining a European capabilities and armaments policy, and shall assist the ***Commission and*** the Council in evaluating the improvement of military capabilities.

4. Decisions relating to the common security and defence policy, including those initiating a mission as referred to in this Article, shall be adopted by the Council acting unanimously ***on a proposal from the High Representative of the Union for Foreign Affairs and Security Policy or an initiative from a Member State.*** The High Representative may propose the use of both national resources and Union instruments, ***together with the Commission where appropriate.***	4. Decisions relating to the common security and defence policy shall be adopted by the Council acting unanimously ***on a proposal from the Commission, which*** may propose the use of both State resources and Union instruments.
5. The Council may entrust the execution of a task, within the Union framework, to a group of Member States in order to protect the Union's values and serve its interests. The execution of such a task shall be governed by Article 44.	5. The Council may entrust the execution of a task, within the Union framework, to a group of States in order to protect the Union's values and serve its interests. The execution of such a task shall be governed by Article 420.
6. Those Member States whose military capabilities fulfil higher criteria and which have made more binding commitments to one another in this area with a view to the most demanding missions shall establish permanent structured cooperation within the Union framework. Such cooperation shall be governed by Article 46. It shall not affect the provisions of Article 43.	6. Those States whose military capabilities fulfil higher criteria and which have made more binding commitments to one another in this area with a view to the most demanding missions shall establish permanent structured cooperation within the Union framework. Such cooperation shall be governed by Article 422.
7. If a Member State is the victim of armed aggression on its territory, the other Member States shall have towards it an obligation of aid and assistance by all the means in their power, in accordance with Article 51 of the United Nations Charter. ***This shall not prejudice the specific character of the security and defence policy of certain Member States.***	7. If a State is the victim of armed aggression on its territory, the other States shall have towards it an obligation of aid and assistance by all the means in their power, in accordance with Article 51 of the United Nations Charter.
Commitments and cooperation in this area shall be consistent with commitments under the North Atlantic Treaty Organisation, which, for those States which are members of it, remains the foundation of their collective defence and the forum for its implementation.	

Article 43	Article 419 (ex-Article 43 TEU)
1. The tasks referred to in Article 42(1), in the course of which the Union may use civilian and military means, shall include joint disarmament operations, humanitarian and rescue tasks, military advice and assistance tasks, conflict prevention and peace-keeping tasks, tasks of combat forces in crisis management, including peace-making and post-conflict stabilisation. All these tasks may contribute to the fight against terrorism, including by supporting third countries in combating terrorism in their territories.	1. The tasks referred to in Article 418(1), in the course of which the Union may use civilian and military means, shall include joint disarmament operations, humanitarian and rescue tasks, military advice and assistance tasks, conflict prevention and peace-keeping tasks, tasks of combat forces in crisis management, including peace-making and post-conflict stabilisation. All these tasks may contribute to the fight against terrorism, including by supporting third countries in combating terrorism in their territories.
2. The Council shall adopt decisions relating to the tasks referred to in paragraph 1, defining their objectives and scope and the general conditions for their implementation. The High Representative of the Union for Foreign Affairs and Security Policy, ***acting under the authority of the Council and in close and constant contact with the Political and Security Committee***, shall ensure coordination of the civilian and military aspects of such tasks.	2. The Council shall adopt decisions relating to the tasks referred to in paragraph 1, ***on proposals of the Commission***, defining their objectives and scope and the general conditions for their implementation. The Foreign Minister shall ensure coordination of the civilian and military aspects of such tasks.
Article 44	Article 420 (ex-Article 44 TEU)
1. Within the framework of the decisions adopted in accordance with Article 43, the ***Council*** may entrust the implementation of a task to a group of Member States which are willing and have the necessary capability for such a task. Those Member States, in ***association*** with the High Representative of the Union for Foreign Affairs and Security Policy, shall agree among themselves on the management of the task.	1. Within the framework of the decisions adopted in accordance with Article 419, the ***Union*** may entrust the implementation of a task to a group of States which are willing and have the necessary capability for such a task. Those States, in ***close cooperation*** with the Foreign Minister, shall agree on the management of the task.

2. Member States participating in the task shall keep the Council regularly informed of its progress on their own initiative or at the request of another Member State. Those States shall inform the Council immediately should the completion of the task entail major consequences or require amendment of the objective, scope and conditions determined for the task in the decisions referred to in paragraph 1. In such cases, the Council shall adopt the necessary decisions.	2. States participating in the task shall keep the ***Commission and*** the Council regularly informed of its progress on their own initiative or at the request of another State. Those States shall inform the ***Commission and*** the Council immediately should the completion of the task entail major consequences or require amendment of the objective, scope and conditions determined for the task in the decisions referred to in paragraph 1. In such cases, the Council, ***on a proposal of the Commission***, shall adopt the necessary decisions.
Article 45	Article 421 (ex-Article 45 TEU)
1. The European Defence Agency referred to in Article 42(3), subject to the authority of the Council, shall have as its task to:	1. The European Defence Agency, subject to the authority of the ***Commission***, shall have as its task to:
(a) ***contribute to identifying*** the Member States' military capability objectives and evaluating observance of the capability commitments given by the Member States;	(a) ***identify*** the States' military capability objectives and evaluating observance of the capability commitments given by the States;
(b) promote harmonisation of operational needs and adoption of effective, compatible procurement methods;	(b) promote harmonisation of operational needs and adoption of effective, compatible procurement methods;
(c) propose multilateral projects to fulfil the objectives in terms of military capabilities, ensure coordination of the programmes implemented by the Member States and management of specific cooperation programmes;	(c) propose multilateral projects to fulfil the objectives in terms of military capabilities, ensure coordination of the programmes implemented by the States and management of specific cooperation programmes;
(d) support defence technology research, and coordinate and plan joint research activities and the study of technical solutions meeting future operational needs;	(d) support defence technology research, and coordinate and plan joint research activities and the study of technical solutions meeting future operational needs;
(e) ***contribute to identifying*** and, if necessary, implementing any useful measure for strengthening the industrial and technological base of the defence sector and for improving the effectiveness of military expenditure.	(e) ***identify*** and, if necessary, implement any useful measure for strengthening the industrial and technological base of the defence sector and for improving the effectiveness of military expenditure.

2. The European Defence Agency shall be open to all Member States wishing to be part of it. ***The Council, acting by a qualified majority, shall adopt a decision defining the Agency's statute, seat and operational rules.*** That decision should take account of the level of effective participation in the Agency's activities. Specific groups shall be set up within the Agency bringing together Member States engaged in joint projects. The Agency shall carry out its tasks in liaison with the Commission where necessary.	2. ***The European Parliament and the Council, acting in accordance with the ordinary legislative procedure, shall establish*** the European Defence Agency. The Agency shall be open to all States wishing to be part of it. That decision should take account of the level of effective participation in the Agency's activities. Specific groups shall be set up within the Agency bringing together States engaged in joint projects. The Agency shall carry out its tasks in liaison with the Commission where necessary.
Article 46	Article 422 (ex-Article 46 TEU)
1. Those Member States which wish to participate in the permanent structured cooperation referred to in Article 42(6), which fulfil the criteria and have made the commitments on military capabilities set out in the Protocol on permanent structured cooperation, shall notify their intention to the ***Council and to the High Representative of the Union for Foreign Affairs and Security Policy.***	1. Those States which wish to participate in the permanent structured cooperation, which fulfil the criteria and have made the commitments on military capabilities set out in the Protocol No 8 on permanent structured cooperation, shall notify their intention to the ***Commission.***
2. Within three months following the notification referred to in paragraph 1 the Council shall adopt a decision establishing permanent structured cooperation and determining the list of participating Member States. The Council shall act by a qualified majority after consulting the ***High Representative.***	2. Within three months following the notification referred to in paragraph 1 the Council shall adopt a decision establishing permanent structured cooperation and determining the list of participating States. The Council shall act ***on a proposal of the Commission*** by a qualified majority after consulting ***the European Parliament.***
3. Any Member State which, at a later stage, wishes to participate in the permanent structured cooperation shall notify its intention to the ***Council and to the High Representative.***	3. Any State which, at a later stage, wishes to participate in the permanent structured cooperation shall notify its intention to the ***Commission.***

The Council shall adopt a decision confirming the participation of the Member State concerned which fulfils the criteria and makes the commitments referred to in Articles 1 and 2 of the Protocol on permanent structured cooperation. The Council shall act by a qualified majority after consulting the ***High Representative***. Only members of the Council representing the participating Member States shall take part in the vote.

A qualified majority shall be defined in accordance with Article 238(3)(a) of the Treaty on the Functioning of the European Union.

The Council shall adopt a decision confirming the participation of the State concerned which fulfils the criteria and makes the commitments referred to in Articles 1 and 2 of Protocol No 8. The Council shall act ***on a proposal of the Commission*** by a qualified majority, after consulting ***the Parliament***. Only members of the Council representing the participating States shall take part in the vote.

A qualified majority shall be defined in accordance with Article 14(4).

4. If a participating Member State no longer fulfils the criteria or is no longer able to meet the commitments referred to in Articles 1 and 2 of the Protocol on permanent structured cooperation, the Council may adopt a decision suspending the participation of the Member State concerned.

The Council shall act by a qualified majority. Only members of the Council representing the participating Member States, with the exception of the Member State in question, shall take part in the vote.

A qualified majority shall be defined in accordance with Article 238(3)(a) of the Treaty on the Functioning of the European Union.

4. If a participating State no longer fulfils the criteria or is no longer able to meet the commitments referred to in Articles 1 and 2 of the Protocol, the Council may adopt a decision suspending the participation of the State concerned.

The Council shall act ***on a proposal of the Commission*** by a qualified majority, ***after consulting the Parliament***. Only members of the Council representing the participating States, with the exception of the State in question, shall take part in the vote.

A qualified majority shall be defined in accordance with Article 14(4).

5. Any participating Member State which wishes to withdraw from permanent structured cooperation shall notify its intention to the ***Council***, which shall take note that the Member State in question has ceased to participate.

5. Any participating State which wishes to withdraw from permanent structured cooperation shall notify its intention to the ***Commission***, which shall ***inform the Council and Parliament*** that the State in question has ceased to participate.

6. ***The decisions and recommendations of the Council within the framework of permanent structured cooperation, other than those provided for in paragraphs 2 to 5, shall be adopted by unanimity. For the purposes of this paragraph, unanimity shall be constituted by the votes of the representatives of the participating Member States only.***	
Article 205	[delete]

COMMON COMMERCIAL POLICY

CHAPTER FOUR

The scope of the commercial policy is widened from foreign direct investment to include all investment, which will reduce the number of over-complicated 'mixed' EU and intergovernmental agreements (Article 424(1)).

Article 206	Article 423 (ex-Article 206 TFEU)
By establishing a customs union in accordance with Articles 28 to 32, the Union shall contribute, in the common interest, to the harmonious development of world trade, the progressive abolition of restrictions on international trade and on foreign direct investment, and the lowering of customs and other barriers.	By establishing a customs union in accordance with Articles 269 to 273, the Union shall contribute, in the common interest, to the harmonious development of world trade, the progressive abolition of restrictions on international trade and on foreign direct investment, and the lowering of customs and other barriers.
Article 207	Article 424 (ex-Article 207 TFEU)
1. The common commercial policy shall be based on uniform principles, particularly with regard to changes in tariff rates, the conclusion of tariff and trade agreements relating to trade in goods and services, and the commercial aspects of intellectual property, foreign ***direct*** investment, the achievement of uniformity in measures of liberalisation, export policy and measures to protect trade such as those to be taken in the event of dumping or subsidies. The common commercial policy shall be conducted in the context of the principles and objectives of the Union's external action.	1. The common commercial policy shall be based on uniform principles, particularly with regard to changes in tariff rates, the conclusion of tariff and trade agreements relating to trade in goods and services, and the commercial aspects of intellectual property, foreign investment, the achievement of uniformity in measures of liberalisation, export policy and measures to protect trade such as those to be taken in the event of dumping or subsidies. The common commercial policy shall be conducted in the context of the principles and objectives of the Union's external action.

2. The European Parliament and the Council, acting by means of regulations in accordance with the ordinary legislative procedure, shall adopt the measures defining the framework for implementing the common commercial policy.

3. Where agreements with one or more third countries or international organisations need to be negotiated and concluded, Article 218 shall apply, subject to the special provisions of this Article.

The Commission shall make recommendations to the Council, which shall authorise it to open the necessary negotiations. The Council and the Commission shall be responsible for ensuring that the agreements negotiated are compatible with internal Union policies and rules.

The Commission shall conduct these negotiations in consultation with a special committee appointed by the Council to assist the Commission in this task and within the framework of such directives as the Council may issue to it. The Commission shall report regularly to the special committee and to the European Parliament on the progress of negotiations.

4. For the negotiation and conclusion of the agreements referred to in paragraph 3, the Council shall act by a qualified majority.

For the negotiation and conclusion of agreements ***in the fields of trade in services and the commercial aspects of intellectual property, as well as foreign direct investment, the Council shall act unanimously where such agreements include provisions for which unanimity is required for the adoption of internal rules.***

2. The European Parliament and the Council, acting by means of regulations in accordance with the ordinary legislative procedure, shall adopt the measures defining the framework for implementing the common commercial policy.

3. Where agreements with one or more third countries or international organisations need to be negotiated and concluded, Article 439 shall apply, subject to the special provisions of this Article.

The Commission shall make recommendations to the Council, which shall authorise it to open the necessary negotiations. The Commission shall be responsible for ensuring that the agreements negotiated are compatible with internal Union policies and rules.

The Commission shall conduct these negotiations in consultation with a special committee appointed by the Council to assist the Commission in this task and within the framework of such directives as the Council may issue to it. The Commission shall report regularly to the special committee and to the European Parliament on the progress of negotiations.

4. For the negotiation and conclusion of the agreements referred to in paragraph 3, the Council shall act by a qualified majority.

For the negotiation and conclusion of agreements ***which include provisions for which the special legislative procedure is required for the adoption of internal rules, the Council shall act in accordance with its voting rules under the special legislative procedure.***

The Council shall ***also*** act unanimously for the negotiation and conclusion of agreements:	The Council shall act unanimously for the negotiation and conclusion of agreements:
(a) in the field of trade in cultural and audiovisual services, where these agreements risk prejudicing the Union's cultural and linguistic diversity;	(a) in the field of trade in cultural and audiovisual services, where these agreements risk prejudicing the Union's cultural and linguistic diversity;
(b) in the field of trade in social, education and health services, where these agreements risk seriously disturbing the national organisation of such services and prejudicing the responsibility of Member States to deliver them.	(b) in the field of trade in social, education and health services, where these agreements risk seriously disturbing the national organisation of such services and prejudicing the responsibility of the States to deliver them.
5. The negotiation and conclusion of international agreements in the field of transport shall be subject to Title VI of Part Three and to Article 218.	5. The negotiation and conclusion of international agreements in the field of transport shall be subject to Article 433.
6. The exercise of the competences conferred by this Article in the field of the common commercial policy shall not affect the delimitation of competences between the Union and the Member States, and shall not lead to harmonisation of legislative or regulatory provisions of the Member States in so far as the Treaties exclude such harmonisation.	6. The exercise of the competences conferred by this Article in the field of the common commercial policy shall not affect the delimitation of competences between the Union and the States, and shall not lead to harmonisation of legislative or regulatory provisions of the States in so far as the Fundamental Law excludes such harmonisation.

INTERNATIONAL RELATIONS

CHAPTER FIVE

Here we insist that EU states which wish to conduct their own supplementary international policies with third countries must at the least inform the Commission in advance. The purpose is to integrate more closely residual national development aid policies with the Union's common policy.

The Commission takes over from the Council the power to impose sanctions against third countries, subject to revocation by either chamber of the legislature (Article 430).

DEVELOPMENT COOPERATION	DEVELOPMENT COOPERATION
Article 208	Article 425 (ex-Article 208 TFEU)
1. Union policy in the field of development cooperation shall be conducted within the framework of the principles and objectives of the Union's external action. The Union's development cooperation policy and that of the Member States complement and reinforce each other.	1. Union policy in the field of development cooperation shall be conducted within the framework of the principles and objectives of the Union's external action. The Union's development cooperation policy and that of the States ***shall*** complement and reinforce each other.
Union development cooperation policy shall have as its primary objective the reduction and, in the long term, the eradication of poverty. The Union shall take account of the objectives of development cooperation in the policies that it implements which are likely to affect developing countries.	Union development cooperation policy shall have as its primary objective the reduction and, in the long term, the eradication of poverty. The Union shall take account of the objectives of development cooperation in the policies that it implements which are likely to affect developing countries.
2. The Union and the Member States shall comply with the commitments and take account of the objectives they have approved in the context of the United Nations and other competent international organisations.	2. The Union and the States shall comply with the commitments and take account of the objectives they have approved in the context of the United Nations and other competent international organisations.

Article 209	Article 426 (ex-Article 209 TFEU)
1. The European Parliament and the Council, acting in accordance with the ordinary legislative procedure, shall adopt the measures necessary for the implementation of development cooperation policy, which may relate to multiannual cooperation programmes with developing countries or programmes with a thematic approach.	1. The European Parliament and the Council, acting in accordance with the ordinary legislative procedure, shall adopt the measures necessary for the implementation of development cooperation policy, which may relate to multiannual cooperation programmes with developing countries or programmes with a thematic approach.
2. The Union may conclude with third countries and competent international organisations any agreement helping to achieve the objectives referred to in Article 21 of the Treaty on European Union and in Article 208 of this Treaty.	2. The Union may conclude with third countries and competent international organisations any agreement helping to achieve the objectives referred to in Articles 406 and 425.
The first subparagraph shall be without prejudice to Member States' competence to negotiate in international bodies and to conclude agreements.	***States intending to negotiate in international bodies and to conclude agreements shall inform the Commission thereof.***
3. The European Investment Bank shall contribute, under the terms laid down in its Statute, to the implementation of the measures referred to in paragraph 1.	3. The European Investment Bank shall contribute, under the terms laid down in its Statute, to the implementation of the measures referred to in paragraph 1.
Article 210	Article 427 (ex-Articles 210 TFEU) .....
Article 211	[delete]

ECONOMIC, FINANCIAL AND TECHNICAL COOPERATION WITH THIRD COUNTRIES	ECONOMIC COOPERATION
Article 212	Article 428 (ex-Article 212 TFEU)
1. Without prejudice to the other provisions of the Treaties, and in particular Articles 208 to 211, the Union shall carry out economic, financial and technical cooperation measures, including assistance, in particular financial assistance, with third countries other than developing countries. Such measures shall be consistent with the development policy of the Union and shall be carried out within the framework of the principles and objectives of its external action. The Union's operations and those of the Member States shall complement and reinforce each other.	1. Without prejudice to the other provisions of the Fundamental Law, and in particular Articles 425 to 427, the Union shall carry out economic, financial and technical cooperation measures, including assistance, in particular financial assistance, with third countries other than developing countries. Such measures shall be consistent with the development policy of the Union and shall be carried out within the framework of the principles and objectives of its external action. The Union's operations and those of the States shall complement and reinforce each other.
2. The European Parliament and the Council, acting in accordance with the ordinary legislative procedure, shall adopt the measures necessary for the implementation of paragraph 1.	2. The European Parliament and the Council, acting in accordance with the ordinary legislative procedure, shall adopt the measures necessary for the implementation of paragraph 1.
3. Within their respective spheres of competence, the Union and the Member States shall cooperate with third countries and the competent international organisations. The arrangements for Union cooperation may be the subject of agreements between the Union and the third parties concerned.	3. Within their respective spheres of competence, the Union and the States shall cooperate with third countries and the competent international organisations. The arrangements for Union cooperation may be the subject of agreements between the Union and the third parties concerned.
The first subparagraph shall be without prejudice to the Member States' competence to negotiate in international bodies and to conclude international agreements.	***States intending to negotiate in international bodies and to conclude agreements shall inform the Commission thereof.***
Article 213	[delete]

HUMANITARIAN AID	HUMANITARIAN AID
Article 214	Article 429 (ex-Article 214 TFEU)
1. The Union's operations in the field of humanitarian aid shall be conducted within the framework of the principles and objectives of the external action of the Union. Such operations shall be intended to provide ad hoc assistance and relief and protection for people in third countries who are victims of natural or man-made disasters, in order to meet the humanitarian needs resulting from these different situations. The Union's measures and those of the Member States shall complement and reinforce each other.	1. The Union's operations in the field of humanitarian aid shall be conducted within the framework of the principles and objectives of the external action of the Union. Such operations shall be intended to provide ad hoc assistance and relief and protection for people in third countries who are victims of natural or man-made disasters, in order to meet the humanitarian needs resulting from these different situations. The Union's measures and those of the States shall complement and reinforce each other.
2. Humanitarian aid operations shall be conducted in compliance with the principles of international law and with the principles of impartiality, neutrality and non-discrimination.	2. Humanitarian aid operations shall be conducted in compliance with the principles of international law and with the principles of impartiality, neutrality and non-discrimination.
3. The European Parliament and the Council, acting in accordance with the ordinary legislative procedure, shall establish the measures defining the framework within which the Union's humanitarian aid operations shall be implemented.	3. The European Parliament and the Council, acting in accordance with the ordinary legislative procedure, shall establish the measures defining the framework within which the Union's humanitarian aid operations shall be implemented.
4. The Union may conclude with third countries and competent international organisations any agreement helping to achieve the objectives referred to in paragraph 1 and in Article 21 of the Treaty on European Union.	4. The Union may conclude with third countries and competent international organisations any agreement helping to achieve the objectives referred to in paragraph 1 and in Article 406.
The first subparagraph shall be without prejudice to Member States' competence to negotiate in international bodies and to conclude agreements.	***States intending to negotiate in international bodies and to conclude agreements shall inform the Commission thereof.***

5. In order to establish a framework for joint contributions from young Europeans to the humanitarian aid operations of the Union, a European Voluntary Humanitarian Aid Corps shall be set up. The European Parliament and the Council, acting by means of regulations in accordance with the ordinary legislative procedure, shall determine the rules and procedures for the operation of the Corps.	5. In order to establish a framework for joint contributions from young Europeans to the humanitarian aid operations of the Union, a European Voluntary Humanitarian Aid Corps shall be set up. The European Parliament and the Council, acting by means of regulations in accordance with the ordinary legislative procedure, shall determine the rules and procedures for the operation of the Corps.
6. The Commission may take any useful initiative to promote coordination between actions of the Union and those of the Member States, in order to enhance the efficiency and complementarity of Union and national humanitarian aid measures.	6. The Commission may take any useful initiative to promote coordination between actions of the Union and those of the States, in order to enhance the efficiency and complementarity of Union and national humanitarian aid measures.
7. The Union shall ensure that its humanitarian aid operations are coordinated and consistent with those of international organisations and bodies, in particular those forming part of the United Nations system.	7. The Union shall ensure that its humanitarian aid operations are coordinated and consistent with those of international organisations and bodies, in particular those forming part of the United Nations system.
RESTRICTIVE MEASURES	RESTRICTIVE MEASURES
Article 215	Article 430 (ex-Article 215 TFEU)
1. Where a decision, adopted in accordance with Chapter 2 of Title V of the Treaty on European Union, provides for the interruption or reduction, in part or completely, of economic and financial relations with one or more third countries, the ***Council, acting by a qualified majority on a joint proposal from the High Representative of the Union for Foreign Affairs and Security Policy and the Commission, shall adopt the necessary measures. It shall inform the European Parliament thereof.***	1. Where a decision adopted ***in the field of common foreign and security policy*** provides for the interruption or reduction, in part or completely, of economic and financial relations with one or more third countries, ***the Commission*** shall adopt the necessary measures.
2. Where a decision adopted in accordance with Chapter 2 of Title V of the Treaty on European Union so provides, the **Council** may adopt restrictive measures ***under the procedure referred to in paragraph 1*** against natural or legal persons and groups or non-State entities.	Where a decision in the field of common foreign and security policy so provides, ***the Commission*** may adopt restrictive measures against natural or legal persons and groups or non-State entities. ***The decisions of the Commission shall enter into force after a period of four weeks if no objection has been expressed either by the European Parliament, acting pursuant to Article 12(8), or by the Council, acting pursuant to Article 14(5).***

3. The acts referred to in this Article shall include necessary provisions on legal safeguards.	2. The acts referred to in this Article shall include necessary provisions on legal safeguards.

INTERNATIONAL AGREEMENTS

CHAPTER SIX

Specific provision has to be made for Associate States to join the international agreements of the Union (Article 431).

The key provision is Article 433 (ex-Article 218 TFEU), where several adjustments are made to simplify and rationalise the procedures. It is made clear that the Commission can prompt the Council to open an international negotiation, even in foreign and security policy matters, and that the Commission is the negotiator on behalf of the Union as a whole. Parliament's consent will now be needed both to authorise and to conclude all international treaties of the EU, including those in the field of CFSP. Decision-making procedures for international treaties must mirror those used for the Union's internal rules.

Similarly, the Commission's role is enhanced in global monetary matters (Article 434).

Article 216	Article 431 (ex-Article 216 TFEU)
1. The Union may conclude an agreement with one or more third countries or international organisations where the Treaties so provide or where the conclusion of an agreement is necessary in order to achieve, within the framework of the Union's policies, one of the objectives referred to in the Treaties, or is provided for in a legally binding Union act or is likely to affect common rules or alter their scope.	1. The Union may conclude an agreement with one or more third countries or international organisations where the Fundamental Law so provides or where the conclusion of an agreement is necessary in order to achieve, within the framework of the Union's policies, one of the objectives referred to in the Fundamental Law, or is provided for in a legally binding Union act or is likely to affect common rules or alter their scope.
2. Agreements concluded by the Union are binding upon the institutions of the Union and on its Member States.	2. Agreements concluded by the Union are binding upon the institutions of the Union and on its States. ***These agreements shall bind an Associate State in accordance with the terms of its specific participation.***

Article 217	Article 432 (ex-Article 217 TFEU)
The Union may conclude with one or more third countries or international organisations agreements establishing an association involving reciprocal rights and obligations, common action and special procedure.	The Union may conclude with one or more third countries or international organisations agreements establishing an association involving reciprocal rights and obligations, common action and special procedure.
Article 218	Article 433 (ex-Article 218 TFEU)
1. Without prejudice to the specific provisions laid down in Article 207, agreements between the Union and third countries or international organisations shall be negotiated and concluded in accordance with the following procedure.	1. Without prejudice to the specific provisions laid down in Article 424, agreements between the Union and third countries or international organisations shall be negotiated and concluded in accordance with the following procedure.
2. The Council shall authorise the opening of negotiations, adopt negotiating directives, authorise the signing of agreements and conclude them.	2. ***Acting in accordance with the ordinary legislative procedure, on a proposal from the Commission, the European Parliament and*** Council shall authorise the opening of negotiations, adopt negotiating directives, authorise the signing of agreements and conclude them.
3. The Commission, ***or the High Representative of the Union for Foreign Affairs and Security Policy where the agreement envisaged relates exclusively or principally to the common foreign and security policy***, shall submit ***recommendations*** to the Council, which shall adopt a decision authorising the opening of negotiations ***and, depending on the subject of the agreement envisaged, nominating the Union negotiator or the head of the Union's negotiating team.***	3. The Commission shall submit ***proposals*** to the Council, which shall adopt a decision authorising the opening of negotiations. ***The Commission shall conduct the negotiations.***
4. ***The Council may address directives to the negotiator and designate a special committee in consultation with which the negotiations must be conducted.***	

5. The Council, on a proposal by the ***negotiator***, shall adopt a decision authorising the signing of the agreement and, if necessary, its provisional application before entry into force.

6. The Council, on a proposal by the ***negotiator***, shall adopt a decision concluding the agreement.

Except where agreements relate exclusively to the common foreign and security policy, the Council shall adopt the decision concluding the agreement:

(a) after obtaining the consent of the European Parliament in the following cases:

- ***(i) association agreements;***
- ***(ii) agreement on Union accession to the European Convention for the Protection of Human Rights and Fundamental Freedoms;***
- ***(iii) agreements establishing a specific institutional framework by organising cooperation procedures;***
- ***(iv) agreements with important budgetary implications for the Union;***
- ***(v) agreements covering fields to which either the ordinary legislative procedure applies, or the special legislative procedure where consent by the European Parliament is required.***

The European Parliament and the Council may, in an urgent situation, agree upon a time-limit for consent.

4. The Council, on a proposal by the ***Commission***, shall adopt a decision authorising the signing of the agreement. If its provisional application before entry into force is necessary, ***the decision can only be adopted after obtaining the consent of the European Parliament***.

5. The Council, on a proposal by the ***Commission***, shall adopt a decision concluding the agreement ***after obtaining the consent of the European Parliament***.

The European Parliament shall deliver its ***decision*** within a time-limit which the ***Commission*** may set depending on the urgency of the matter. In the absence of ***a decision*** within that time-limit, the Council may act.

(b) ***after consulting the European Parliament in other cases.*** The European Parliament shall deliver its ***opinion*** within a time-limit which the ***Council*** may set depending on the urgency of the matter. In the absence of ***an opinion*** within that time-limit, the Council may act.

7. When concluding an agreement, the Council may, ***by way of derogation from paragraphs 5, 6 and 9***, authorise the negotiator to approve on the Union's behalf modifications to the agreement where it provides for them to be adopted by a simplified procedure or by a body set up by the agreement. The Council may attach specific conditions to such authorisation.

8. The Council shall act by a qualified majority throughout the procedure.

However, ***it shall act unanimously when the agreement covers a field for which unanimity is required for the adoption of a Union act as well as for association agreements and the agreements referred to in Article 212 with the States which are candidates for accession. The Council shall also act unanimously for the agreement*** on accession of the Union to the European Convention for the Protection of Human Rights and Fundamental Freedoms; the decision concluding this agreement shall enter into force after it has been approved by the Member States in accordance with their respective constitutional requirements.

9. The ***Council, on a proposal from the Commission or the High Representative of the Union for Foreign Affairs and Security Policy***, shall adopt a decision suspending application of an agreement and establishing the positions to be adopted on the Union's behalf in a body set up by an agreement, when that body is called upon to adopt acts having legal effects, with the exception of acts supplementing or amending the institutional framework of the agreement.

6. When concluding an agreement, the Council may authorise the Commission to approve on the Union's behalf modifications to the agreement where it provides for them to be adopted by a simplified procedure or by a body set up by the agreement. The Council may attach specific conditions to such authorisation.

7. The Council shall act by a qualified majority throughout the procedure.

However, ***for the negotiation and conclusion of agreements which include provisions for which the special legislative procedure is required for the adoption of internal rules, the Council shall act in accordance with Article 14(5).***

The decision concluding the agreement on accession of the Union to the European Convention for the Protection of Human Rights and Fundamental Freedoms shall enter into force after it has been approved by the States in accordance with their respective constitutional requirements.

8. The ***Commission*** shall adopt a decision suspending application of an agreement and establishing the positions to be adopted on the Union's behalf in a body set up by an agreement, when that body is called upon to adopt acts having legal effects, with the exception of acts supplementing or amending the institutional framework of the agreement.

10. The European Parliament shall be immediately and fully informed at all stages of the procedure.	9. The European Parliament shall be immediately and fully informed at all stages of the procedure. ***In cases where the Council acts according to its rules under the special legislative procedure, the Parliament shall vote to give its consent by a majority of its component Members.***
11. A Member State, the European Parliament, the Council or the Commission may obtain the opinion of the Court of Justice as to whether an agreement envisaged is compatible with the Treaties. Where the opinion of the Court is adverse, the agreement envisaged may not enter into force unless it is amended or the Treaties are revised.	10. A State, the European Parliament, the Council or the Commission may obtain the opinion of the Court of Justice as to whether an agreement envisaged is compatible with the Fundamental Law. Where the opinion of the Court is adverse, the agreement envisaged may not enter into force unless it is amended or the Fundamental Law is revised.
Article 219	Article 434 (ex-Article 219 TFEU)
1. By way of derogation from Article 218, the ***Council***, either on a recommendation from the European Central Bank or on a recommendation from the ***Commission*** and after consulting the European Central Bank, in an endeavour to reach a consensus consistent with the objective of price stability, may conclude formal agreements on an exchange-rate system for the euro in relation to the currencies of third States. ***The Council shall act unanimously after consulting the European Parliament and in accordance with the procedure provided for in paragraph 3.*** The ***Council*** may, either on a recommendation from the European Central Bank or on a recommendation from the Commission, and after consulting the European Central Bank, in an endeavour to reach a consensus consistent with the objective of price stability, adopt, adjust or abandon the central rates of the euro within the exchange-rate system. The President of the Council shall inform the European Parliament of the adoption, adjustment or abandonment of the euro central rates.	1. By way of derogation from Article 433, the ***Commission***, either on a recommendation from ***the Council or*** the European Central Bank, and after consulting the European Central Bank, in an endeavour to reach a consensus consistent with the objective of price stability, may conclude formal agreements on an exchange-rate system for the euro in relation to the currencies of third States. The ***Commission*** may, either on a recommendation from ***the Council or*** the European Central Bank, and after consulting the European Central Bank, in an endeavour to reach a consensus consistent with the objective of price stability, adopt, adjust or abandon the central rates of the euro within the exchange-rate system. The President of the ***Commission*** shall inform the European Parliament ***and the Council*** of the adoption, adjustment or abandonment of the euro central rates.

2. In the absence of an exchange-rate system in relation to one or more currencies of third States as referred to in paragraph 1, the ***Council***, either on a recommendation from the ***Commission*** and after consulting the European Central Bank or on a recommendation from the European Central Bank, may formulate general orientations for exchange-rate policy in relation to these currencies. These general orientations shall be without prejudice to the primary objective of the ESCB to maintain price stability.	2. In the absence of an exchange-rate system in relation to one or more currencies of third States as referred to in paragraph 1, the ***Commission***, after consulting ***the European Parliament, the Council and*** the European Central Bank or on a recommendation from the European Central Bank, may formulate general orientations for exchange-rate policy in relation to these currencies. These general orientations shall be without prejudice to the primary objective of the ESCB to maintain price stability.
3. By way of derogation from Article 218, where agreements concerning monetary or foreign exchange regime matters need to be negotiated by the Union with one or more third States or international organisations, the ***Council***, on a recommendation from the ***Commission*** and after consulting the European Central Bank, shall decide the arrangements for the negotiation and for the conclusion of such agreements. These arrangements shall ensure that the Union expresses a single position. ***The Commission shall be fully associated with the negotiations.***	3. By way of derogation from Article 433, where agreements concerning monetary or foreign exchange regime matters need to be negotiated by the Union with one or more third States or international organisations, the ***Commission***, after consulting ***the Council and*** the European Central Bank, shall decide the arrangements for the negotiation and for the conclusion of such agreements. These arrangements shall ensure that the Union expresses a single position.
4. Without prejudice to Union competence and Union agreements as regards economic and monetary union, Member States may negotiate in international bodies and conclude international agreements.	4. Without prejudice to Union competence and Union agreements as regards economic and monetary union, States may negotiate in international bodies and conclude international agreements. ***States intending so to negotiate in shall inform the Commission thereof.***
THE UNION'S RELATIONS WITH INTERNATIONAL ORGANISATIONS AND THIRD COUNTRIES AND UNION DELEGATIONS	INTERNATIONAL ORGANISATIONS
Articles 220–221	Articles 435–436 (ex-Articles 220–221 TFEU) .....

SOLIDARITY

CHAPTER SEVEN

The final chapter deals with the procedures concerning solidarity in the case of disasters. The role of the Commission and Parliament are enhanced in the protection of the security interest of the Union.

SOLIDARITY CLAUSE	SOLIDARITY
Article 222	Article 437 (ex-Article 222 TFEU)
1. The Union and its Member States shall act jointly in a spirit of solidarity if a Member State is the object of a terrorist attack or the victim of a natural or man-made disaster. The Union shall mobilise all the instruments at its disposal, including the military resources made available by the Member States, to:	1. The Union and its States shall act jointly in a spirit of solidarity if a State is the object of a terrorist attack or the victim of a natural or man-made disaster. The Union shall mobilise all the instruments at its disposal, including the military resources made available by the States, to:
(a) – prevent the terrorist threat in the territory of the ***Member States***;	(a) – prevent the terrorist threat in the territory of the ***Union***;
– protect democratic institutions and the civilian population from any terrorist attack;	– protect democratic institutions and the civilian population from any terrorist attack;
– assist a Member State in its territory, at the request of its political authorities, in the event of a terrorist attack;	– assist a State in its territory, at the request of its political authorities, in the event of a terrorist attack;
(b) assist a Member State in its territory, at the request of its political authorities, in the event of a natural or man-made disaster.	(b) assist a State in its territory, at the request of its political authorities, in the event of a natural or man-made disaster.

2. Should a Member State be the object of a terrorist attack or the victim of a natural or man-made disaster, the other ***Member States*** shall assist it at the request of its political authorities. To that end, the Member States shall coordinate between themselves ***in the Council.***	2. Should a State be the object of a terrorist attack or the victim of a natural or man-made disaster, ***the Union institutions and*** the other States shall assist it at the request of its political authorities. To that end, ***the Commission shall coordinate the assistance.***
3. The arrangements for the implementation by the Union of the solidarity clause shall be defined ***by a decision adopted by the Council acting on a joint proposal by the Commission and the High Representative of the Union for Foreign Affairs and Security Policy. The Council shall act in accordance with Article 31(1) of the Treaty on European Union where this decision has defence implications. The European Parliament shall be informed.***	3. The arrangements for the implementation by the Union of the solidarity clause shall be defined ***in regulations laid down by the European Parliament and the Council, acting on a proposal by the Commission, in accordance with the special legislative procedure.***
For the purposes of this paragraph and without prejudice to Article 240, the Council shall be assisted by the Political and Security Committee with the support of the structures developed in the context of the common security and defence policy and by the Committee referred to in Article 71; the two committees shall, if necessary, submit joint opinions.	For the purposes of this paragraph and without prejudice to Article 38, the Council shall be assisted by the Political and Security Committee with the support of the structures developed in the context of the common security and defence policy and by the Committee referred to in Article 380; the two committees shall, if necessary, submit joint opinions.
4. The European Council shall regularly assess the threats facing the Union in order to enable the Union and its Member States to take effective action.	4. The European Council shall regularly assess the threats facing the Union in order to enable the Union and its States to take effective action.

IN WITNESS WHEREOF, the undersigned Plenipotentiaries have signed this Fundamental Law.

Done at ....

PROTOCOLS

We make no proposal to alter Protocol Nos 1 or 2 on the role of national parliaments. Interparliamentary cooperation between the European Parliament and national parliaments is bedding down. To date, the requisite number of national parliaments has not been found to trigger the 'yellow card' against a draft law on the grounds of an alleged breach of the principle of subsidiarity.

Protocol No 3 comprises a radically amended version of the 1976 Act which, already having the status of EU primary law, introduced direct elections to the European Parliament. The new Protocol reflects the new mandate of MEPs, made by the Lisbon treaty, as being 'representatives of the citizens of the Union' (Article 1). Article 3 defines what is meant by the principle of degressive proportionality. Article 4 empowers the Parliament to establish an arithmetical formula for seat apportionment. Article 5 introduces the concept of electing a certain number of MEPs in a pan-EU constituency from transnational lists. An EU electoral authority will be established to oversee the conduct of elections to the Parliament.

No changes are proposed at this stage to the Statutes of the ECJ, ECB or EIB (Protocol Nos 4, 5 and 6, respectively).

Protocol No 7 modernises the 1965 Protocol on privileges and immunities with respect to the rights and duties of MEPs. The new regime reflects the supranational autonomy of the European Parliament.

Protocol No 8, on permanent structured cooperation in defence, includes the concept of the battlegroup.

Protocol No 9 fleshes out the concept of Associate Membership of the Union (Article 136). Article 2 lays down the obligations of Associate Members. Article 3 provides for the relationship between the associate and full member states. Articles 4 and 5 lay down the institutional engagement of associates.

We propose no change to Protocol No 10 except to the title to include the factor of excessive debt as well as deficit. No change is proposed to the euro convergence criteria in Protocol No 11. Protocol No 12 is amended to reflect the fact that economic governance of the euro states is pitched by the Fundamental Law within the context of enhanced cooperation.

Protocol No 18 sets out the procedure for the entry into force of the Fundamental Law and a contingency plan for what happens if unanimity of ratification is not achieved. In short, EU member states which do not wish to take the federal step forward will be expected either to adopt associate membership status or to leave the Union altogether. They will be discouraged from blocking deeper integration by and for those who want it.

A number of Lisbon Protocols are deleted either because they are redundant or because they contradict the general approach taken in the Fundamental Law that all EU members are expected to join the euro and to play a full part in all aspects of integration. Opt-outs and derogations are discouraged in favour of the more formal, and less destabilising, associate membership. It remains for the three countries concerned, Denmark, Ireland and the UK, to make their choices.

We delete ex-Protocol No 6 of Lisbon to reflect the new system for decisions on the location of seats (Article 120).

PROTOCOLS	PROTOCOLS
Protocol No 1 on the role of National Parliaments in the European Union	**Protocol No 1** ***The Role of State Parliaments*** .....
Protocol No 2 on the application of the Principles of Subsidiarity and Proportionality	**Protocol No 2** ***The Application of the Principles of Subsidiarity and Proportionality*** .....
ACT **concerning the election of the members of the European Parliament by direct universal suffrage**	**Protocol No 3** ***Seat Apportionment and Electoral Procedure of the European Parliament***
Article 1	Article 1 (ex-Article 1 Electoral Act)
1. In each Member State, members of the European Parliament shall be elected on the basis of proportional representation, using the list system or the single transferable vote.	1. Members of the European Parliament shall be elected ***as representatives of the citizens of the Union*** on the basis of proportional representation, using the list system or the single transferable vote.

Article 2

In accordance with its specific national situation, each Member State may establish constituencies for elections to the European Parliament or subdivide its electoral area in a different manner, without generally affecting the proportional nature of the voting system.

Article 3

Member States may set a minimum threshold for the allocation of seats. At national level this threshold may not exceed 5 per cent of votes cast.

Article 4

Each Member State may set a ceiling for candidates' campaign expenses.

Article 5

1. The five-year term for which members of the European Parliament are elected shall begin at the opening of the first session following each election.

It may be extended or curtailed pursuant to the second subparagraph of Article 10 (2).

2. The term of office of each member shall begin and end at the same time as the period referred to in paragraph 1.

Article 6

1. Members of the European Parliament shall vote on an individual and personal basis. They shall not be bound by any instructions and shall not receive a binding mandate.

2. Members of the European Parliament shall enjoy the privileges and immunities applicable to them by virtue of the Protocol of 8 April 1965 on the privileges and immunities of the European Communities.

Article 2
(ex-Article 2 Electoral Act)

Each State may establish constituencies for elections to the European Parliament or subdivide its electoral area in a different manner, without generally affecting the proportional nature of the voting system.

Article 3

1. For the purpose of the apportionment of seats among States in accordance with the principle of degressive proportionality pursuant to Article [12(3)] of the Fundamental Law, the ratio between the population and the number of seats of each State, before rounding to whole numbers, shall vary in relation to their respective populations in such a way that each Member elected in a more populous State represents more citizens than each Member elected in a less populous State and also, conversely, that no less populous State has more seats than a more populous State.

2. Where a State accedes to the Union during a parliamentary term, it shall be allocated seats which will be added to the number of seats provided for in Article [12(2)] on a transitional basis for the remainder of that parliamentary term.

Article 4

The European Parliament and the Council, acting in accordance with the special legislative procedure, shall establish a fair, durable and transparent system for the apportionment of the seats in the Parliament per State. The system will take account of demography, the principle of degressive proportionality as set forth in Article 3(1), and the election of a certain number of Members in accordance with the provisions of Article 5.

Article 7

1. The office of member of the European Parliament shall be incompatible with that of:

- member of the government of a Member State,

- member of the Commission of the European Communities,

- Judge, Advocate-General or Registrar of the Court of Justice of the European Communities or of the Court of First Instance,

- member of the Board of Directors of the European Central Bank,

- member of the Court of Auditors of the European Communities,

- Ombudsman of the European Communities,

- member of the Economic and Social Committee of the European Community and of the European Atomic Energy Community,

- member of the Committee of the Regions,

- ***member of committees or other bodies set up pursuant to the Treaties establishing the European Community and the European Atomic Energy Community for the purposes of managing the Communities' funds or carrying out a permanent direct administrative task,***

- member of the Board of Directors, Management Committee or staff of the European Investment Bank,

- active official or servant of the institutions of the European Communities or of the specialised bodies attached to them or of the European Central Bank.

Article 5

1. Pursuant to Article [12(3)] of the Fundamental Law, there shall be one additional constituency formed of the entire territory of the Union from which shall be elected a certain number of Members. The number of such Members to be elected from the single European seat at the next elections shall be determined before the end of the fourth calendar year of the parliamentary term.

This decision on the number of such Members shall be taken on a proposal of the Parliament by the Council, acting by qualified majority, and with the consent of Parliament, which shall act by a majority of its component Members.

2. The European Parliament and the Council, acting in accordance with the ordinary legislative procedure, shall establish a European electoral authority to conduct and verify the electoral process of the European Union constituency.

3. The transnational lists of candidates for election in the European Union constituency shall be registered with the European electoral authority by the European political parties. The lists shall be admissible only if composed of candidates resident in at least one third of the States.

4. Each elector shall have two votes, one that may be cast for the election of Members in the State and one supplementary vote that may be cast for the European Union-wide list. Seats shall be allocated from the European lists in accordance with the Sainte-Laguë method.

Article 6
(ex-Article 3 Electoral Act)

States may set a minimum threshold for the allocation of seats. At national level this threshold may not exceed 5 per cent of votes cast.

2. ***From the European Parliament elections in 2004, the office of member of the European Parliament shall be incompatible with that of member of a national parliament.***

By way of derogation from that rule and without prejudice to paragraph 3:

– ***members of the Irish National Parliament who are elected to the European Parliament at a subsequent poll may have a dual mandate until the next election to the Irish National Parliament, at which juncture the first subparagraph of this paragraph shall apply;***

– ***members of the United Kingdom Parliament who are also members of the European Parliament during the five-year term preceding election to the European Parliament in 2004 may have a dual mandate until the 2009 European Parliament elections, when the first subparagraph of this paragraph shall apply.***

3. ***In addition, each Member State may, in the circumstances provided for in Article 8, extend rules at national level relating to incompatibility.***

4. Members of the European Parliament to whom paragraphs 1, 2 and 3 become applicable in the course of the five-year period referred to in Article 5 shall be replaced in accordance with Article 13.

Article 8

Subject to the provisions of this Act, the electoral procedure shall be governed in each Member State by its national provisions.

These national provisions, which may if appropriate take account of the specific situation in the Member States, shall not affect the essentially proportional nature of the voting system.

There shall be no minimum threshold for the allocation of seats from the European Union constituency.

Article 7
(ex-Article 4 Electoral Act)

The limitation of campaign expenses of candidates and political parties shall be laid down in delegated acts.

Article 8
(ex-Articles 5, 10 & 11 Electoral Act)

1. Elections to the European Parliament shall be held ***in May***; for all States this date shall fall within the same period starting on a ***Saturday*** morning and ending on the Sunday. ***The European Parliament and the Council, acting in accordance with the ordinary legislative procedure, shall determine the date of the polling days of the next election before the end of the fourth calendar year of the parliamentary term.***

2. States may not officially make public the results of their count until after the close of polling in the State whose electors are the last to vote within the polling period.

3. The five-year term for which Members of the European Parliament are elected shall begin at the opening of the first session following each election. The Parliament shall meet, without requiring to be convened, on the first Tuesday after expiry of an interval of one month from the end of the polling period.

The powers of the Parliament shall cease upon the opening of the first sitting of the new Parliament.

Article 9 No one may vote more than once in any election of members of the European Parliament.	Article 9 (ex-Article 6 Electoral Act) 1. Members of the European Parliament shall vote on an individual and personal basis. They shall not be bound by any instructions and shall not receive a binding mandate. 2. Members of the European Parliament shall ***have the rights and obligations laid down in the Members' Statute and*** the Protocol on the privileges and immunities of the European ***Union***.
Article 10 1. Elections to the European Parliament shall be held ***on the date and at the times fixed by each Member State; for all Member States this date shall fall within the same period starting on a Thursday morning and ending on the following Sunday.*** 2. Member States may not officially make public the results of their count until after the close of polling in the Member State whose electors are the last to vote within the period referred to in paragraph 1.	Article 10 (ex-Article 7 Electoral Act) 1. The office of Member of the European Parliament shall be incompatible with that of: ***– member of a State or of a regional parliament or assembly with legislative powers,*** – member of the government of a State, – member of the European Commission, – Judge, Advocate-General or Registrar of the European Court of Justice, – member of the Board of Directors of the European Central Bank, – member of the Court of Auditors, – Ombudsman, – member of the Economic and Social Committee, – member of the Committee of the Regions, – active official or servant ***of an institution, agency or body of the European Union***. 2. Members of the European Parliament to whom paragraph 1 becomes applicable in
Article 11 1. ***The Council, acting unanimously after consulting the European Parliament, shall determine the electoral period for the first elections.*** 2. Subsequent elections shall take place in the corresponding period in the last year of the five-year period referred to in Article 5. ***Should it prove impossible to hold the elections in the Community during that period, the Council acting unanimously shall, after consulting the European Parliament, determine, at least one month before the end of the five-year term referred to in Article 5, another electoral period which shall not be more than two months before or one month after the period fixed pursuant to the preceding subparagraph.*** 3. ***Without prejudice to Article 196 of the Treaty establishing the European Community and Article 109 of the Treaty establishing the European Atomic Energy Community***, the European Parliament shall meet, without requiring to be convened, on the first	

Tuesday after expiry of an interval of one month from the end of the electoral period.

4. The powers of the European Parliament shall cease upon the opening of the first sitting of the new European Parliament.

Article 12

The European Parliament shall verify the credentials of members of the European Parliament. For this purpose it shall take note of the results declared officially by the Member States and shall rule on any disputes which may arise out of the provisions of this Act other than those arising out of the national provisions to which the Act refers.

Article 13

1. A seat shall fall vacant when the mandate of a member of the European Parliament ends as a result of resignation, death or withdrawal of the mandate.

2. Subject to the other provisions of this Act, each Member State shall lay down appropriate procedures for filling any seat which falls vacant during the five-year term of office referred to in Article 5 for the remainder of that period.

3. Where the law of a Member State makes explicit provision for the withdrawal of the mandate of a member of the European Parliament, that mandate shall end pursuant to those legal provisions. The competent national authorities shall inform the European Parliament thereof.

4. Where a seat falls vacant as a result of resignation or death, the President of the European Parliament shall immediately inform the competent authorities of the Member State concerned thereof.

the course of the five-year period referred to in ***Article 8*** shall be replaced in accordance with ***Article 15 or 16.***

Article 11
(ex-Article 8 Electoral Act)

Subject to the provisions of this Protocol, the electoral procedure shall be governed in each State by its ***own*** provisions.

These provisions shall not affect the essentially proportional nature of the voting system.

Article 12
(ex-Article 9 Electoral Act)

Without prejudice to Article 5(4), no one may vote more than once in any election of members of the European Parliament.

Article 13
(ex-Article 12 Electoral Act)

The European Parliament shall verify the credentials of ***the Members of Parliament on the basis*** of the results declared officially by the ***European electoral authority and by the States, respectively***. It shall rule on any disputes which may arise.

Article 14
(ex-Article 13(1) Electoral Act)

A seat shall fall vacant when the mandate of a member of the European Parliament ends as a result of resignation, death or withdrawal of the mandate.

Article 15
(ex-Article 13(2-4) Electoral Act)

1. In the case of the Members elected in the States, and subject to the other provisions of this Protocol, each State shall lay down appropriate procedures for filling any seat which falls vacant during the five-year term of office referred to in Article 8 for the remainder of that period.

Article 14

Should it appear necessary to adopt measures to implement this Act, the Council, acting unanimously on a proposal from the European Parliament after consulting the Commission, shall adopt such measures after endeavouring to reach agreement with the European Parliament in a conciliation committee consisting of the Council and representatives of the European Parliament.

Article 15

This Act is drawn up in the Danish, Dutch, English, Finnish, French, German, Greek, Irish, Italian, Portuguese, Spanish and Swedish languages, all the texts being equally authentic.

Annexes I and II shall form an integral part of this Act.

Article 16

The provisions of this Act shall enter into force on the first day of the month following that during which the last of the notifications referred to in the Decision is received.

Udfærdiget i Bruxelles, den tyvende september nitten hundrede og seksoghalvfjerds.

Geschehen zu Brüssel am zwanzigsten September neunzehnhundert-sechsundsiebzig.

Done at Brussels on the twentieth day of September in the year one thousand nine hundred and seventy-six.

Fait à Bruxelles, le vingt septembre mil neuf cent soixante-seize.

Arna dhéanamh sa Bhruiséil, an fichiú lá de mhí Mhéan Fómhair, míle naoi gcéad seachtó a sé.

2. Where the law of a State provides for a temporary replacement of a member of its State Parliament on maternity leave, that State may decide that such provisions are to apply mutatis mutandis to the Members of the European Parliament elected in that State.

3. Where the law of a State makes explicit provision for the withdrawal of the mandate of a Member of the European Parliament elected in that State, that mandate shall end pursuant to those legal provisions. Such legal provisions shall not be adopted with retroactive effect. The competent State authorities shall inform the European Parliament thereof.

4. Where a seat of a Member elected in the States falls vacant as a result of resignation or death, the President of the European Parliament shall immediately inform the competent authorities of the State concerned thereof.

Article 16

1. In the case of the Members elected for the European Union constituency, and subject to the other provisions of this Protocol, appropriate procedures for the filling of any vacancy for the remainder of the five-year term of office referred to in Article 8 shall be laid down in delegated acts.

2. Where the law of the Union makes explicit provision for the withdrawal of the mandate of a Member of the European Parliament elected on the European Union-wide list, that mandate shall end pursuant to those legal provisions. The electoral authority shall inform the European Parliament thereof.

3. Where a seat of a Member elected for the European Union constituency falls vacant as a result of resignation or death, the President of the European Parliament shall immediately inform the electoral authority thereof.

Fatto a Bruxelles, addì venti settembre millenovecentosettantasei. *Gedaan te Brussel, de twintigste september negentienhonderd zesenzeventig.*	
ANNEX I *The United Kingdom will apply the provisions of this Act only in respect of the United Kingdom.*	
ANNEX II *Declaration on Article 14* *As regards the procedure to be followed by the Conciliation Committee, it is agreed to have recourse to the provisions of paragraphs 5, 6 and 7 of the procedure laid down in the joint declaration of the European Parliament, the Council and the Commission of 4 March 1975.*	
Protocol No 3 on the statute of the Court of Justice of the European Union	**Protocol No 4** The Statute of the Court of Justice of the European Union .....
Protocol No 4 on the statute of the European System of Central Banks and of the European Central Bank	**Protocol No 5** The Statute of the European System of Central Banks and of the European Central Bank .....
Protocol No 5 On the statute of the European Investment Bank	**Protocol No 6** The Statute of the European Investment Bank .....
Protocol No 6 on the location of the seats of the institutions and of certain bodies, offices, agencies and departments of the European Union	[delete]

Protocol No 7 on the privileges and immunities of the European Union **Articles 1–6**	**Protocol No 7** ***The Privileges and Immunities of the European Union*** Articles 1–6 .....
Article 7 No administrative or other restriction shall be imposed on the free movement of Members of the European Parliament travelling to or from the place of meeting of the European Parliament. Members of the European Parliament shall, in respect of customs and exchange control, be accorded: (a) by their own government, the same facilities as those accorded to senior officials travelling abroad on temporary official missions; (b) by the government of other Member States, the same facilities as those accorded to representatives of foreign governments on temporary official missions.	Article 7 No administrative or other restriction shall be imposed on the free movement of Members of the European Parliament. Members of the European Parliament shall, in respect of customs and exchange control, be accorded: (a) by their own government, the same facilities as those accorded to senior officials travelling abroad on temporary official missions; (b) by the government of other States, the same facilities as those accorded to representatives of foreign governments on temporary official missions.
Article 8 Members of the European Parliament shall not be subject to any form of inquiry, detention or legal proceedings in respect of opinions expressed or votes cast by them in the performance of their ***duties.***	Article 8 Members of the European Parliament shall ***at no time*** be subject to any form of inquiry, detention or legal proceedings in respect of ***any action taken,*** votes cast ***or statement made in the exercise of their mandate.*** ***The European Parliament shall decide, on the application of a Member, whether an action was taken or a statement was made in the exercise of his or her mandate.*** ***The European Parliament shall lay down provisions for the implementation of this Article in its rules of procedure.***

Article 9 *During the sessions of the European Parliament, its Members shall enjoy:* *(a) in the territory of their own State, the immunities accorded to members of their parliament;* *(b) in the territory of any other Member State, immunity from any measure of detention and from legal proceedings.* *Immunity shall likewise apply to Members while they are travelling to and from the place of meeting of the European Parliament.* *Immunity cannot be claimed when a Member is found in the act of committing an offence and shall not prevent the European Parliament from exercising its right to waive the immunity of one of its Members.*	Article 9 *1. Any restriction of a Member's personal freedom shall be permitted only with the consent of the European Parliament, except where he or she is caught in the act of committing an offence.* *2. The seizure of a Member's documents or electronic records or the searching of his or her person, office or place of residence or interception of his or her mail or telephone calls may be ordered only with the consent of the European Parliament.* *3. A Member shall be entitled to decline to give evidence about information which that Member has obtained in the exercise of his or her mandate or about persons from or to whom he or she has obtained or given such information.* *4. Investigations or criminal proceedings against a Member shall be suspended at the request of the European Parliament.* *5. Consent pursuant to paragraph 2 shall be applied for only by a State authority competent under the law of that State.* *Consent pursuant to paragraph 2 or suspension pursuant to paragraph 4 may be granted conditionally, or for a limited period or on a restricted basis.*
Articles 10–22	Articles 10–22 .....
Protocol No 8 Relating to Article 6(2) of the Treaty on European Union on the accession of the Union to the European Convention on the Protection of Human Rights and Fundamental Freedoms	[delete]

Protocol No 9 on the decision of the Council relating to the implementation of Article 16(4) of the Treaty on European Union and Article 238(2) of the Treaty on the Functioning of the European Union between 1 November 2014 and 31 March 2017 on the one hand, and as from 1 April 2017 on the other	[delete]
Protocol No 10 on permanent structured cooperation established by Article 42 of the Treaty on European Union	**Protocol No 8** **Permanent Structured Cooperation in Defence** .....
Article 1 The permanent structured cooperation referred to in Article 42(6) of the Treaty on European Union shall be open to any Member State which undertakes, from the date of entry into force of the Treaty of Lisbon, to: (a) proceed more intensively to develop its defence capacities through the development of its national contributions and participation, where appropriate, in multinational forces, in the main European equipment programmes, and in the activity of the Agency in the field of defence capabilities development, research, acquisition and armaments (European Defence Agency), and (b) have the capacity to supply by 2010 at the latest, either at national level or as a component of multinational force groups, targeted combat units for the missions planned, structured at a tactical level as a battlegroup, with support elements including transport and logistics, capable of carrying out the tasks referred to in Article 43 of the Treaty on European Union, within a period of five to 30 days, in particular in response to requests from the United Nations Organisation, and which can be sustained for an initial period of 30 days and be extended up to at least 120 days.	Article 1 The permanent structured cooperation referred to in Article [42(6)] of the Fundamental Law shall be open to any State which undertakes to: (a) proceed more intensively to develop its defence capacities through the development of its national contributions and participation, where appropriate, in multinational forces, in the main European equipment programmes, and in the activity of the European Defence Agency in the field of defence capabilities development, research, acquisition and armaments; (b) have the capacity to supply, either at State level or as a component of multinational force groups, targeted combat units for the missions planned, structured at a tactical level as a battlegroup, with support elements including transport and logistics, capable of carrying out the tasks referred to in Article [43], within a period of five to 30 days, in particular in response to requests from the United Nations Organisation, and which can be sustained for an initial period of 30 days and be extended up to at least 120 days;

	(c) establish a battlegroup under European command comprising three or more States in accordance with a Union law which shall lay down the modalities of military command, political control, financing, recruitment, armament, and deployment.
Article 2	Article 2 .....
Protocol No 11 on Article 42 of the Treaty on European Union	[delete]
	Protocol No 9 *Associate Membership of the Union* Article 1 *1. This Protocol lays down guidelines for the negotiation and conclusion of an agreement admitting any European state to associate membership of the Union, pursuant to Article 137. The agreement will set out the terms, conditions, scope and limits of associate membership and the adjustments to the law of the Union which such association entails. The agreement may be of limited duration.*
	Article 2 *The agreement shall commit the Associate State to respect and promote the values and principles of the Union, as laid down in Article 2. The Associate State shall not obstruct the Union from pursuing and accomplishing its goals and objectives, as laid down in Article 3. It shall be bound to respect the principle of sincere cooperation, pursuant to Article 4(3). It shall respect and promote the Charter of Fundamental Rights.*

Article 3

1. The agreement shall specify in which of the Union's policies and functions the Associate State is to participate, and the terms and conditions, financial and institutional, which shall apply to that participation.

2. Participation by an Associate State in the internal market, in whole or in part, may not risk the operation of the market.

3. Participation by an Associate State in the external action of the Union or in an international agreement of the Union shall not prejudice the cohesion or limit the scope of the Union's position.

4. Associate States may have service agreements with the Commission or the agencies of the Union for the delivery of policy in certain specified fields. These arrangements may contain reciprocal rights and obligations as well as the possibility of undertaking activities jointly.

Article 4

1. Members of the government and parliament of an Associate State shall be invited to participate in meetings of the European Parliament, European Council and Council, respectively, as and when appropriate for the purposes of implementing the agreement.

2. Officials representing the government of an Associate State may participate in relevant consultative processes of the European Commission and in appropriate committees which dispose of delegated acts and implementing measures.

3. The modalities of the participation of representatives of Associate States shall be laid down by each institution in its own rules of procedure.

	Article 5 ***1. Associate States shall acknowledge the jurisdiction of the Court of Justice.*** ***An Associate State may intervene in cases before the Court of Justice. It may institute third-party proceedings to contest a judgment rendered without its being heard, where the judgment is prejudicial to its rights.*** ***2. Associate States shall nominate judges to the Court of Justice and General Court on the same terms and conditions, and according to the same procedures, as a judge nominated by a State having full membership of the Union.*** ***Judges from Associate States shall not sit in cases where the law of the Union does not apply specifically to the Associate State concerned.***
	Article 6 ***An associate membership agreement may be suspended, in whole or in part, in accordance with the procedures laid down in Article 133.***
Protocol No 12 on the excessive deficit procedure	**Protocol No 10** The Excessive ***Debt and*** Deficit Procedure .....
Protocol No 13 on the convergence criteria	**Protocol No 11** The ***euro*** convergence criteria .....

Protocol No 14 on the euro group	**Protocol No 12** ***The Eurogroup***
THE HIGH CONTRACTING PARTIES, DESIRING to promote conditions for stronger economic growth in the European Union and, to that end, to develop ever-closer coordination of economic policies within the euro area, CONSCIOUS of the need to lay down special provisions for ***enhanced dialogue*** between the Member States whose currency is the euro, pending the euro becoming the currency of all Member States of the Union, ***HAVE AGREED UPON the following provisions, which shall be annexed to the Treaty on European Union and to the Treaty on the Functioning of the European Union:***	Article 1 Conscious of the need to lay down special provisions for ***closer integration*** between the States whose currency is the euro, ***those States agree to establish enhanced cooperation between themselves***, pending the euro becoming the currency of all States of the Union. ***They shall act in accordance with the enhanced cooperation provisions of the Fundamental Law save where that Law and this Protocol otherwise provide.***
Article 1 The Ministers of the Member States whose currency is the euro shall meet ***informally. Such meetings shall take place***, when necessary, to discuss questions related to the specific responsibilities they share with regard to the single currency. The Commission shall take part in the meetings. The European Central Bank shall be invited to take part in such meetings, which shall be prepared by the representatives of the Ministers with responsibility for finance of the Member States whose currency is the euro and of the Commission.	Article 2 (ex-Article 1) The ministers of the States whose currency is the euro ***form the Eurogroup. They*** shall meet when necessary to discuss questions related to the specific responsibilities they share with regard to the single currency. The Commission shall take part in the meetings. The European Central Bank shall be invited to take part in such meetings, which shall be prepared by the representatives of the Ministers with responsibility for finance of the States whose currency is the euro and of the Commission.
Article 2 The Ministers of the Member States whose currency is the euro shall elect a president for two and a half years, by a majority of those Member States.	Article 3 ***Meetings of the Eurogroup shall be chaired by the Chair of the Council of Economic and Financial Affairs.*** ***The Eurogroup will agree and publish its rules of procedure.***
Protocol No 15 on certain provisions relating to the United Kingdom of Great Britain and Northern Ireland	[delete]

Protocol No 16 on certain provisions relating to Denmark	[delete]
Protocol No 17 on Denmark	[delete]
Protocol No 18 on France	**Protocol No 13** on France .....
Protocol No 19 on the Schengen *acquis* integrated into the framework of the European Union	[delete]
Protocol No 20 on the application of certain aspects of Article 26 of the Treaty on the Functioning of the European Union to the United Kingdom and to Ireland	[delete]
Protocol No 21 on the position of the United Kingdom and Ireland in respect of the area of freedom, security and justice	[delete]
Protocol No 22 on the position of Denmark	[delete]
Protocol No 23 on external relations of the Member States with regard to the crossing of external borders	[delete]
Protocol No 24 on asylum of nationals of Member States of the European Union	**Protocol No 14** on asylum of nationals of Member States of the European Union .....

Protocol No 25 on the exercise of shared competence	[delete]
Protocol No 26 on services of general interest	**Protocol No 15** on services of general interest .....
Protocol No 27 on the internal market and competition	[delete]
Protocol No 28 on economic, social and territorial cohesion	[delete]
Protocol No 29 on the system of public broadcasting in the Member States	**Protocol No 16** on the system of public broadcasting in the Member States .....
Protocol No 30 on the application of the Charter of Fundamental Rights of the European Union to Poland and to the United Kingdom	[delete]
Protocol No 31 concerning imports into the European Union of petroleum products refined in the Netherlands Antilles	[delete]
Protocol No 32 on the acquisition of property in Denmark	[delete]
Protocol No 33 concerning Article 157 of the Treaty on the Functioning of the European Union	[delete]
Protocol No 34 on special arrangements for Greenland	**Protocol No 17** on special arrangements for Greenland .....

Protocol No 35 on Article 40.3.3 of the Constitution of Ireland	[delete]
Protocol No 36 on transitional provisions …..	**Protocol No 18** Transitional Provisions *1. This Fundamental Law shall be ratified in accordance with Article 48(4) of the Treaty on European Union.* *2. Pursuant to Article 48(5) of the Treaty on European Union, if, two years after the signature of the Fundamental Law, four fifths of the States have ratified it and one or more States have encountered difficulties in proceeding with ratification, the matter shall be referred to the European Council.* *3. At that stage, and in accordance with Article 30(4) of the Vienna Convention on the Law of Treaties (1969), the Fundamental Law will be deemed to govern the relations between those States which have completed ratification according to their respective constitutional requirements.* *4. The European Council shall invite any State which has not completed the ratification of the Fundamental Law either to apply to become an Associate State of the Union in accordance with the same procedures as those laid down in Article 137 of the Fundamental Law or to notify its intention to secede from the Union in accordance with Article 50 of the Treaty on European Union (Article 138 of the Fundamental Law).*
Protocol No 37 on the financial consequences of the expiry of the ECSC Treaty and on the research fund for coal and steel	[delete]

TABLES OF EQUIVALENCES

FUNDAMENTAL LAW	*OLD TREATIES*
PART I – CONSTITUTIONAL PROVISIONS	
Article 1	Article 1 TEU
Article 2	Article 2 TEU
Article 3	Article 3 TEU
Article 4	Article 4 TEU
Article 5	Article 5 TEU
Article 6	Article 6 TEU
	Article 8 TEU (repealed)
Article 7	Article 9 TEU
Article 8	Article 10 TEU
Article 9	Article 11 TEU
Article 10	Article 12 TEU
Article 11	Article 13 TEU
Article 12	Article 14 TEU
Article 13	Article 15 TEU
Article 14	Articles 16 TEU & 238 TFEU
Article 15	Article 17 TEU
	Article 18 TEU (repealed)
Article 16	Article 19 TEU
	Preamble TFEU (repealed)
	Article 1 TFEU (repealed)
Article 17	Article 2 TFEU
Article 18	Article 3 TFEU
Article 19	Article 4 TFEU
	Article 5 TFEU (repealed)
Article 20	Article 6 TFEU
Article 21	Article 352 TFEU
Article 22	new
Article 23	Article 223 TFEU
Article 24	Article 224 TFEU
Article 25	Article 225 TFEU
Article 26	Article 226 TFEU
Article 27	Article 227 TFEU
Article 28	Article 228 TFEU
Article 29	Article 229 TFEU
Article 30	Article 230 TFEU

FUNDAMENTAL LAW	OLD TREATIES
Article 31	Article 231 TFEU
Article 32	Article 232 TFEU
Article 33	Article 233 TFEU
Article 34	Article 234 TFEU
Article 35	Article 235 TFEU
	Article 236 TFEU (repealed)
Article 36	Article 237 TFEU
	Article 238 TFEU (repealed)
Article 37	Article 239 TFEU
Article 38	Article 240 TFEU
Article 39	Article 241 TFEU
	Article 242 TFEU (repealed)
Article 40	Article 243 TFEU
	Article 244 TFEU (repealed)
Article 41	Article 245 TFEU
Article 42	Article 246 TFEU
Article 43	Article 247 TFEU
Article 44	Article 248 TFEU
Article 45	Article 249 TFEU
Article 46	Article 250 TFEU
Article 47	Article 251 TFEU
Article 48	Article 252 TFEU
Article 49	Article 253 TFEU
Article 50	Article 254 TFEU
Article 51	Article 255 TFEU
Article 52	Article 256 TFEU
Article 53	Article 257 TFEU
Article 54	Article 258 TFEU
Article 55	Article 259 TFEU
Article 56	Article 260 TFEU
Article 57	Article 261 TFEU
	Article 262 TFEU (repealed)
Article 58	Article 263 TFEU
Article 59	Article 264 TFEU
Article 60	Article 265 TFEU
Article 61	Article 266 TFEU
Article 62	Article 267 TFEU
Article 63	Article 268 TFEU
Article 64	Article 269 TFEU
Article 65	Article 270 TFEU
Article 66	Article 271 TFEU
Article 67	Article 272 TFEU
Article 68	Article 273 TFEU
Article 69	Article 274 TFEU

FUNDAMENTAL LAW	*OLD TREATIES*
	Article 275 TFEU (repealed)
	Article 276 TFEU (repealed)
Article 70	Article 277 TFEU
Article 71	Article 278 TFEU
Article 72	Article 279 TFEU
Article 73	Article 280 TFEU
Article 74	Article 281 TFEU
Article 75	Article 282 TFEU
Article 76	Article 283 TFEU
Article 77	Article 284 TFEU
Article 78	Article 285 TFEU
Article 79	Article 286 TFEU
Article 80	Article 287 TFEU
Article 81	Article 288 TFEU
Article 82	Article 289 TFEU
Article 83	Article 290 TFEU
Article 84	Article 291 TFEU
Article 85	Article 292 TFEU
Article 86	Article 293 TFEU
Article 87	Article 294 TFEU
Article 88	new
Article 89	Article 295 TFEU
Article 90	Article 296 TFEU
Article 91	Article 297 TFEU
Article 92	Article 298 TFEU
Article 93	Article 299 TFEU
Article 94	Article 300 TFEU
Article 95	Article 301 TFEU
Article 96	Article 302 TFEU
Article 97	Article 303 TFEU
Article 98	Article 304 TFEU
Article 99	Article 305 TFEU
Article 100	Article 306 TFEU
Article 101	Article 307 TFEU
Article 102	Article 308 TFEU
Article 103	Article 309 TFEU
Article 104	Article 20 TEU
Article 105	Article 326 TFEU
Article 106	Article 327 TFEU
Article 107	Article 328 TFEU
Article 108	Article 329 TFEU
Article 109	Article 330 TFEU
Article 110	Article 331 TFEU
Article 111	Article 332 TFEU

FUNDAMENTAL LAW	*OLD TREATIES*
Article 112	Article 333 TFEU
Article 113	Article 334 TFEU
Article 114	Articles 47 TEU & 335 TFEU
Article 115	Article 336 TFEU
Article 116	Article 337 TFEU
Article 117	Article 338 TFEU
Article 118	Article 339 TFEU
Article 119	Article 340 TFEU
Article 120	Article 341 TFEU
Article 121	Article 342 TFEU
Article 122	Article 343 TFEU
Article 123	Article 344 TFEU
Article 124	Article 345 TFEU
Article 125	Article 346 TFEU
Article 126	Article 347 TFEU
Article 127	Article 348 TFEU
Article 128	Article 349 TFEU
Article 129	Article 350 TFEU
Article 130	Article 351 TFEU
	Article 353 TFEU (repealed)
Article 131	Article 355 TFEU
Article 132	Article 356 TFEU
	Article 357 TFEU (repealed)
	Article 358 TFEU (repealed)
Article 133	Article 7 TEU
Article 134	Article 354 TFEU
Article 135	Article 48 TEU
Article 136	Article 49 TEU
Article 137	new
Article 138	Article 50 TEU
Article 139	new
Article 140	Article 51 TEU
Article 141	Article 52 TEU
Article 142	Article 53 TEU
Article 143	Article 54 TEU
Article 144	Article 55 TEU
PART II – CHARTER OF FUNDAMENTAL RIGHTS	
	Preamble (repealed)
Article 145	Article 1 CFR
Article 146	Article 2 CFR
Article 147	Article 3 CFR
Article 148	Article 4 CFR
Article 149	Article 5 CFR

FUNDAMENTAL LAW	*OLD TREATIES*
Article 150	Article 6 CFR
Article 151	Article 7 CFR
Article 152	Article 8 CFR
Article 153	Article 9 CFR
Article 154	Article 10 CFR
Article 155	Article 11 CFR
Article 156	Article 12 CFR
Article 157	Article 13 CFR
Article 158	Article 14 CFR
Article 159	Article 15 CFR
Article 160	Article 16 CFR
Article 161	Article 17 CFR
Article 162	Article 18 CFR
Article 163	Article 19 CFR
Article 164	Article 20 CFR
Article 165	Article 21 CFR
Article 166	Article 22 CFR
Article 167	Article 23 CFR
Article 168	Article 24 CFR
Article 169	Article 25 CFR
Article 170	Article 26 CFR
Article 171	Article 27 CFR
Article 172	Article 28 CFR
Article 173	Article 29 CFR
Article 174	Article 30 CFR
Article 175	Article 31 CFR
Article 176	Article 32 CFR
Article 177	Article 33 CFR
Article 178	Article 34 CFR
Article 179	Article 35 CFR
Article 180	Article 36 CFR
Article 181	Article 37 CFR
Article 182	Article 38 CFR
Article 183	Article 39 CFR
Article 184	Article 40 CFR
Article 185	Article 41 CFR
Article 186	Article 42 CFR
Article 187	Article 43 CFR
Article 188	Article 44 CFR
Article 189	Article 45 CFR
Article 190	Article 46 CFR
Article 191	Article 47 CFR
Article 192	Article 48 CFR
Article 193	Article 49 CFR

FUNDAMENTAL LAW	*OLD TREATIES*
Article 194	Article 50 CFR
Article 195	Article 51 CFR
Article 196	Article 52 CFR
Article 197	Article 53 CFR
Article 198	Article 54 CFR
PART III – FINANCES OF THE UNION	
Article 199	Article 310 TFEU
Article 200	Article 311 TFEU
Article 201	new
Article 202	new
Article 203	Article 312 TFEU
Article 204	new
Article 205	Article 313 TFEU
Article 206	Article 314 TFEU
Article 207	Article 315 TFEU
Article 208	Article 316 TFEU
Article 209	Article 317 TFEU
Article 210	Article 318 TFEU
Article 211	Article 319 TFEU
Article 212	Article 320 TFEU
Article 213	Article 321 TFEU
Article 214	Article 322 TFEU
Article 215	Article 323 TFEU
Article 216	Article 324 TFEU
Article 217	Article 325 TFEU
PART IV – ECONOMIC AND MONETARY UNION	
Article 218	Article 119 TFEU
Article 219	Article 120 TFEU
Article 220	Article 121 TFEU
Article 221	Article 122 TFEU
Article 222	Article 123 TFEU
Article 223	Article 124 TFEU
Article 224	Article 125 TFEU
Article 225	Article 126 TFEU
Article 226	Article 127 TFEU
Article 227	new
Article 228	Article 128 TFEU
Article 229	Article 129 TFEU
Article 230	Article 130 TFEU
Article 231	Article 131 TFEU
Article 232	Article 132 TFEU
Article 233	Article 133 TFEU

FUNDAMENTAL LAW	*OLD TREATIES*
Article 234	Article 134 TFEU
Article 235	Article 135 TFEU
Article 236	Article 136 TFEU
Article 237	Article 137 TFEU
Article 238	Article 138 TFEU
Article 239	new
Article 240	Article 139 TFEU
Article 241	new
Article 242	Article 140 TFEU
Article 243	Article 141 TFEU
Article 244	Article 142 TFEU
Article 245	Article 143 TFEU
Article 246	Article 144 TFEU
PART V – THE POLICIES OF THE UNION	
Article 247	Article 7 TFEU
Article 248	Article 8 TFEU
Article 249	Article 9 TFEU
Article 250	Article 10 TFEU
Article 251	Article 11 TFEU
Article 252	Article 12 TFEU
Article 253	Article 13 TFEU
Article 254	Article 14 TFEU
Article 255	Article 15 TFEU
Article 256	Article 16 TFEU
Article 257	Article 17 TFEU
Article 258	Article 18 TFEU
Article 259	Article 19 TFEU
Article 260	Article 20 TFEU
Article 261	Article 21 TFEU
Article 262	Article 22 TFEU
Article 263	Article 23 TFEU
Article 264	Article 24 TFEU
Article 265	Article 25 TFEU
Article 266	Article 26 TFEU
Article 267	new
Article 268	Article 27 TFEU
Article 269	Article 28 TFEU
Article 270	Article 29 TFEU
Article 271	Article 30 TFEU
Article 272	Article 31 TFEU
Article 273	Article 32 TFEU
Article 274	Article 33 TFEU
Article 275	Article 34 TFEU

FUNDAMENTAL LAW	*OLD TREATIES*
Article 276	Article 35 TFEU
Article 277	Article 36 TFEU
Article 278	Article 37 TFEU
Article 279	Article 45 TFEU
Article 280	Article 46 TFEU
Article 281	Article 47 TFEU
Article 282	Article 48 TFEU
Article 283	Article 49 TFEU
Article 284	Article 50 TFEU
Article 285	Article 51 TFEU
Article 286	Article 52 TFEU
Article 287	Article 53 TFEU
Article 288	Article 54 TFEU
Article 289	Article 55 TFEU
Article 290	Article 56 TFEU
Article 291	Article 57 TFEU
Article 292	Article 58 TFEU
Article 293	Article 59 TFEU
Article 294	Article 60 TFEU
Article 295	Article 61 TFEU
Article 296	Article 62 TFEU
Article 297	Article 63 TFEU
Article 298	Article 64 TFEU
Article 299	Article 65 TFEU
Article 300	Article 66 TFEU
Article 301	Article 101 TFEU
Article 302	Article 102 TFEU
Article 303	Article 103 TFEU
Article 304	Article 104 TFEU
Article 305	Article 105 TFEU
Article 306	Article 106 TFEU
Article 307	Article 107 TFEU
Article 308	Article 108 TFEU
Article 309	Article 109 TFEU
Article 310	Article 110 TFEU
Article 311	Article 111 TFEU
Article 312	Article 112 TFEU
Article 313	Article 113 TFEU
Article 314	Article 114 TFEU
	Article 115 TFEU (repealed)
Article 315	Article 116 TFEU
Article 316	Article 117 TFEU
Article 317	Article 118 TFEU
Article 318	Articles 145 & 147 TFEU

FUNDAMENTAL LAW	*OLD TREATIES*
Article 309	Article 146 TFEU
	Article 147 TFEU (repealed)
Article 320	Article 148 TFEU
Article 321	Article 149 TFEU
Article 322	Article 150 TFEU
Article 323	Article 151 TFEU
Article 324	Article 152 TFEU
Article 325	Article 153 TFEU
Article 326	Article 154 TFEU
Article 327	Article 155 TFEU
Article 328	Article 156 TFEU
Article 329	Article 157 TFEU
Article 330	Article 158 TFEU
Article 331	Article 159 TFEU
	Article 160 TFEU (repealed)
	Article 161 TFEU (repealed)
Article 332	Article 162 TFEU
Article 333	Article 163 TFEU
Article 334	Article 164 TFEU
Article 335	Article 165 TFEU
Article 336	Article 166 TFEU
Article 337	Article 167 TFEU
Article 338	Article 168 TFEU
Article 339	Article 169 TFEU
Article 340	Article 38 TFEU
Article 341	Article 39 TFEU
Article 342	new
Article 343	Article 40 TFEU
Article 344	Article 41 TFEU
Article 345	Article 42 TFEU
Article 346	Article 43 TFEU
Article 347	Article 44 TFEU
	Article 90 TFEU (repealed)
Article 348	Article 91 TEFU
	Article 92 TFEU (repealed)
Article 349	Article 93 TFEU
	Article 94 TFEU (repealed)
	Article 95 TFEU (repealed)
Article 350	Article 96 TFEU
	Article 97 TFEU (repealed)
	Article 98 TFEU (repealed)
	Article 99 TFEU (repealed)
	Article 100 TFEU (repealed)
Article 351	Article 170 TFEU

FUNDAMENTAL LAW	*OLD TREATIES*
Article 352	Article 171 TFEU
Article 353	Article 172 TFEU
Article 354	Article 173 TFEU
Article 355	Article 174 TFEU
Article 356	Article 175 TFEU
Article 357	Article 176 TFEU
Article 358	Article 177 TFEU
Article 359	Article 178 TFEU
Article 360	Article 179 TFEU
Article 361	Article 180 TFEU
Article 362	Article 181 TFEU
Article 363	Article 182 TFEU
Article 364	Article 183 TFEU
Article 365	Article 184 TFEU
Article 366	Article 185 TFEU
Article 367	Article 186 TFEU
Article 368	Article 187 TFEU
Article 369	Article 188 TFEU
Article 370	Article 189 TFEU
Article 371	Article 190 TFEU
Article 372	Article 191 TFEU
Article 373	Article 192 TFEU
Article 374	Article 193 TFEU
Article 375	Article 194 TFEU
Article 376	new
	Article 195 TFEU (repealed)
PART VI – FREEDOM, SECURITY AND JUSTICE WITHIN THE UNION	
Article 377	Article 67 TFEU
	Article 68 TFEU (repealed)
	Article 69 TFEU (repealed)
Article 378	Article 70 TFEU (repealed)
Article 379	Article 71 TFEU
Article 380	Article 72 TFEU
Article 381	Article 73 TFEU
Article 382	Article 74 TFEU
Article 383	Article 75 TFEU
	Article 76 TFEU (repealed)
Article 384	Article 77 TFEU
Article 385	Article 78 TFEU
Article 386	Article 79 TFEU
Article 387	Article 80 TFEU
Article 388	Article 81 TFEU

FUNDAMENTAL LAW	*OLD TREATIES*
Article 389	Article 82 TFEU
Article 390	Article 83 TFEU
Article 391	Article 84 TFEU
Article 392	Article 85 TFEU
Article 393	Article 86 TFEU
Article 394	Article 87 TFEU
Article 395	Article 88 TFEU
Article 396	Article 89 TFEU
Article 397	Article 196 TFEU
Article 398	Article 197 TFEU
PART VII – ASSOCIATION OF THE OVERSEAS TERRITORIES	
Article 399	Article 198 TFEU
Article 400	Article 199 TFEU
Article 401	Article 200 TFEU
Article 402	Article 201 TFEU
Article 403	Article 202 TFEU
Article 404	Article 203 TFEU
Article 405	Article 204 TFEU
PART VIII – THE EXTERNAL ACTION OF THE UNION	
Article 406	Articles 8 & 21 TEU
Article 407	Article 22 TEU
	Article 23 TEU (repealed)
Article 408	Article 24 TEU
Article 409	Article 25 TEU
Article 410	Article 26 TEU
Article 411	Article 27 TEU
	Article 28 TEU (repealed)
	Article 29 TEU (repealed)
	Article 30 TEU (repealed)
Article 412	Article 31 TEU
Article 413	Article 32 TEU
	Article 33 TEU (repealed)
Article 414	Article 34 TEU
	Article 35 TEU (repealed)
Article 415	Article 36 TEU
Article 416	Article 37 TEU
	Article 38 TEU (repealed)
	Article 39 TEU (repealed)
	Article 39 TEU (repealed)
Article 417	Article 41 TEU
Article 418	Article 42 TEU

FUNDAMENTAL LAW	*OLD TREATIES*
Article 419	Article 43 TEU
Article 420	Article 44 TEU
Article 421	Article 45 TEU
Article 422	Article 46 TEU
	Article 205 TFEU (repealed)
Article 423	Article 206 TFEU
Article 424	Article 207 TFEU
Article 425	Article 208 TFEU
Article 426	Article 209 TFEU
Article 427	Article 210 TFEU
	Article 211 TFEU (repealed)
Article 428	Article 212 TFEU
	Article 213 TEFU (repealed)
Article 429	Article 214 TFEU
Article 430	Article 215 TFEU
Article 431	Article 216 TFEU
Article 432	Article 217 TFEU
Article 433	Article 218 TFEU
Article 434	Article 219 TFEU
Article 435	Article 220 TFEU
Article 436	Article 221 TFEU
Article 437	Article 222 TFEU
PROTOCOLS	
Protocol No 1	Protocol No 1
Protocol No 2	Protocol No 2
Protocol No 3	1976 Act
Protocol No 4	Protocol No 3
Protocol No 5	Protocol No 4
Protocol No 6	Protocol No 5
	Protocol No 6 (repealed)
Protocol No 7	Protocol No 7
	Protocol No 8 (repealed)
	Protocol No 9 (repealed)
Protocol No 8	Protocol No 10
	Protocol No 11 (repealed)
Protocol No 9	new
Protocol No 10	Protocol No 12
Protocol No 11	Protocol No 13
Protocol No 12	Protocol No 14
	Protocol No 15 (repealed)
	Protocol No 16 (repealed)
	Protocol No 17 (repealed)
Protocol No 13	Protocol No 18
	Protocol No 19 (repealed)

FUNDAMENTAL LAW	*OLD TREATIES*
	Protocol No 20 (repealed)
	Protocol No 21 (repealed)
	Protocol No 22 (repealed)
	Protocol No 23 (repealed)
Protocol No 14	Protocol No 24
	Protocol No 25 (repealed)
Protocol No 15	Protocol No 26
	Protocol No 27 (repealed)
	Protocol No 28 (repealed)
Protocol No 16	Protocol No 29
	Protocol No 30 (repealed)
	Protocol No 31 (repealed)
	Protocol No 32 (repealed)
	Protocol No 33 (repealed)
Protocol No 17	Protocol No 34
	Protocol No 35 (repealed)
Protocol No 18	Protocol No 36
	Protocol No 37 (repealed)

Last Words

by Thomas Fischer und Joachim Fritz-Vannahme, Bertelsmann Stiftung

For many observers of the current political debate about Europe's future, publishing a constitutional draft for a federal Europe at this point in time seems highly ambitious at best – or even unrealistic at worst. Alerted by the sharp decrease in public support for the European project since the beginning of the Euro crisis, even those political decision-makers who are in favour of further deepening integration consider another reform of the EU Treaty to be an incalculable political risk.

Most of them are still suffering from the extremely cumbersome exercise of giving life to the Lisbon Treaty. The memory of this long and arduous journey is too fresh in their minds to already embark on the next fundamental revision of the EU's primary law. From the perspective of the so-called pragmatists, pleading now for a qualitative constitutional leap towards a federal Europe is coming close to denying a reality characterized by the resurging idea of national sovereignty.

With reference to the subsidiarity principle, a growing number of member – state governments seem to seriously question the EU Treaty's objective of "an ever closer Union". By launching its "Balance of Competences Review" aiming at the repatriation of EU powers, the British government has been the forerunner in this trend. Another striking example is the Dutch government, which has recently published its "wish list" naming those policy areas where the Netherlands does not want to see additional power transferred to the EU.

Whether due to so-called pragmatism or the conviction that the creation of the "United States of Europe" would point in the wrong direction, the project of a federal constitution for Europe apparently has to face strong headwinds in the current political debate.

Against this backdrop, the reader of this book may wonder why the Bertelsmann Stiftung has joined forces with the Spinelli Group to publish the draft for "A Fundamental Law of the European Union". The reason is not that we agree on every detail of the proposal or that we have fallen victim to pro-European idealism. On the contrary, we think that heading for our foundation's leitmotif of the "United States of Europe" is a much more pragmatic position these days than shying away from ambitious treaty reforms.

We share the conviction of the Spinelli Group that by voicing support for a federal EU constitution, we are making a much more important contribution to the much-needed democratic debate on Europe's future than those who desperately avoid the notion of federalism and vaguely talk about deeper integration or the advantages of a political union. With the publication of this book, we primarily want to provoke an open dispute about competing political options between supporters and opponents of the idea of the "United States of Europe" and provide a sort of sounding board that allows for the mapping of alternative ideas about how to shape the future EU.

To put it slightly differently, we are driven by the deep conviction that Europe will not progress if the public and political debate gets stuck in TINA ("There is no alternative") thinking. Although we support large parts of the Spinelli Group's constitutional draft and its philosophy, we see the primary purpose of its publication as triggering an open process of deliberation which allows those alternatives to win for which the best arguments are put forward.

From our viewpoint, one of the key merits of the Spinelli Group's blueprint for the constitutional architecture of a federal Europe is that it clarifies from the very beginning its main purpose: According to the authors, "All the reforms proposed are aimed at strengthening the capacity of the EU to act". Completely in line with their understanding of federalism, we do not promote a centralized European superstate but "a constitutional union in which different levels of democratic government are coordinate, not subordinate".

Regarding political priorities, we share the Group's conclusion that completing Economic and Monetary Union (EMU) is the key challenge for Europe's policymakers and that "more of the same" will not be sufficient to achieve this objective. Several aspects of EMU featuring high on Europe's current political agenda already raise the question of to what extent they will be possible without changing the EU Treaty.

Actually, the Treaty on Stability, Coordination and Governance (better known as the "Fiscal Compact"), which aims to foster fiscal discipline and structural reforms, provides for its incorporation into the EU Treaty before the end of 2017. The introduction of a fiscal capacity or a "solidarity mechanism" for Eurogroup members based upon bilateral contracts between single member states and the EU institutions might require revisions of the EU's primary law.

The same applies to the need to extend democratic control by the European Parliament to the European Central Bank in its new role as Single Bank Supervisory Authority and – at least in the longer run – for the creation of a European Banking Resolution Fund and a European Deposit Guarantee Scheme. And if it should prove necessary to introduce new mechanisms for the mutualisation of debts at the EMU level, such as a European Debt Redemption Fund or a European Debt Agency, the German Constitutional Court has clearly decided that this will not be possible without changes to the "no bail-out" clause of the Lisbon Treaty.

Against this backdrop, we think the Spinelli Group is perfectly right in highlighting that the installation of a true "economic government of the fiscal union" in Part IV of the Fundamental Law constitutes the main innovation in their constitutional draft. Most of the reform proposals presented there, such as the introduction of the new post of Treasury Minister to foster the Commission's role as the EU's fiscal and economic government, the measures suggested to make sure that member states observe stronger fiscal discipline or the introduction of a special fiscal capacity for the Euro countries, we can fully support.

Beyond that, we welcome the proposed extension of the Treaty rules on enhanced cooperation to the eurozone. This would allow for a multi-speed Europe that does not run the risk of growing fragmentation between the ins, pre-ins and outs of EMU. Without this remedy, eurozone members might be increasingly tempted to fall back on separate intergovernmental agreements outside the EU Treaty, such as the Fiscal Compact or the Treaty on the European Stability Mechanisms, to live up to the functional requirements resulting from the single currency.

Since we are convinced that, in parallel, the Treaty objective of a socially balanced market economy has to be implemented more efficiently within and across member states, we agree with the Spinelli Group that the role of the Commission and the European Parliament in formulating employment and macro-economic policy guidelines ought to be strengthened and that the Treaty's horizontal social clause should be tightened.

Beyond that, the other proposals presented in the Fundamental Law to "refresh" European powers in the fields of energy, agriculture and common fisheries, the internal market, competition, transport, R&D, environmental protection and climate change, justice and home affairs, and external affairs also make, by and large, sense from our point of view – as far as the EU's capacities to act more efficiently are concerned. Details still have to be further discussed, of course.

Our overall impression is that the Fundamental Law of the European Union is perfectly fit for the purpose of re-initiating the debate on the EU's future constitution and, if another European Convention should be set up within the next few years, of contributing to the preparation of the next Treaty reform. For that reason, we have decided to publish this book jointly with the Spinelli Group.

The Bertelsmann Stiftung will, however, further elaborate on some questions which the present publication can only touch upon. The authors of the Fundamental Law basically assume that EU institutions will become "more responsive to the needs and aspirations of the people they serve" if the EU's capacity to act (i.e. its "output legitimacy") is strengthened and if its institutional setup is further developed along the lines of a fully fledged federal two-chamber system – made up of the European Parliament and the Council – with the European Commission turning into a democratic constitutional government.

The basic intention of the Spinelli Group may also be circumscribed along the lines of the official motto of the Union, which the Fundamental Law provides for: "Unity in diversity". First of all, the group seeks to strengthen unity to overcome excessive diversity. This approach is hardly surprising given that the authors of the constitutional draft are Members of the European Parliament. From their perspective, more unity – that is, the allocation of additional powers at the EU level – is crucial for restoring citizens' trust in the European integration project. This, however, will only be possible if, at the same time, there is more democratic accountability and legitimacy of European policymaking.

Accordingly, the Fundamental Law includes a number of excellent proposals for democratic reform. To provide for a clearer separation of powers, the Council (as second legislative chamber) is deprived of its executive powers which are transferred to the European Commission as democratic government of the Union. The Fundamental Law co-decision between Parliament and Council applies throughout – including in those areas where the Council currently enjoys the right to legislate alone.

The European Commission President is made more accountable to the European Parliament, and the role of the President of the European Council is limited to directing and coordinating the affairs of the Council. Last but not least, a certain number of deputies of the European Parliament ought to be elected from a pan – European constituency in future, which shall also contribute to the emergence of truly European parties.

These institutional reforms are complemented by treaty changes aiming to foster democratic legitimacy by upgrading the status of European citizenship. In this context, the most significant innovations are – from our viewpoint – the incorporation of the EU's Charter of Fundamental Rights into the Treaty text, the simplification of access to the European Court of Justice for individuals, the extension of the voting rights of EU citizens living in EU member states other than their own to national parliamentary elections, and the widening of the scope of the European Citizens' Initiative to include political agenda-setting.

We do not doubt that this package of reform measures would contribute to making the democratic foundations of EU institutions much more solid. Nevertheless, we think that they are only insufficiently apt to solve the profound dilemma the European Union has to face: On the one hand, from a purely functional perspective, there are rather strong arguments in favour of transferring additional powers to the Union level. On the other hand, however, political and public acceptance in member states is fading away the more the Union interferes in fields of national high politics constituting the core of nation-statism and the closely related construct of national sovereignty.

This dilemma is not at all new. Since the Maastricht Treaty and the introduction of the EMU at the latest, it has been an increasingly difficult exercise to find the right balance between the requirements of efficient policymaking and the political preferences of citizens. However, since the outbreak of the Eurocrisis, this dilemma has assumed a completely new quality. The most ambitious European project, the single currency, which had been perceived since its introduction as a success story by most European citizens, has turned into one of the most controversially discussed issues in the political and public debate about the EU. In the meantime, the surge of Euroscepticism we have witnessed in recent years has spread to the EU as a whole and triggered much more fundamental national debates about the added value of European integration.

It goes without saying that representatives of national governments – in their role as members of the Council or the European Council – are particularly affected by this growing gap between efficient EU policies and predominant public attitudes at home. Former Eurogroup President Jean-Claude Juncker has perfectly summarized their difficult position. When responding to the question of why the Europeans only have halfhearted answers to the sovereign debt crisis, he said:

"We all know what to do; we just don't know how to get re-elected after we've done it."

The Spinelli Group implicitly refers to this problem in its Fundamental Law by stating that "at the level of the heads of governments, meeting in the European Council, the response to the financial and economic crisis has tended to be too little too late." At the same time, this is exactly the reason why the authors strongly plead for replacing the intergovernmental model of decision-making with a federal EU government. Nevertheless, this approach can only be part of the solution. It does not give a persuasive answer to the question of how to tackle the issue of increasingly divergent public policy preferences and the revival of the subsidiarity principle in the political debates at the member-state level.

It is against this background that, from our point of view, the success and viability of the European project will largely depend on the ability to develop a completely new system of federal checks and balances tailor-made to keep a sound balance between efficiency requirements at the EU level and public acceptance at the national level.

Accordingly, this will be one of the key priorities in our foundation's work on Europe's future for the next few years. Amongst other issues, it might be particularly worthwhile in this context to have a closer look at the role of national parliaments in European policymaking and at potential patterns of interparliamentary collaboration between them and the European Parliament. With regard to this crucial issue, the Fundamental Law of the European Union hardly goes beyond the status quo of the Lisbon Treaty. Hence, we would be delighted if we could cooperate with the Spinelli Group to further elaborate on the future role of national parliaments in EU decision-making.

When talking about the future of the EU, we are actually talking about the question of how to provide for a functioning democracy able to cope efficiently with the internal and global challenges Europe is currently facing. This is the key issue we have to address – and we urgently need answers. With the publication of the Fundamental Law of the European Union, the Spinelli Group and the Bertelsmann Stiftung give a possible response to this essential question.